# COME AND SEE

# COME AND SEE

*An Eastern Orthodox Perspective on Contextualization*

*Edward Rommen*

WILLIAM CAREY
LIBRARY

*Come and See: An Eastern Orthodox Perspective on Contextualization*



Published by William Carey Library
1605 E. Elizabeth Street
Pasadena, CA 91104 | www.missionbooks.org

Melissa Hicks, editor
Brad Koenig, copyeditor
Hugh Pindur, graphic design
Rose Lee-Norman, indexer

William Carey Library is a ministry of the U.S. Center for World Mission
Pasadena, CA | www.uscwm.org
Printed in the United States of America

17 16 15 14 13     5 4 3 2 1BP 600

---

Library of Congress Cataloging-in-Publication Data

Rommen, Edward, 1947-
Come and see : an Eastern Orthodox perspective on contextualization / Edward Rommen.
pages cm
ISBN 978-0-87808-534-7
1. Christianity and culture. 2. Missions--Theory. 3. Orthodox Eastern Church--Doctrines. I. Title.
BR115.C8R657 2013
261--dc23

2012044577

# Contents

# Foreword

"The evangelistic task is to introduce the person of Christ … This is the most fundamental principle in the process of contextualization." These statements come from the concluding chapter of this book. And this book is one of the most significant of many recent works on contextualization.

That having been said, readers will probably expect me to overview what the author has written and tell why it is significant. I will not proceed in that fashion for two reasons. First, the author has already summarized the book in his introduction. Second, the significance of this work stems from Dr. Rommen's expertise but also the uniqueness of his objective—namely, to explore the potential of the gospel, the role of the sacraments, and the use of cyberspace in effecting the kind of contextualization that will enable people to know the Lord Jesus personally and intimately.

Rommen's book is not an easy read, nor is its message easy to grasp, much less put into practice. However, I think that process will be helped along by the relating of several biographical vignettes.

I first met Ed during his student days at Trinity Evangelical Divinity School in the 1960s. Under the leadership of Dean Kenneth Kantzer, TEDS attracted many of the brightest and most dedicated students of theology and mission at the time, Ed among them. As a student, Ed's Norwegian parentage and background in the Norwegian Evangelical Free Church became apparent in a variety of ways but, far from being restrictive, they proved to be advantageous later on when Ed and his wife, Ainee, served as Free Church missionaries in Germany.

It was in a missionary capacity that Ed Rommen's extraordinary abilities to master the German language and culture, and to work effectively both independently and in concert with leaders and lay members of the Evangelical Free Church of Germany, became most apparent. Following several successful church plants, Rommen was invited by Free Church leaders to join the faculty of their denominational seminary at Ewersbach. Somewhat later, when the Berlin Wall came down, he was appointed to a leading role in making preparation for the reunification of the Free Churches of East and West Germany.

Not being of a mind to pass up an opportunity to enhance his own learning and skills, Ed completed a doctor of theology program at the prestigious University of Munich while simultaneously engaged in these various ministries. In the end, however, a serious asthmatic condition that steadily worsened in the German environment necessitated the return of the Rommen family to the States.

Back home, Dr. Rommen engaged the minds and hearts of his students while serving on the faculties of Trinity Evangelical Divinity School and then Columbia Biblical Seminary. Eventually, however, Ed and Ainee were to make a decision that would change the course of their ministry dramatically. Involvement with several Columbia-area evangelical churches they deemed to be altogether too "free," "unchurchly," and *laissez faire* caused the Rommens to distance themselves from that kind of evangelicalism. Instead, they associated with a local congregation of the Orthodox Church—a church in which they felt enabled to retain orthodox doctrine without sacrificing sensibilities of worship and witness.

One thing led to another. Before long, their giftedness and devotion to Christ having been recognized in this new ecclesiastical context, the Rommens were afforded special responsibilities and opportunities for significant service. Eventually, Dr. Rommen was called to be the priest of Holy Transfiguration Orthodox Church in Raleigh-Durham, North Carolina. For a number of years now he has also served as adjunct professor at Duke Divinity School.

With this as background, let me return to the primary thesis of *Come and See: An Eastern Orthodox Perspective on Contextualization*. Namely, that the kind of contextualization called for in promulgating the biblical gospel leads to more than correct information about the Christ of the gospel; it also leads to a personal and life-changing relationship with the Christ who *is* the gospel. Now in making this very important distinction, I rather think that Dr. Rommen undervalues somewhat the contribution of our early book *Contextualization: Meanings, Methods, and Models*. True, in that we attempted to display various aberrant contextualized theologies while explicating and illustrating a kind of contextualization we deemed more faithful to Scripture, our book primarily had to do with information *about* Christ and the gospel. But I think that exercise was, and is, very useful in much the same way as knowing the few facts *about* Dr. Rommen offered above can and should prove helpful to understanding his book. But let it serve to enhance and in no way diminish the quintessential importance of trusting and knowing Christ personally and of the kind of contextualization of Christian witness, worship, and works that help effect that relationship. Two interrelated illustrations—one more existential in nature and the other more theological—will give some indication of what I have in mind here.

First, students of mission especially want to give attention to the ways in which the Rommens' "dis-ease" and perhaps even *angst* with evangelical worship in America may have contributed to their acceptance and effectiveness among evangelicals in Germany. I refer to the Rommens' genuine disdain for the noncreedal, nonliturgical and, at times, somewhat "freewheeling" nature of many worship services in America and, on the flipside, their corresponding appreciation for the more ordered, liturgical, and doctrinally robust nature of corporate worship in evangelical churches in Germany. I myself have had occasion to experience the profound difference between celebrations of, for example, the Lord's Supper in many Free Churches in the United States and its celebration in Free Churches in Germany. The latter tend to be, not only more frequent, but also more solemn and symbolically significant. Dr. Rommen would be the first to admit that this frequency, uniformity, and solemnity can—and sometimes does—result in rote observance and empty form. But, if I understand him correctly, his contention would be that, contextualized and administered properly, this ordinance/sacrament has the potential to bring members of the body of Christ into a much more intimate relationship with the Christ who is the gospel.

Second, we must ask whether or not Scripture will uphold Rommen's contention? I am not a sacramentarian, nevertheless I think that we must answer that question in the affirmative. A careful examination of Paul's words concerning the observance of the Lord's Supper in his first letter to the Corinthian church (1 Cor 11:17–34) reveals that the Supper is indeed a "remembrance" (in the sense of "recollection") of the Lord's death, *but it is much more than that.* The "more" is epitomized in two related Greek verbs employed by New Testament writers and usually translated as "remember": *mimneskomai* and *mnemoneuo.* These verbs sometimes convey the simple meaning of remembering or bringing to mind the events of the past. At other times, however, the "remembering" is intended to evoke a present response, whether in thankful prayer (1 Thess 1:3), a proper attitude (John 2:22; Eph 2:11), or an appropriate action (Gal 2:10; Rev 2:5). Accordingly, the related noun *anamnesis*, as used by Paul in the Corinthian passage before us (1 Cor 11:24,25), entails not merely participation in a commemorative meal, *but also recognition of the Lord's personal and "present presence" among his people and a corporate proclamation of "the Lord's death till He comes" (1 Cor 11:25,26 NKJV)!*

Yes, Dr. Rommen's book will do much good evangelistically, spiritually, theologically, ecclesiastically. All who are truly Christian—and many yet to become truly Christian—are surely in his debt.

David J. Hesselgrave, PhD
professor emeritus of Mission
Trinity Evangelical Divinity School
Deerfield, Illinois

# Introduction

In 1989 David Hesselgrave and I coauthored *Contextualization: Meanings, Methods, and Models.*[1] At the time, contextualization of the gospel was hotly debated, and there was no end to new proposals and experimentation. There were innovative translations of the Bible for repressed minorities,[2] culturally driven modifications of the Roman Mass for use in sub-Saharan Africa,[3] Lutheran political theology in Germany,[4] and Catholic liberation theology in Latin America.[5] In the midst of all this activity questions were raised as to the legitimacy of certain models. Were they faithful to the gospel or did they represent a syncretistic compromise of the truth? So in our book we made an effort to provide a framework(s)—philosophical, anthropological, linguistic, and theological—for evaluating specific cases of proposed contextualization. In the process we came to the conclusion that contextualization is best viewed as

> the attempt to communicate the *message* of the person, works, Word, and will of *God* in a way that is faithful to God's revelation, especially as it is put forth in the teachings of Holy *Scripture*, and that is meaningful to

---

1 David J. Hesselgrave and Edward Rommen, *Contextualization: Meanings, Methods, and Models* (Grand Rapids: Baker Book House, 1989).

2 Clarence Jordon, *The Cotton Patch Version of Matthew and John* (New York: Association, 1973); Caanan Banana, "The Lord's Prayer—in the Ghetto," in *Mission Trends No. 3: Third World Theologies; Asian, African, and Latin American Contributions to a Radical, Theological Realignment in the Church*, ed. Gerald Anderson and Thomas F. Stransky (New York: Paulist, 1976), 156–57.

3 Bertsch, Ludwig, ed. *Der neue Meßritus im Zaire*, vol. 18, *Theologie der Dritten Welt* (Freiburg, Germany: Herder, 1993).

4 Jürgen Moltmann, *A Theology of Hope* (New York: Harper & Row, 1967).

5 Jose Miguez Bonino, *Doing Theology in a Revolutionary Situation* (Philadelphia: Fortress, 1975).

> respondents in their respective cultural and existential contexts. Contextualization is both verbal and nonverbal and has to do with theologizing; Bible translation, interpretation, and application; Incarnational lifestyle; evangelism; Christian instruction; church planting and growth; church organization; worship style—indeed with all those activities involved in carrying out the Great Commission.[6]

This definition gave us a workable starting point for evaluating a wide array of proposals. For us the message was paramount. What we were evaluating was information and its transmission. Regardless of a specific contextualization's source, we wanted to be sure that the information it contained about Christ was true to the Scriptures and understandable in the recipient's culture.

As I look back on that project, over twenty years later, it occurs to me that, while we did respond reasonably well to the basic contours of the immediate discussion, we were bound by a number of theological, ecclesial, procedural, and historical constraints that limited our creativity and caused us to underemphasize several aspects of the process that I now believe are essential to a proper understanding of the contextualization of the gospel.

*Theologically*, we were, as already stated, committed to a frame of reference that viewed the gospel primarily as information about God. Note that the definition given in 1989 includes the communication of a *message about a person* but not the introduction of the person proper. These, it now seems to me, are two very different things. Certainly we need to mediate information about, among other things, the person of God. But in the case of the gospel, which is so clearly focused on an unmediated relationship between the risen, living, ever-present Lord Jesus Christ (Gal 2:20; 2 Pet 1:4) and the invitee, an indirect presentation via information will prove less than satisfying. Without an unmediated personal encounter there can be no reconciliation, no justification, no new life in Christ. So whatever it is, contextualization involves the mediation, not only of information

6 Hesselgrave and Rommen, *Contextualization*, 200 (italics added).

about God, but the facilitation of a personal encounter with the saving, forgiving, all-present, Lord of life, Jesus Christ.

Take, for example, the account of how the Apostle Nathaniel entered into Jesus' band of disciples (John 1:43–51). As we enter the story, Jesus already had four followers—Andrew and Peter, John and James. Now he is introduced to Philip, perhaps by Andrew and Peter, who lived in the same town. Notice what Philip does next. He goes and finds Nathaniel and gives Nathaniel some information about Jesus, that he is the one "of whom Moses in the law, and the prophets, did write, Jesus of Nazareth, the son of Joseph" (1:45). But Nathaniel, who hasn't met Jesus yet, responds skeptically, as if to say, "You can't expect me to believe that." Obviously information about Jesus was just not enough. What I find most fascinating is that Philip doesn't argue the point. He simply says to come and see for yourself; in other words, come and meet him yourself.

We don't generally think of contextualizing the person we are introducing, even cross-culturally; we simply bring them with us, make the introduction, and allow the negotiation of intimacy between the two to take its natural course. The person being introduced has to be real, observable, and present. Today, of course, we face the challenge of a physically absent Christ. In what sense is he or can he be made real, observable, and present in the contemporary context? This is part of what I want to explore in this book.

*Ecclesially*, our original effort was largely limited to a Free Church frame of reference. As a result we made little use of the idea of the church's tradition, and we did not ask about the ways in which it might limit or facilitate the process of contextualization. Here, we are not speaking simply of the ways in which things have been done historically within the various streams of Christianity, but rather that whole dynamic body of doctrine and practice that was handed down by Christ to the apostles and, under the guidance of the Holy Spirit, by them to successive generations of the church. In the previous work we hinted at tradition's usefulness by devoting a chapter to the work of the earliest Christian apologists, but there was no consideration of the ways in which those early models might inform and even limit the scope of contemporary contextualization. Look again at our 1989 definition. It includes a whole array of ecclesial components such as church administration and worship styles. Yet it offered little help in discerning the usefulness of one structure, one understanding of worship, over against its alternatives. The question I would now like to ask is, have certain structures and practices been handed down by the Christ and the apostles, passed on through the centuries across cultural boundaries, and preserved by the church? If so, to what extent are they binding today? What must we continue to preserve? Do we have unlimited freedom to choose or change those structures?

Our initial ecclesial orientation also limited us to a more-or-less nonsacramental, nonliturgical mode of churchly being. While we did explore the limits of changing the form and content of the Lord's Supper (mentioned only once in the original book), we made little mention of the sacrament's relationship to the overall mission of the church. If we had ranged beyond our own Free Church heritage, we would have had to explore the close connection between the Liturgy, in particular the Eucharist, and the mission of the church.

*Procedurally*, we gave little attention to the conditions under which contextualization was to take place. I think that we were so interested in the contents (the information) and the mechanics of the operation itself that we neglected to explore the nature of the persons involved. We spent a great deal of time discussing layers of nested contexts and the path of information from one mind to another, all as if the participants, especially the recipients, were marginal, passive actors in a process that forced compliance by virtue of the veracity of the information and the cleverness of the technique. In this present work I would like to examine the nature of personhood, the concept of interpersonal communion, and the ways in which a personal encounter with both Christ and the contextualizer can be facilitated.

*Historically*, we could not include an account of the radically different context of the Internet, since it was just then beginning to take shape. In 1989, computer-mediated communication (CMC) was in its infancy. Since then cyberspace has become so prominent a feature of late modern life, that we can no longer ignore it as a field of contextualization. Almost every religion on the planet has taken to the Internet to propagate its teachings. Many of them have established what they call "communities of faith," within which one is able to pray, worship, and nurture intimate relationships. Email, chat groups and, more recently, blogs and social networking sites have attracted millions of participants. While academic studies of cyberspace are just now coming in, researchers seem to agree that CMC has fundamentally changed the way in which we communicate.[7] It seems to have changed and depersonalized what we mean by intimacy, community, identity, and friendship.[8] If that is true, what will contextualization of the gospel look like in this context? How can an introduction to the person of Jesus Christ be issued in this environment?

These then are some of the issues that arise when I revisit our original book in the light of its understandable limitations and the fundamental changes to the ways in which we communicate. These concerns quite naturally lead to the layout of the present project. Before I can speak to the specifics of contextualization, I need to make clear what I mean by the gospel-as-person, by communion, and by personhood, not only by defining the ideas, but also by demonstrating that they are securely anchored in divine revelation. In chapter 1 I will begin by reviewing something of creation's character and the relationship between the Creator and creation: in particular I will survey the doctrines of the Trinity, creation out of nothing, and the Incarnation. This survey will reveal the nature of the Trinity as a tri-hypostatic personal unity possessed of communion, a dynamic state of mutual interpenetration (*perichoresis*) or participation, fully partaking of one another's love without confusion. Moving on to the creation of human beings, I will show them to be hypostatic repetitions of God's own person and, as such, predisposed to personal communion, and open to the Incarnation as God's personal intervention in the world. So if the world, and in particular human beings, were created for personal interaction with both the divine and the creaturely, then awareness of the divine is preinscribed in their very being, and the presence of Christ in their midst brings the deifying and redemptive potential of that communion to their

7 Sherry Turkle, *The Second Self: Computers and the Human Spirit*, 20th anniversary ed. (Cambridge, MA: MIT Press, 2005); Lorne L. Dawson and Douglas E. Cowan, eds., *Religion Online: Finding Faith on the Internet* (New York: Routledge, 2004).

8 One researcher went as far as to suggest that "the use of the word 'friend' on social networking sites is a dilution and a debasement." Christine Rosen, "Virtual Friendship and the New Narcissism," *New Atlantis* 17 (Summer 2007): 28.

very persons. In other words, the incarnate, second Person of the Trinity is salvation and deification. The gospel is a person.

With that established, I will then take a look at the idea of human personhood. What do we mean when we say that someone is a person? What are the conditions under which we can legitimately refer to another entity as person? In particular I will examine the ways in which human beings reflect personhood in their dual, finite/infinite mode of existence, their faculty of belief, their ability to self-actualize (agency), and their commitment to second-order beliefs (beliefs about beliefs, morality).

What then are the implications of these insights for the task of contextualization? If the gospel is primarily information, then the task of evangelism is the proclamation of a particular message, and contextualization is the adaptation of that message to each socioreligious context it encounters. But if the gospel is a person, then the task of evangelism is to introduce that person, and contextualization is the process of creating a context within which the invitation can be meaningfully issued. In that case, spending time adjusting the content and repackaging the message would at best be a secondary concern and at worst an avoidable diversion. What is there to adjust? If we want to introduce a person, we insist on some kind of open, face-to-face encounter. We want the person to be known in her own right and not as a product of some cross-cultural spin. In most cases that person-to-person encounter generates its own sphere of engagement, a field of interaction in which the participants, using available resources, negotiate and nurture their own unique relationship. If that is true, then the primary task of contextualization is to establish an invitational core context, which is host to the presence of the Divine Person, and is defined with the help of personhood-engaging gifts of ecclesial tradition, which enables conditions that facilitate communion and engages extra-ecclesial fields of personal presence.

As I am using the term, a "context" is a set of facts or circumstances that surround a situation or an event. In the case of missions, the context's event is the invitation to Christ, while the facts and circumstances surrounding and regulating that event are provided by the church. The term "field" refers to the space around a radiating body within which it can exert force on similar bodies. Within a field of personal presence, one person radiates presence, which moves other persons to reciprocate in some fashion. As such, fields of human presence exist within contexts. In the context of the church there is a primary field of divine-human encounter generated by the presence of Christ. This context also provides a field of encounter for the faithful and their guests. Moreover it reaches out (by means of witnesses) into extra-ecclesial contexts accessing or creating fields of personal presence in order to invite individuals to "come and see" the primary field of Christ's presence.

In the second chapter I examine sacrament as a place of divine presence, the essential field of divine-human encounter. The Eucharist, as practiced within the context of the church, is of special importance since it is said to involve the very real presence of Christ. It is the postpaschal place of Christ's self-manifestation, and because it is a tangible and regular presence, this becomes a place of divine-human encounter today. The Eucharist also represents the universality of Christ's sacrifice as something having been accomplished for the whole world. In what sense is the sacrament itself celebrated on behalf of the whole world? If we can show a relationship between communion and the salvation of the world, that the real manifestation of Christ is being offered for personal encounter with the world, then one has to ask if and how the sacrament should be deliberately incorporated into our understanding of proclaiming the gospel. Baptism is to be viewed similarly, since it is explicitly mentioned by our Lord in connection with the evangelization of the world (Matt 28:18). Baptism is another place where the living Christ personally manifests himself. If Christ is truly present, baptism becomes another field of encounter in which he can be introduced.

The third chapter will present ecclesial tradition as the means for establishing the core invitational context. The facts that, in this case, surround the invitation are, on the one hand, the various gifts of tradition and, on the other hand, the four conditions of human personhood. Taken together these elements define a framework in which the finitude/infinitude, beliefs, agency, and morality of persons can reside; a place where both the potential and the limitations of human beings can be brought into conformity with divine intent; and a place where an invitation to Christ can be issued and accepted. In defining the context of mission within the possibilities and constraints of tradition, we can take comfort in knowing that we are being guarded and guided by boundaries that have been established by God in the church throughout the ages. So in this chapter I will examine the nature of tradition and show how it engages personhood, helps us avoid error, and frees us to act with confidence by placing limits on the content, form, and shape of the core context.

The fourth chapter will examine how the core context, once established, facilitates the conditions of communion necessary for issuing the invitation. For one person to introduce another person to Christ, they will have to navigate three distinct fields of personal encounter. The first field is that of divine-human communion, such that the one issuing the invitation knows the person being introduced; i.e., Christ. This relationship can be defined as a state of spirituality, the inviter's unbroken relationship to the Divine Person, enabling intact and fully functioning personal being, and it obviously takes place within the context of the church. The second field is the environment of trust and freedom that is established between the person mediating the introduction and the person to whom the introduction is being made. This is the field of interhuman communion, of mutual presence established by mutual self-transcendence, love, and freedom, and will probably take place in an extra-ecclesial setting. The third field is the divine-human communion that develops as the invitee joins in the transcending of the physical and temporal limits of human being and fully apprehends the presence of the Divine Person, again within the context of the church.

In the fifth chapter I enter the realm of computer-mediated communication (CMC) as one of the extra-ecclesial fields of personal presence into which the core context reaches. The Internet has become so widely available that today it may well be considered our primary form of communication. In spite of its somewhat illusory nature, cyberspace presents an amazing opportunity for the dissemination of information. At the same time it poses unique challenges, since it takes place in the absence of many of the cues we take for granted in face-to-face communication. Here there are no (or few) facial expressions, no body language, little in terms of those aspects of communication that radiate off the participants. How then can the gospel-as-person be communicated in this depersonalized medium? Is it really a field of personal presence? How do you introduce a person in this context? What do identity, friendship, intimacy, community look like in this environment? In this chapter I will examine the ways in which the core context might engage cyberspace.

To conclude I will sketch out the parameters of an approach to contextualization that will take advantage of the personal nature of the created world and account for its fallenness. This will not come in the form of detailed, methodological suggestions, but rather as general principles that will help us facilitate a context of encounter in which the living Lord can be effectively introduced to those with whom he seeks communion, and in which the nascent relationships can be nurtured. This, it seems to me, is the very *telos* of contextualization.

Finally, I would like to say something about the spirit in which I offer these reflections. For most of my life I have been involved in the evangelical missions movement. I served as a cross-cultural missionary, and I taught missiology and theology at several evangelical schools both in Europe and North America. During those years I received some of the greatest treasures of my life, a personal faith in the risen Lord Jesus Christ, an unshakable confidence in and love for the Scriptures, and a burning desire to make him know to others. When, after a long period of searching, I moved to the Orthodox Church, it was not because I was rejecting my own heritage, but because I believed I had found a hitherto untapped source of spiritual life and theological insight. The ancient teachings made my faith come alive with new understanding and with a confidence rooted in abiding continuity of the church. So, when I made the move east, I was not turning away from something, but rather embracing the next step in my own spiritual journey, building on the solid foundation of the things I had already been given.

For that reason, this book is not an apologetic for the Orthodox way. It is rather an attempt to give something back. What I am saying is that I have discovered and want to make accessible a whole world of thought which I believe could make a significant contribution to our understanding of the mission of the church. I am not trying to convert the reader, but I am trying to challenge us all to take a look at our theological and missiological assumptions and to learn from each other. This, of course, is always a difficult task; it takes considerable effort, which the reader will soon discover. This task is made even more difficult by the general lack of familiarity with the teachings and the piety of the Orthodox Church. In order to assist the reader I will, starting with chapter 1, provide definitions of key theological and philosophical terms in the footnotes. I should also point out that there is today no reason to apologize for including Orthodox sources in our study. In fact,

> Orthodoxy has deeply influenced some of the most important Protestant theologians working today. Geoffrey Wainwright, Sarah Coakley, Rowan Williams and John Milbank (from Great Britain); Wolfhart, Jurgen Moltman and Miroslav Wolf (from central Europe); Robert Jenson, Eugene Rogers and Kathryn Tanner (from the U.S.)—these and many others have turned to Orthodox sources. It is difficult now to do serious theological work without extensive reference to ancient and modern Orthodox sources.[9]

What I would like to do here is take this already-active exchange of theological ideas and move it into the realm of missiology. As I have said, I believe that Orthodox practice and thought could stimulate fruitful discussion and lead to new missiological insights. While my own experience is limited to North America and Europe, it is my hope that these explorations will help others to recast their approach to the other spheres of fontier missions, such as the worlds of the Hindus, the Buddhists, and the Muslims. So it is against the backdrop of what I have already learned from my abiding friend David Hesselgrave and so many others that I revisit the work we did so many years ago—all in all an effort to learn how to more effectively introduce the person of Christ to a world in need of his love.

9 Jason Byassee, "Looking East: The Impact of Orthodox Theology," *Christian Century*, December 28, 2004, 24.

Chapter 1

# Contextualization and the Challenge of the Gospel-as-person

By this point the reader has to be wondering just what I mean by the gospel-as-person. After all, doesn't the word "gospel" mean the "good news" about the work of Christ, the drawing near of God's kingdom (Matt 9:35)? And isn't it our responsibility to proclaim that message about Christ throughout the world? Obviously! But I wonder if we have not been so preoccupied with the information that we have sometimes failed to introduce the Savior. Perhaps our concern for the rational (or even scriptural) integrity of the message has caused us to miss the importance of the mystical (mysterious) relationship that the message is supposed to facilitate. While it may seem a bit one-sided, my emphasis on the person of Christ is justified both by the Scriptures and by the need for a dynamic balance between information and personal relationship. Mark 1:1 speaks of "the beginning of the gospel of Jesus Christ, the Son of God." Saint Paul writes of the gospel of God, the Son, and Christ (Rom 1:1,9,16). The "of" in these cases cannot mean "about," as if the message were merely descriptive or simply the possession of the second Person of the Trinity. The reality to which these passages point is a message embodied by, made real by the person of Christ. It is information in which we participate personally (Eph 3:6), through which we are saved (Eph 1:13), by which we are made one in Christ (1 Cor 4:15). So I choose to emphasize and explore that personal aspect of the gospel by considering the theological roots of the gospel-as-person, the unique nature of human personhood, and the challenges that this perspective brings to the missional task of the church.

## 1. Theological Roots of the Gospel-as-person

My understanding of the gospel-as-person is rooted in the doctrines of (a) the Trinity, as tri-hypostatic, personal unity[10]; (b) creation of human beings as a hypostatic repetition of God's own person/image[11]; (c) the Incarnation as God's personal intervention in the world, by which divine-human unity was made possible and by which the becoming of humanity is refocused on its fulfillment in Christ; and (d) the Ascension/Pentecost as the completion of the Incarnation with Christ's ascent to heaven and the possibility of his continued presence, a divine presence-in-absence, as mediated by the descended Holy Spirit.

### *a. The Trinity as Personal, Tri-hypostatic Unity*

Orthodox Christians confess that God exists as one nature (essence) in three persons.[12] That is, the divine essence is *hypostasized* as Father, Son, and Holy Spirit.[13] This tri-hypostatic union is sustained by a self-giving (kenotic) love.[14] The Father begets the Son, who reveals the Father, and from the Father there proceeds the Holy Spirit, who rests on the Son and facilitates the revelation of the Father through the *Son*.

This kenotic communion is the mode of God's existence. This intertrinitarian communion is the essence and the life of God who exists eternally as three, as relationship fulfilled, simple, without motion, devoid of becoming. There is nothing toward which God is progressing, no

---

10 *Hypostasis* is the Greek word the Fathers of the first and second ecumenical councils used to identify the three Persons of the Trinity. They maintained that God existed as one essence (the word used was *osia*) and in three persons (*hypostases*). Thus we speak of a tri-hypostatic unity.

11 The *repetition* of God in his creatures does not imply the essential divinity of the creatures, but rather the idea that they bear something of the image of God; that is, he has built into them something of himself.

12 Orthodox Church in America, *The Priest's Service Book*, trans. Archbishop Dmitri (Dallas: Diocese of the South, 2003), 142–43.

13 The usage of the term "hypostasize" changed dramatically in the fourth century from an emphasis on substance to an emphasis on person. Cf. Jean Zizioulas and Paul McPartland, *Communion and Otherness: Further Studies in Personhood and the Church* (New York: T & T Clark, 2006), 214.

14 *Kenosis* is the Greek word used to describe Christ emptying himself to take on the form of a slave (Phil 2:7). So in theological usage the term refers to the self-emptying, selfless, condescension of Christ in order to save the created order.

temporality that could be measured by time; he has no spatial dimension that might be contrasted with another place. In other words, the tri-hypostatically existing God is all that there *is*. He is the very fullness of personal being.[15]

This focuses our attention on *who* God is as opposed to *what* he is. God does not exist simply as substance (*ousia*), but rather as person (hypostasis)—three persons. The "who-ness" of God is obviously tied to the intertrinitarian relationships; who the Father is is revealed by his relationship to the Son and the Spirit. Thus while each Divine Person freely posits its own being and is self-aware, this is done tri-hypostatically, so that each hypostasis shares equally in the I-ness of divinity without losing individual characteristics. However, that I-ness is not a self-serving existence, but rather the self-emptying freedom of each person in service to the other hypostases. Being this way is not a defining of one's own boundaries, but rather a transcending of those boundaries for the sake of the Others. Self-awareness, then, includes an awareness of what is often called "non-I" ("Other"),[16] which allows for the self-actualization of, or the self-determination of personhood. But again, divine personhood does not exist by itself, but rather in relationship to Other, thus overcoming the I/non-I distinction by sharing essence and I-ness so completely that it is possible to speak of the Divine Person, a divine I, the "who" of divine existence. One thinks here of Jesus' words, "I and my Father are one" (John 10:30) and "I am in the Father, and the Father in me" (John 14:11). There is then within the Trinity a sharing of knowledge which is complete, having no beginning, no ending, no becoming. God *is* as the eternally existing, tri-hypostatic Divine Person—ideas captured in the verses of the *Great Canon* of Saint Andrew of Crete[17]:

---

15 Cf. Jean Zizioulas, *Being as Communion: Studies in Personhood and the Church* (London: Darton, Longman & Todd, 2004).

16 It might seem strange to speak of otherness in God, but the very presence of personhood indicates it. This has been a difficult point for theology, since it seems that this idea undermines the unity of the Trinity. As a result many have given unity an ontological priority over person as if God existed solely as noncontingent, self-explicable, unified substance rather than in the freedom of his capacity as radically other person among radically other persons. See Zizoulas and McPartland, *Communion and Otherness*, 36.

17 Bulgakov mentions the canon in passing. Sergius Bulgakov, *The Bride of the Lamb*, trans. Boris Jakim (Grand Rapids: Eerdmans, 2002), 43.

> Let us glorify the Father, exalt the Son, and faithfully worship the Divine Spirit, inseparable Trinity, Unity in essence, as the Light and Lights, the Life and Lives, giving life and light to the ends of the earth.[18]

### b. *Creation out of Nothing*

If God is the fullness of being, then it is impossible that anything else should exist outside of God. The "nothing" of Genesis 1 cannot be a something into which God deposits creation. It is not a space surrounding, containing, complementing, or limiting God. "'Out of nothing' means … that there is no matter or force that could contain the possibility of the world and could assure the world a place *alongside* God, *outside of* or *apart from* God."[19]

> It is impossible to imagine that, *before* creation, there "was" a nothing that was like a kind of emptiness, a sack into which, the latter, upon creation, all the forms of being were poured. Such a state of divine being *before* or *outside* the creation of the world simply did not exist and could not have existed, just as there was no emptiness and no such sack.[20]

Nor can the biblical phrase "in the beginning" be taken as a kind of temporal marker. It is not a point before which there was no time. The whole notion of the beginning of time is absurd since time is simply a measure of temporality, the space between two events, and always presupposes a before and an after. What, then, is the "before" of the beginning? There is none. The beginning is rather the eternal, timeless being of God.

In that sense, creation must arise out of God as an act of self-actualization or self-revelation of his nature. But not as some kind of

---

18 Andrew of Crete, *The Great Canon* (Jordanville, NY: Holy Trinity Monastery, n.d.), 34.

19 Bulgakov, *Bride of the Lamb*, 43.

20 Ibid., 44.

divine first cause.[21] God is not the world's "first mover,"[22] since he exists above the world and is not part of its being, and he is not a "first cause," since the mechanistic idea of cause and effect violates the personal nature of divine being. God did not cause the world; he created it. As Bulgakov puts it, creation is released into an existence of its own from the depths of God's own being, an act of divine love, divine self-determination

> by which the hypostatic God, eternally possessing this divine world as his own nature,[23] *releases* it from the depths of hypostatic being into *self-being*, makes it the cosmos in the truest sense, *creates* the world "out of nothing," that is, out of Himself, out of his own divine content.[24]

This line of thinking has been characterized as a form of panentheism,[25] a recently rearticulated view of God's relationship to the world,[26] according to which "the Being of God includes and penetrates the whole universe,

---

21 The notion of cause is difficult in connection with the eternality of God, since it presupposes a cause of the cause as well as a spatio-temporal context within which causality operates. According to Bulgakov, "The doctrine of God as the *cause* of the world, which acts upon the world but also interacts with it in some way, is only a monstrous misunderstanding, a theological temptation which replaces the revelation of the living and personal God with the doctrine of an impersonal mechanism of causality." Ibid., 220.

22 The idea of a first mover or prime mover was discussed by Thomas Aquinas and before him by Aristotle in book 12 of his *Metaphysics* as "something which moves other things without itself being moved by anything."

23 Indeed a number of the Fathers did explore and develop the idea of the divine world. Saint Gregory of Nazianzen uses the phrase "images of the world"; i.e., God's thoughts of the world. Or "when he willed it, the Creator gave substance to and produced his eternally preexisting knowledge of beings." Maximus Confessor, "The Four Hundred Chapters on Love," in *Maximus Confessor: Selected Writings*, ed. George Berthold (New York: Paulist Press, 1985), 75–76.

24 Bulgakov, *Bride of the Lamb*, 48.

25 Knight presents Eastern Christian teaching as a strong form of panentheism. Christopher C. Knight, "Emergence, Naturalism, Panenthesim: An Eastern Christian Perspective," in *All That Is: A Naturalistic Faith for the Twenty-First Century; A Theological Proposal with Responses from Leading Thinkers in the Religion-Science Dialogue*, ed. A. R. Peacocke and Philip Clayton (Minneapolis: Fortress, 2007), 83.

26 Michael W. Brierley, "Naming a Quiet Revolution: The Pantheistic Turn in Modern Theology," in *In Whom We Live and Move and Have Our Being: Panentheistic Reflections on God's Presence in a Scientific World*, ed. Philip Clayton and A. R. Peacocke (Grand Rapids: Eerdmans, 2004).

so that every part of it exists in God and (as against pantheism) that God's being is more than, and is not exhausted by, the universe."[27]

I believe that we can allow this characterization to stand as long as it is qualified. An acceptable form of panentheism will not lead to an ontological physicalism[28] nor to an emergentist monism[29] that entirely eliminates the divine from the world by assuming that "everything can be broken down into whatever physicists deem ultimately to constitute matter/energy … No extra entities or forces, other than the basic four forces of physics."[30] This reductionist approach simply replaces the concept of God with that of matter and energy, and brackets the question of divine immanence. Moreover, panentheism should not be taken to imply a naturalism (theistic or otherwise) that replaces God's personal action in the world with the laws of nature or limits that influence to an occasional redirection of those laws. To suggest that God continually and only creates through natural processes, allowing new realities to emerge,[31] confuses the God-given ability/freedom of creation to self-actualize with divine action itself and eliminates the possibility of divine response to events in the created order. Finally, panentheism must not be construed in such a way as to suggest divine becoming; that is, that God, in his essence, is being changed by the evolution of the created order. We may well speak of God's self-limiting and self-emptying act of creation, but to, for that reason, throw over the idea of divine impassibility, as if divinity contained even the "slightest trace of time, generation, and emergence,"[32] would

---

27 A. R. Peacocke and Philip Clayton, *All That Is: A Naturalistic Faith for the Twenty-First Century; A Theological Proposal with Responses from Leading Thinkers in the Religion-Science Dialogue* (Minneapolis: Fortress Press, 2007), 22.

28 Philip Clayton and P. C. W. Davies, *The Re-Emergence of Emergence: The Emergentist Hypothesis from Science to Religion* (New York: Oxford University Press, 2006), 2.

29 Cf. Peacocke and Clayton, *All That Is*, 12–16.

30 Ibid., 12.

31 A hypothesis that envisions the continual (re)combination of particles and aggregates into evermore complex systems which posses novel properties irreducible to and unpredictable from the lower-level entities and which exert downward causation affecting their lower-level constituents. Clayton and Davies, *Re-Emergence of Emergence*, 2.

32 Alexei V. Nesteruk, "The Universe as Hypostatic Inherence in the Logos of God: Panentheism in the Eastern Orthodox Perspective," in *In Whom We Live and Move and Have Our Being*, ed. Philip Clayton and Arthur Peacocke (Grand Rapids: Eerdmans, 2004), 169.

be to deny the absolute transcendence of God and render panentheism inconceivable in an Orthodox context.

Panentheism, even when qualified as above, still leaves unresolved the tension between the immanence and the transcendence of God. Yet that immanence and transcendence is precisely what the Holy Scriptures teach. Consider the words of the prophet Jeremiah, "I am a God who is near, says the Lord, and not a God afar off. If someone shall be hidden in secret places, is it not I that shall also see him? Do I not fill heaven and earth? says the Lord" (Jer 23:23,24 LXX). The Psalmist puts it this way. "Where could I go from Your Spirit? Or flee from Your face? If I should ascend into heaven, You would be there; If I should descend into Hades, You would be there" (Ps 138 (139):7–8 LXX). And Saint Paul affirms that "he is before all things, and by him all things consist" (Col 1:17). How then can this dual truth of divine transcendence and immanence be articulated? Two complementary paths have been explored by the Eastern Church. One involves the distinction between the *Logos* and the *logoi* of creation. The other is based on the difference between God's essence and his energies.

The first of these was developed primarily by Saint Maximus the Confessor (580–662). Maximus begins with the creation of all things by Christ the *Logos* (John 1:1–3). Each created entity is preexistent as *logos* (word or thought) in God, all of which are summarized and unified by the *Logos.*[33] It is this preexistence in God's thought that "safeguards their unity in Him." At the same time, the "differentiation and the mobility of created beings, also ordered by God, safeguard their independence and individual existence,"[34] each having been given its own *logos*, "which is God's intention for that thing, its inner essence, that which makes it distinctively itself and at the same time draws it toward the divine realm."[35]

33 Cf. Andrew Louth, "The Cosmic Vision of Saint Maximos the Confessor," in *In Whom We Live and Move and Have Our Being: Panentheistic Reflections on God's Presence in a Scientific World*, ed. Philip Clayton and A. R. Peacocke (Grand Rapids: Eerdmans, 2004).

34 Lars Thunberg, *Microcosm and Mediator: The Theological Anthropology of Maximus the Confessor*, 2nd ed. (Chicago: Open Court, 1995), 75.

35 Kallistos Ware, "God Immanent yet Transcendent: The Divine Energies according to Saint Gregory Palamas," in *In Whom We Live and Move and Have Our Being: Panentheistic Reflections on God's Presence in a Scientific World*, ed. Philip Clayton and A. R. Peacocke (Grand Rapids: Eerdmans, 2004), 160.

The *logoi* are both created (as in each created entity) and uncreated (as subsisting eternally in God's will). As such the *Logos* is at once the transcendent source of created being and the immanent presence of divine intention.

The second path distinguishes between God's essence and his energies.[36] Saint John of Damascus (ca. 676–787), for example, begins with the fact that God, who is without form, immaterial and uncircumscribed, has no spatial dimension. "For He is His own place, filling all things and being above all things, and Himself maintaining all things."[37] Yet we can speak of God being or acting in this or that place, if by that we mean those places where God's energy becomes manifest. "For He penetrates everything without mixing with it, and imparts to all His energy."[38] Similarly, both Saint Basil and Saint Gregory of Nyssa teach that "in the world *only the Divine energies*, the active forces of the Divine goodness, are manifested and operate."[39]

It was Saint Gregory Palamas (1296–1359) who did the most to develop this idea, and his approach was accepted as the teaching of the church by councils in 1347 and 1351. According to Palamas, "The divine essence and the divine energy are everywhere inseparably present," remaining totally undivided. At the same time, however, he states that no created being can participate in God's essence. If that is the case, how can created being be united with God and become partakers of the divine nature (2 Pet 1:4)? The answer can be found in a threefold distinction.[40]

36 The idea of the energies of God does not imply that God is some kind of energy being, but rather that God is able to manifest himself in time and space by means of his energies. This is often compared to the energy of a fire, which can make a piece of iron glow red without at the same time being the fire itsef. What then is the difference between the fire and the glowing energy in the iron? In other words, energy is a projection of God into the created world. Another analogy is that between the sun and light. We see the sun as the source of light and warmth and are still able to distinguish between the sun itself and the warmth and light it emits.

37 John of Damascus, Ch. 13 in "An Exact Exposition of the Orthodox Faith," in *Hilary of Poitiers; John of Damascus*, vol. 9 of *A Select Library of the Nicene and Post-Nicene Fathers of the Christian Church*, 2nd series, ed. Philip Schaff and Henry Wace (Grand Rapids: Eerdmans, 1975), http://www.ccel.org/ccel/schaff/ npnf209.iii. iv.i.xiii.html.

38 Ibid.

39 Cited by Georges Florovsky, "The Idea of Creation in Christian Philosophy," Holy Trinity Orthodox School, http://www.holytrinitymission.org/books/english/theology_creation_florovsky_e.htm (italics in the original).

40 Ware, "God Immanent yet Transcendent," 163.

> Three realities pertain to God: essence, energy, and the triad of divine hypostases. As we have seen, those privileged to be united to God so as to become one spirit with Him—as St. Paul said, "He who cleaves to the Lord is one spirit with Him" (1 Cor 6:17)—are not united to God with respect to His essence, since all the theologians testify that with respect to his essence God suffers no participation. Moreover, the hypostatic union is fulfilled only in the case of the Logos, the God-man. Thus, those privileged to attain union with God are united to Him with respect to his energy; and the "spirit," according to which they cleave to God and are one with Him, is and is called the uncreated energy of the Holy Spirit, but not the essence of God.[41]

Accordingly there are three types of union/participation: the inner-trinitarian unity according to *essence* that unites the three persons of the Godhead, the union according to *hypostasis* that united humanity and divinity in the single person of Jesus Christ, and the union according to *energy* by means of which a human being can be made one with God without losing his own distinctiveness. These energies, then, are "the deifying powers which proceed from God and come down to us, creating substance, giving life, and granting wisdom."[42] Even though we are not able to penetrate the essence of God, we are able to perceive and participate in the energies. This is how God descends and makes himself known while remaining absolutely transcendent. This is how God can remain wholly other and still be present and continuously active in the world.

Releasing the world to *be* on its own was not simply an extension of his own eternal being; the result of that would have been something eternal and divine, since he is already everything that exists. So the only way God could have created the world would have been to release it into

---

41 Saint Gregory Palamas, "Topics of Natural and Theological Science and on the Moral and Ascetic Life: One Hundred and Fifty Texts," in *The Philokalia: The Complete Text*, vol. 4, comp. Saint Nikodimos of the Holy Mountain and Saint Makarios of Corinth, trans. and ed. G. E. H. Palmer, Philip Sherrard, and Kallistos Ware (London: Faber & Faber, 1995), 380.

42 Saint Gregory Palamas, *The Triads*, The Classics of Western Spirituality (Mahwah, NJ: Paulist, 1983), 94.

a limited, subeternal, telocentric mode of existence within God.[43] The best way to describe this limitation is to speak of creation's potential or its becoming. In other words, creation is not perfect or complete[44]; it has not yet reached its divinely predetermined destiny. It is constantly moving toward that goal as evidenced in creation's freedom to self-actualize.

In this ability to self-actualize, creation bears the stamp of the Creator, revealing God and possessing a limited creative faculty. We note that in the Genesis account the earth brings forth, the waters bring forth, and the animals procreate (Gen 1:12,21,22). For that reason it is possible to see the six days of creation as a progressive self-actualization of creation under God's direction, one unified act of the triune God, which continues until creation has reached its appointed end in Christ.

One aspect of creation that is special is the creation of human beings. Note that this happens in connection with a specific, midcreation "decision" by which the Godhead chooses to create humankind in his own image and after his likeness (Gen 1:26). So this aspect of creation is indeed special. But not only in that the earth gives rise to the body, but in the inbreathing of divine breath, by which the human being becomes a person. Again we have the idea of God releasing something of himself, of his person, in order to create. Put differently, God replicates himself in human being. Human beings (and angels) are the only creatures that are a hypostasization of the divine will. Thus human beings take on the *personal* character of the Trinity. "God is the creator of his own living images, persons according to his image in its tri-hypostatic character."[45]

> In the creation of persons, of hypostatic spirits, human and angelic, God repeats Himself, as it were, creates *co-I's* for Himself in his hypostatic image, breathing into them the breath of his own divine life … This creation is transcendent and unfathomable for the human understanding in as much as it takes place beyond our being, and our very being is

---

43 "Telocentric" is a mode of existence centered on the achievement of some ultimate *telos* or destiny, in this case true communion with God.

44 Of course, this should not be taken to mean that the prelapsarian human being was already subject to death and lust, those came after the Fall as the natural consequences of sin.

45 Bulgakov, *Bride of the Lamb*, 87.

> conditioned by God's creative act. But our thought is capable of encompassing the idea of the *living participation* of the creaturely I in the divine spirit.[46]

The idea that God has created man in his own image[47] tells us something about who man is and not simply *what* he is. As person the human being cannot exist in isolation; he exists in communion and for that reason each person is something unique and unrepeatable.[48] The claim to personhood is a claim to uniqueness; "I" exists only once as an individual, personalized concretization of human being. As such the human being is inherently valuable, loved, and created in the image of God.

> The idea of the inviolability of the human being as such, so closely connected with our current concept of the person, originates in the Old Testament, where it appears in connection with the creation of the human being in God's image. Because of being created in the image of God, the human being, every human being, shares in God's own sanctity ... Thus, the origin of our idea of the inviolability of the human being as person lies in the biblical belief in Creation. The dignity belonging to every human being as such is founded in the divine intention for humanity. In other words, the statement about the human being's creation in the image of God must be read as a statement about human *destiny*.[49]

Uniqueness, however, does not imply perfection. Like the rest of creation humankind is imperfect, but unlike its fellow creatures the human has the potential to become like God, not in God's nature, but in the fullness of his person.[50] Humanity is given the possibility to *be* uniquely,

---

46 Ibid.

47 Or as Zizioulas insists, in the image of the Trinity, *imago Trinitatis*. Zizioulas and McPartland, *Communion and Otherness*, 248.

48 Ibid., 166–67.

49 Wolfhart Pannenberg and Niels Henrik Gregersen, *The Historicity of Nature: Essays on Science and Theology* (West Conshohocken, PA: Templeton Foundation Press, 2008), 124.

50 This idea is summarized in the great Eucharistic prayer of the Liturgy of Saint

with a creative faculty, and the real possibility of self-actualization. This freedom is considered by some to be the core aspect of human personhood. Harry Frankfurt suggests that the "essential difference between persons and other creatures is to be found in the structure of a person's will."[51] The defining characteristic is the ability to have second-order volitions, which takes place when a person "wants simply to have a certain desire or when he wants a certain desire to be his will."[52]

But this freedom carries with it the potential for both good and evil, not as necessities but as possibilities. Unwilling to acknowledge the source of their own I-ness, the self-aware human being understandably tends to think that the ground of their existence is their ability or freedom to posit their own being and claim uniqueness. Although this is an illusion, being on their own, they pretend to posit their own existence, or rather simply assume it by bracketing the question of their own ontology and assume their unrepeatability, all the while ignoring their indebtedness, their relationship to the Creator. Yet "absolute uniqueness is indicated only through an affirmation arising freely from a relationship [with God] which constitutes by its unbrokenness the ontological ground of being for each person."[53]

It is precisely this freedom, this ability to self-actualize, that has led to an open revolt against contingency and dependency. Using their own being as the starting point, human beings simply ignore the link to divine being. In being for themselves, they disrupt the communion with non-I (all Others). Even though they all share equality of I-ness, the lack of kenotic communion or loving interaction damages the integral nature of humankind (multi-hypostatic unity of humanity),[54] transforming non-I

---

Basil the Great: "When thou hadst fashioned man, taking dust from the earth, and hadst honored him with thine own image, O God, thou didst set him in a paradise of plenty, promising him life immortal and the enjoyment of eternal good things in the observance of thy commandments." Orthodox Church in America, *The Priest's Service Book*, 202.

51 Harry G. Frankfurt, "Freedom of the Will and the Concept of a Person," in *What Is a Person?*, ed. Michael F. Goodman, Contemporary Issues in Biomedicine, Ethics, and Society (Clifton, NJ: Humana, 1988), 128.

52 Ibid., 132.

53 Zizioulas and McPartland, *Communion and Otherness*, 111.

54 One of the foundational ideas of the Russian religious renaissance of the late nineteenth century. Integral man, humanity, is conceived of as the unity of the multi-hypostatic race of human beings. Vladimir Sergeyevich Solovyov and Boris Jakim, *Lectures on Divine Humanity* (Hudson, NY: Lindisfarne, 1995).

into a threat and making it more difficult if not impossible for them to realize their potential in God—godlikeness. Thus they fail to reach the fullness of communion, deification,[55] or living participation, either with the world of other human beings or the Divine Person. They are becoming, but in this case moving away from, a divinely given *telos*.

It is this presence of movement that introduces temporality to the created realm, measured as time—the passage from one point to the next. Even though humanity has its origin in the extratemporal timelessness of divine being (i.e., exists within and not alongside of the divine), it cannot be said that human existence is coeternal with God. However, we might say that it is infinite, not in the sense of an endless, purposeless prolongation, but rather a never-ending, irrevocable movement toward fulfillment in the eternality of God. Moreover, this temporality is hierarchical; that is, there are several levels or types of time. There is ordinary time, used for the administration of and exercise of dominion over the created order (Gen 1:26–30). There is the special, blessed time of the Sabbath, when God rested from his labors (Gen 2:1–3), as would all his children. Then there is the special and intimate time of direct communion with God, God meeting Adam and Eve in the evening in the garden (Gen 3:8) as he would meet with them later through the Incarnation and the Eucharist.

The same thing might also be said for space. In God there is no spatial dimension; however, the movement of human becoming limits creaturely existence spatially. Like temporality this spatial dimension is measured as space between discrete points. Short of its fulfillment in God who will be all in all, creation needs a place to be, a realm in which it can express its freedom to self-actualize. Since creation issues forth from the being of God, space is real, not an illusion. And by virtue of divine kenosis,

---

55 The idea of godlikeness is rooted in the distinction made between image and likness in Genesis 1:26. Having been created in the image of God, the human being has the potential of becoming like God. Obviously not like him in essence, but rather in character; i.e, to reach a union or communion with God that is so complete that it could be said of us that we are like God or that we partake of his nature (2 Pet 1:4). For this reason Saint Irenaeus—"Against Heresies," in *Ante-Nicene Fathers*, vol. 1, ed. Alexander Roberts and James Donaldson (Peabody, MA: Hendrikson, 1995)—and others "played" with human language by saying that God became man in order to help us become gods. It is from that usage that we get current terminology, *theosis* or *deification*, from the word for "God," indicating a process by which we become more and more like him, which is the ultimate purpose and destiny of human being.

space, like temporality will provide a context for becoming until it has reached entelechy.[56]

The mystery of the human realm is that it is created in the image of the divine person of God, and for that reason it exists in a multi-hypostatic, relational context which is both united and differentiated by individuality. According to Zizioulas, personhood can be viewed as both *ecstasis* and *hypostasis* of being. *Ecstasis* is "a movement toward communion which transcends the boundaries of the 'self' and thus to freedom."[57] *Hypostasis* is the bearer of its nature in its totality. We see that the notion of person is to be found only in God and that the human personhood is never satisfied until it exists as an image of God.[58] For that reason personhood cannot be understood in terms of qualities it possesses but rather in the way it relates to others.[59] The whole of creation was made in such a way as to facilitate the personal interaction between the Creator and his creatures.

### c. *The Incarnation as Divine Intervention*

We normally and correctly associate the Incarnation with the redemption of humankind. Indeed the death and resurrection of the incarnate Christ has achieved victory over the twin curses of sin and death. Yet the Incarnation does not seem to be a divine afterthought, a kind of alternative action occasioned by human fallenness. Quite to the contrary, the Scriptures clearly teach that the Incarnation was "predetermined before the creation of the world"[60] (1 Cor 2:7; Eph 1:4; 1 Pet 1:19,20), before the Fall.

> These texts make clear that the coming of the Son into the world is not only an act of God's *providential* government of the world, an act proceeding from God's interaction with the world. It is also God's primordial grace, existing before the creation of the world, that is, constituting the

56 "Time is real because it has eternity itself as its content." Bulgakov, *Bride of the Lamb*, 61.

57 Zizioulas and McPartland, *Communion and Otherness*, 213.

58 Ibid., 215.

59 Ibid., 212.

60 Sergius Bulgakov, *The Lamb of God*, trans. Boris Jakim (Grand Rapids: Eerdmans, 2008), 168.

> very foundation and goal of the world. One can even say that God created the world in order to become incarnate in it, that he created it for the sake of his Incarnation.[61]

If the Fall was not a necessity but merely a possibility of freedom, then why would the Incarnation need to be built into the very fabric of creation? Why create a world free to self-actualize and then include the inevitability of divine intervention? To answer that God simply foreknew the consequences of the human abuse of freedom and, in anticipation of it, devised a solution ahead of time, does not resolve the issue, since it does not speak to the ontological nature of the question. The whole concept of foreknowledge is a human concept, an anthropomorphism, which introduces arbitrariness into the Divine, since it implies that God could have chosen between several different ways of providing redemption. The predetermined necessity of the Incarnation points to a divine human relationship that, while it contains the need for redemption, is set in a larger context.

Why then does God want to enter the world? "In what does the inexorable predeterminedness of the Incarnation consist?"[62] We can give at least two answers. On the one hand, the limitedness of humankind makes it impossible for them to reach fulfillment (godlikeness) on their own; they need divine help.[63] On the other hand, God desires to enter into personal communion with human beings and communicate divine life so that creaturely becoming can find its end in complete communion with God.

As stated above, a person cannot be understood in terms of qualities or capabilities it possesses. Yet those qualities are important as they are lived and become ontologically personal through the hypostasis to which they belong.[64] But for that to take place, the relationship to the Creator has to be in order. It is to that end that Christ came into the world, as an

---

61 Ibid., 169.

62 Ibid., 171.

63 This idea is captured by Irenaeus when he insists that Christ became the Son of man "that man also might become the son of God." The Incarnation was God "arranging after a new manner the advent in the flesh, that he might win back (make the property of God) that human nature (*hominem*) which had departed from God." Saint Irenaeus, "Against Heresies," 424.

64 Zizioulas and McPartland, *Communion and Otherness*, 111.

example of the benefits of communion with God and to facilitate that communion.

The roots of this desired communion lie in the idea of providence and the fact that human beings are created in the image of God. Providence is God's ongoing relationship/interaction with the world, whereby he seeks to keep human becoming on its appointed track. It is not the imposition of extracreational force, but rather a kind of interaction that takes place within the world and according to its laws, God helping humanity in spite of its own sinfulness. At the same time there is a divine desire for direct and personal interaction with the world, an entering into the world on its own terms. Incarnation is the pathway to that personal contact. However, the Son of God cannot become incarnate in just any creature, it has to be the human. This is true, in part, because God has already preinscribed himself in the human being by creating him in his own image. In other words, there is a divine-human compatibility, a link, laid down before the foundations of the world, that enables this intimate and personal communion to take place. In that sense, humanity participates in the Incarnation. Of course, for this to happen the divine hypostasis has to be offered to humanity, and it has to be freely received by humanity. This condition was provided by the kenotic act of the Son and accomplished when the Virgin Mary, overshadowed by the Holy Spirit, accepted divinity and provided it with a pure form of human being.[65] Only thus could God enter into the world. And as a result Christ incarnate can be confessed as truly God and truly man.

The context of the Incarnation, then, is larger than its most obvious and concrete benefit; i.e., redemption. It also represents God's desire to commune personally with humankind in order to move creation's becoming along towards its ultimate end, its entelechy. So we have the tri-hypostatic person of God releasing the world to be on its own, breathing the life of personhood into human beings, and entering that world in order to have direct personal communion with humankind. Christ is truly Emmanuel, God with us. And this is the ultimate content of all Christian witness. The whole of the human creaturely domain is inscribed with

65 Unlike the Catholic doctrine of an immaculate conception, the Eastern Church sees Mary as the sinless culmination of the whole of the Old Testament order. A person in whom the curse of original sin had been so weakened so as to have no affect on her life and conduct.

personhood—both divine and human. Establishing and maintaining the divine-human relationship, or communion, is the very essence of becoming; God moving humanity toward its designated end—salvation/deification.[66] For this reason, establishing this relationship-Emmanuel and the human person—becomes the primary goal of mission, evangelism, and contextualization. It is in him that we move and have our being (Acts 17:28), and he has come to us in order to redeem us and in order to deify us. Surely, the gospel is communion with a person and not merely information about a person.

### *d. Ascension/Pentecost: Divine Presence-in-absence*

One more piece has to be added to this picture, since Christ is no longer physically in the world. How then are we to appropriate the things that Christ accomplished in his life, on the Cross, through the Resurrection? How is a personal relationship with one who is absent even possible? With the Ascension and his glorification, he finished his work here and reoccupied his place next to the Father. He prays that the Father will send "another Helper" (John 14:16). This occurred on Pentecost, and if that event is read in the context of Jesus' words at his last discourse, it becomes apparent that what is significant here is not just the admittedly important gifts of the Spirit (they had been manifested in the Old Testament), but rather the personal or hypostatic descent of the third Person of the Trinity. We see evidence of the personal nature of this descent in the way Jesus speaks about the Holy Spirit abiding with the disciples forever, teaching them, and reminding them of all that Christ taught them (John 14:26). The same personal character is evident in references to the Spirit's actions, such as searching, helping, groaning in prayer (Rom 2:10; 8:26), and in the possibility that he can be grieved (Eph 4:30).

If this hypostatic character is indeed the true significance of the Holy Spirit's coming, it becomes clear that it was necessary for the continuation

66 I don't want to debate the difference between salvation and deification. For a Western exposition of deification, see Daniel A. Keating, *Deification and Grace*, Introductions to Catholic Doctrine (Naples, FL: Sapientia, 2007). For an Eastern example, see Panayiotis Nellas, *Deification in Christ: The Nature of the Human Person* (Crestwood, NY: St. Vladimir's Seminary Press, 1997).

of that which was accomplished in the Incarnation; i.e., divine-human communion.

> Christ's departure from the world in the Ascension does not signify his disIncarnation and the cessation of his connection with humanity. This connection is to be actualized and confirmed, as it were, as the life of Christ in humanity and the life of humanity in Christ. And the actualization of this connection, as far as a new manifestation or renewal of Christ's Incarnation, is precisely the descent of the Holy Spirit, sent by the Father in the name of the Son, or (which is the same thing) by the Son from the Father.[67]

While distinct, the Incarnation and the Ascension are both essential parts of the process of human becoming, its divinization.[68] Thus the Incarnation and Pentecost have the same content. The Holy Spirit reveals Christ, and Christ acts in and through the Spirit, and this is now applied to all of humanity.

> The descent of the Spirit therefore signifies the fulfillment of the work of Divine Incarnation in the world and in humanity; and at Pentecost the Holy Spirit descends not upon the Virgin Mary, as at the Annunciation, and not upon Jesus, as at the Epiphany, but upon all of humanity and all of nature.[69]

The most concrete manifestations of the Holy Spirit's descent occur in the church. It is the body of Christ, by virtue of the Spirit's presence. In the church believers are molded into a multi-hypostatic whole through the ministry of the Holy Spirit. It is the Holy Spirit, who is called down to sanctify the elements at the Eucharist, transforming them into the very

---

67 Sergius Bulgakov, *The Comforter*, trans. Boris Jakim (Grand Rapids: Eerdmans, 2004), 271.

68 "Divinization" is another English rendition of the term "deification." It has nothing to do with the common ideas associated with the occult and power encounter. It is rather the idea that we, with the help of God, can progress towards godlikeness.

69 Bulgakov, *The Comforter*, 278.

presence of Christ. The Holy Spirit equips the church with a fullness of gifts enabling the faithful to witness to Christ, making *him* known to the world. This is evidenced throughout the book of Acts, the story of the Spirit facilitating proclamation of the ascended Christ.

So it is the gift of the Holy Spirit which represents a release of divine personhood, a kenotic transcendence of divine boundaries that allows Christ to remain personally present-in-absence. It is precisely in his absence that Christ can now be known by all.

## 2. On Human Personhood

Before I can explore the implications of this perspective for the task of contextualization, I will have to say just a bit more about how I understand the notion of person/personhood and its limits, as well as the idea of personal relationships. As mentioned above, the human being has been created, *hypostasized*, in the image of God and is for that reason a personal being. At this point it is important to emphasize that personhood is not secondary to the existence of some substance (human nature), but is rather the primary mode of human existence. Personhood is not established by a set of qualities, capabilities, or conditions that have been added to human being, "[as] related to ontology—it is not a quality added, as it were, to beings, something that beings 'have' or 'have not' but is *constitutive* of what can be ultimately called a 'being.'"[70] For this reason the fullness of human personal potential can only be derived from an active relationship to the Divine, the ontological foundation of each human being.[71] The notion of person is to be found only in God and that "human personhood is never satisfied with itself until it has become an image *imago Dei*."[72]

> Ultimately, therefore, a particular being is "itself"—and not another one—because of its *uniqueness* which is established in *communion* and which renders a particular being unrepeatable as it forms part of a relational existence in which it is indispensable and irreplaceable. That which, therefore, makes a particular personal

70 Zizioulas and McPartland, *Communion and Otherness*, 213.

71 Ibid., 111.

72 Ibid., 215.

> being itself—and thus be at all—is, in the final analysis *communion, freedom,* and *love* ...[73]

However, as they appear in the spatio-temporal realm, each individual *has* been created in the image of God, each equivaluable and unique. Creaturely personhood, then, is not graduated. We are not dealing with a range from person to nonperson, but rather personhood as a given for each created human entity, each with the same potential for full realization in Christ. Obviously, then, any subjugation of another person justified by a denial of unique and inviable personhood would violate the biblical course I am following. Nevertheless there is movement, there is becoming. If, as I have insisted, the full potential of personal being can only be realized within the context of relationships, there would, at the very least, have to be evidence of a natural movement toward communion with other human beings,[74] and this movement would have to be the most fundamental, the most essential indication of personhood.

In order to make such a move, a person would have to be *self-aware*.[75] This awareness includes a recognition of various dimensions of existence including one's self; that is, the I, the mind and the will, the physical body, and the external world of objects, and in particular the equivaluable other, non-I. A person knows that they exist in contrast to or over against other things and persons. So the ability to distinguish the self from the other entities of creation is part of what we mean by being a person, and it also goes a long way to defining how each person crafts their own identity. Much of how one views the self is determined by interaction with the non-I and the general environment. I, then, is a composite of multiple layers of awareness, which is conceptualized as an indivisible, unique

---

73 Ibid., 214–15.

74 Zizioulas refers to this part of human existence as *ekstasis*, the movement toward communion which transcends the boundaries of self and thus reaches freedom. Ibid., 213.

75 "Human beings possess the casual capacity for *self-reflexivity*. That is, people are able to make themselves the objects of their own reflection and evaluation. In this way, humans are not only conscious animals, but also, importantly, are self-conscious animals ... aware of themselves as objective beings living" in the world. Christian Smith, *What Is a Person? Rethinking Humanity, Social Life, and the Moral Good from the Person Up* (Chicago: University of Chicago Press, 2010), 51. See also Mark R. Leary, *The Curse of the Self: Self-Awareness, Egotism, and the Quality of Human Life* (New York: Oxford University Press, 2004), 3–24.

individual, but which is in fact a temporal, spatially limited construct that is constantly being shifted by ongoing interaction with other individuals, groups, and societies. In that light, a relationship begins with a desire for or an agreement to negotiate intimacy with non-I by sharing knowledge, by shortening the distance between non-I and I; a sharing of one's own self-awareness.

So the first, and perhaps most basic move in the direction of communion is to acknowledge the other, non-I, as a person. While this is often done with little or no forethought, "I" must have, at least in the spatio-temporal realm, some idea of what constitutes the basic characteristics of personhood in order to make such an assessment. While many have attempted such a rudimentary catalogue,[76] the four conditions proposed by Simon Evnine will serve as a convenient starting point for my own remarks.[77]

## a. *Finitude/Infinitude*

> Persons are spatiotemporally located, causally efficacious particulars. This condition does not, by itself, imply that persons must be material beings. It leaves open the possibility that there may be immaterial, but located and causally efficacious beings. But, taken in conjunction with a background of commonly accepted metaphysical views, this condition does imply that persons must be material. I shall assume they are in what follows, though I believe that, if one thinks one can make sense of immaterial persons at all, everything I say will be transposable into

76 One recent approach uses an emergentist model to suggest that thirty increasingly more complex, personal capacities variously combine and emerge to newer and higher levels from "the human body, particularly from the human brain, as it operates in its material and social environment." Smith, *What Is a Person?*, 42. Of course any talk of lower and higher levels of personhood raises justifiable concern and, recognizing this, Smith clarifies: "The critical realist language of *higher* and *lower* should *not* be read literally as referencing spatial relations or evaluatively as judgments of better and worse. Higher is a metaphor highlighting 'movements' of emergence through different strata of the real. This can be simplified by thinking in terms of an 'upwardly moving' process in keeping with established critical realist discourse." Ibid., 33.

77 Simon Evnine, *Epistemic Dimensions of Personhood* (New York: Oxford University Press, 2008).

> that key. In talking of spatiotemporal location, I mean to assert a location within the spatiotemporal universe, and not coextensive with it. Thus, I take the condition to imply that persons are spatiotemporally finite and I take this, in turn, to imply that they are finite in their various capacities, including their epistemic capacities.[78]

To begin with, then, a person is going to have a physical or material presence bounded by time and space. As mentioned above, I believe that God has created human beings within a spatially and temporally limited context. So, to that degree, I agree with Evnine's basic condition of finitude.

However, several important caveats need to be registered. On the one hand, the materiality and finitude of human persons do not represent the fullness of personhood. That is embodied in the condition of becoming. Human beings may well be spatially and temporally limited, but their *telos* points to something beyond both: an expression of the ever-present image of God, the Divine Spirit, which anticipates eternity with God.

On the other hand, the current finitude of humanity does not rule out the existence of divine personhood and the possibility of human communion with it. If that Divine Person is the source of human personhood, having breathed his Spirit into human beings, having created them in his own image, then we must assume the presence of a supramaterial divine element in the human person. This leads to the difficult question of a personal presence in the absence of a material body or what Zizioulas calls the "presence-in-absence paradox."[79]

I recently missed six weeks of a semester because of surgery. During my time recuperating at home, I tried to maintain contact with my students by listening to recordings of their discussions, sharing in email and online chat sessions, and the like. It seems as though the efforts were appreciated, and a colleague, who led a group in my absence, said to me after, "You are the most present absent professor I have ever known." Like artists and musicians, whose presence is mediated through their work (a creative expression of themselves), I sustained a dynamic presence among the students by releasing something of myself into the void created

78 Ibid., 10–11.

79 Zizioulas and McPartland, *Communion and Otherness*, 219.

by physical absence. My person was projected invisibly, perceived and engaged by the students, allowing for a degree of communion.

This phenomenon indicates the possibility of different modes or even degrees of presence. An object is present through its physical, empirical features and thus becomes part of the observable context. Persons are, at least in part, known in the same way and are present by means of the boundaries of their physical being. However, a physically present person can and often is depersonalized[80]; that is, reduced in the mind of the subject to the status of a thing and treated as if they were a nonperson[81] by having the potential for communion denied or simply ignored. So the mere presence of empirical boundaries does not constitute full personal presence. But neither does its absence eliminate the presence of personhood, since personal presence is established by the transcending of those very boundaries.

> Insofar, therefore, as the human person is an entity whose being or particularity is realized by way of transcendence of its boundaries in an event of communion, its personhood reveals itself as *present*. But in so far as the human person is a being whose particularity is established *also* by its boundaries (a body), personhood realizes this presence as *absence*.[82]

The implications of this are that "the two components must be maintained *simultaneously* if justice is to be done to the mystery of human personhood,"[83] and that physical absence is not necessarily an impediment to knowing, communing with, another personal being. This is particularly important in the case of knowing the Divine Person. In the Incarnation the Divine Person was physically present, transcended his own boundaries and, after the Ascension, remains present precisely in his absence through the Holy Spirit and the sacraments. By ascending,

---

80 Edward Rommen, *Get Real: On Evangelism in the Late Modern World* (Pasadena: William Carey Library, 2010), 60.

81 Of course this cannot actually happen since the individual so depersonalized is a person by virtue of being.

82 Zizioulas and McPartland, *Communion and Otherness*, 219.

83 Ibid.

sending the Holy Spirit, and establishing the church, Christ released to us something of his own being, his tri-hypostatic self which mediates, projects, his person and enables communion. It is not without reason that the church is called his body, his witness in the world; that the sacraments sanctified by the Holy Spirit are his presence among us; and that he said it was expedient for him to ascend and send the Comforter (John 16:7).

## *b. Belief*

> Belief is this. I will be linking the notion of personhood to various views in epistemology that are typically expressed in terms of concepts and beliefs. One or both of the further conditions on personhood I will mention themselves imply that persons necessarily are the subjects of belief. They may also imply that persons must possess concepts. But, partially for the sake of clarity, or as parts of a pre-emptive defense of those further conditions, I will require, as an independent condition, that persons necessarily possess concepts and have beliefs. I doubt whether something could have beliefs as its only kind of mental state. In any case, I shall assume that, in having beliefs, a creature must also have those other kinds of mental states, such as desires and intentions, that form part of the same folk-psychological explanatory apparatus as beliefs.[84]

The idea of belief expresses the human ability to hold some cognitive content to be true. It presupposes the presence of concepts—mental spaces in which this content resides. This, in turn, points to the presence of logical thought processes, which lead to the conviction that certain things follow, are true. Moreover, these beliefs are not held in isolation but are taken together to form a conceptual framework or plausibility structure to which the person is committed and within which further discriminations are made.

---

84 Evnine, *Epistemic Dimensions of Personhood*, 11.

Most of us would like to think that our beliefs are either self-evident, or justified by empirical evidence or by some indubitable logical process.[85] However, beliefs held for those reasons are always arrived at within a larger context of belief, a conceptual framework according to which we accept certain evidence and arguments as valid or true. If, for example, I accept as true the statement "God exists," I might defend that conviction by arguing from the concepts of order and beauty, to the empirically evident order and beauty of the created world, and then to the necessary existence of a benevolent Creator, God. But what is apparent here is that I accept the validity of the argument based on prior commitments to the concepts of beauty and order, to the methods of observing the world, and to the reasonableness of my requirement of a Creator. The argument and evidence has to meet criteria that I have already established, which according to my expectations are likely to be true. So my insistence on the existence of God is based on a set of assumptions and beliefs that cannot be empirically verified or established with certainty. These "trusted premises, postulated axioms [and] presuppositions ... provide the suppositional grounds on which any sense of justification, proof, or verification for a given knowledge system are built."[86] It should also be noted that in the case of my assertion that God exists, another person, with another set of presuppositions, could just as easily reject the assertion, giving a different explanation of the evidence I have marshaled. Belief and disbelief are both part of this condition of personhood.

My personal argument and conclusions will also be bolstered by relationships to a community that shares the same set of presuppositions. I know myself to be in good company when I argue from the beauty of God's creation to God's existence, since that is the exact point made by the psalmist, not to mention the countless generations of the faithful, who maintain that "the heavens declare the glory of God" (Ps 19:1). Others rest sure in their rejection of this belief, knowing that it may well be held by the vast majority of, let us say, the academic and scientific communities to which they belong.

---

85 See Michael Polanyi, *Personal Knowledge: Towards a Post-Critical Philosophy* (Chicago: University of Chicago Press, 1958).

86 Christian Smith, *Moral, Believing Animals: Human Personhood and Culture* (Oxford: Oxford University Press, 2003), 46.

There is, then, a very personal dimension to the act of believing. Because a person is a being that can believe, even in the absence of empirical verification, and because persons are likely to conform their beliefs to those of the community to which they belong, there is no simply logical, evidentiary, scientific, or mathematical way of adjudicating the vast differences between conflicting beliefs without appealing to the underlying frames of conceptual reference, which are themselves not universal.

### c. *Agency*

> This asserts that persons are necessarily agents. Agency includes not only the performance of individual intentional actions but also engaging in relatively long-term plans and projects and deliberating about actions, plans, and projects.[87]

As already indicated, God released humankind to exist on its own within the limited temporal and spatial context of becoming. Within that context human beings reflect the divine image in, among other ways, their freedom to translate desire into concrete action; that is, to self-actualize. This is accomplished by the free exercise of God-given faculties such as rationality, love, and creativity, whereby the individual is able to choose what she does, says, or thinks.[88] Agency, then, is a function of human will and takes the basic form of desire-satisfaction.

As long as this is done in a matrix of relationships characterized by self-transcendence, kenotic love, and complete freedom (that is, as long as the desires of the will are focused on the other), human agency reflects its divine counterpart and contributes to becoming, moving toward humanity's *telos*. However, in the absence of unbroken relationships to the

87 Evnine, *Epistemic Dimensions of Personhood*, 14.

88 As already noted, for some this freedom of will is the primary characteristic or condition of personhood. Harry G. Frankfurt writes, "It seems to be particularly characteristic of humans … that they are able to form what I shall call 'second-order' desires … Besides wanting and choosing and being moved to do this or that, men also want to have (or not to have) certain desires and motives. No animal other than man … appears to have the capacity for reflective self-evaluation that is manifested in the formation of 'second-order desires.'" "Freedom of the Will," 128–29.

Divine and other persons' desire-satisfaction, agency itself mutates into an exercise of self-love. In this realm of self-centeredness, this reduced mode of being, others are seen as challenges to self-actualization and are either held at a distance, destroyed, or possessed. Without the non-I of divinity and the other of humanity, the I is isolated, and the very freedoms that should mark personhood—love, interaction, procreation, creativity—are distorted or even lost. Note, for example, how many late modern couples, loving only themselves, choose not to transcend their own desire for pleasure, personal freedom, and convenience and refuse the gift of life, communion, to another generation. Absent communion, personhood is distorted, and the whole array of God-given faculties is transmuted into gluttony, avarice, unspeakable sensualities; in short, all the passions against which the Fathers warned.[89]

While self-love represents a distortion, it does not eradicate the image of the personal Creator inscribed in the human spirit. Agency, even in the guise of self-love, remains a condition of personhood and in some cases does lead to expressions of love, unmercenary behavior, and self-sacrifice. However, to reach its full potential, its intended purpose, personal agency has to be transformed by communion with the Divine and instructed in the ways of self-transcendence, love, and freedom.

## *d. Morality*

> This is the ability to have beliefs about beliefs, both one's own and other people's. The ability to have beliefs about beliefs is a clear prerequisite for the kinds of social practices within which the concept of a person lives. To give a very simple example, a legal system has to have room for considering not just what people do but what they believe they are doing. Having beliefs about beliefs, in this situation and in other, more quotidian ones, is part of being able to explain persons' actions. So, having second-

89 John Cassian, "On the Eight Vices," in *The Philokalia: The Complete Text*, vol. 1, comp. Saint Nikodimos of the Holy Mountain and Saint Makarios of Corinth, trans. and ed. G. E. H. Palmer, Philip Sherrard, and Kallistos Ware (London: Faber & Faber, 1983), 73–93.

> order beliefs must be accompanied by having second-order desires, intentions, and so on.[90]

This condition of personhood is the foundation of human morality. It facilitates an evaluation of actions (agency) within a matrix of beliefs and obligations to which one is already committed. It is an orientation which is, or so it is believed, not determined by one's own desires and preferences, but is rather an independent moral structure by which self-actualization itself can be judged.[91] Christians would generally accept the rightness of loving one's enemy (Matt 5:44), and they do so based on a prior commitment to the authority of Jesus Christ. Possessed of this conviction, they evaluate or judge their own actions as well as those of others, even those who do not hold to the same obligation. In so doing they are supported by the members of their own Christian community. And if others accept the judgment in sufficient numbers, they lay the foundation for a generalized moral structure or social practice, which becomes part of the prevailing culture, and underscores the independence the precept is thought to have over the desires of individuals. Such structures can come to exist even in the absence of a commitment to the underlying belief; in this case, the authority of Jesus. Again we see both affirmation and tension in the overlapping requirements of individually held beliefs and those held by the various networks of interlocution in which the individual is embedded. Since second-order beliefs are a condition of personhood, the obligations accepted by others can and often do differ greatly. As is the case with beliefs, there is no simply mechanistic way of reconciling these differences. In either case, second-ordinality allows for a set of assumptions, beliefs, and expectations that exist as "internal" frames of reference and as "external" structures of social practice. "There is nowhere a human [person] can go to escape moral order. There is no way to be human except through moral order."[92]

---

90 Evnine, *Epistemic Dimensions of Personhood*, 15.

91 Smith, *Moral, Believing Animals*, 54.

92 Ibid., 148.

# 3. On Contextualization

In light of what I have said thus far, it becomes apparent that the task of evangelism is introducing the person of Christ to individual human beings who enter into communion with God, enabling them to fulfill the potential of their personhood. Doing this does not involve adapting information to a particular context, but rather establishing the context prescribed by God for the presence of Christ wherever we happen to be among the peoples of the world. Contextualization does not merely react; it creates, it establishes *a new invitational core context which (a) is host to the presence of the Divine Person, (b) is defined with the help of personhood-engaging gifts of ecclesial tradition, (c) enables conditions that facilitate communion, and (d) engages extra-ecclesial fields of personal presence.*

These several components of the process are not to be taken as a sequence. They are interrelated, mutually dependent elements of one dynamic, living unity that I am calling contextualization. They will all have to be present, operating coterminously. To speak of one (the church) is to speak of the others (the gifts of tradition). To speak of ecclesial holiness (chapter 2) is to speak of the believer's life in Christ (chapter 4). Issues and themes will bleed across my chapters, defying absolutely clean divisions. This is not a program to be implemented, but rather a life to be lived in Christ. Yet the logic of the process does allow me to identify certain nodes, concentrations of content, that when analyzed reveal the movement of the entire process. That process, when taken as a whole, is what I mean by contextualization—creating a context in which an invitation to a personal relationship with the ascended Christ can be issued.

## *a. A Context that Is Host to the Divine Person (Chapter 2)*

Obviously, if we are going to introduce someone to Christ, Christ has to be present. Here we are faced with the challenge of the physical absence of Christ. How is Christ to be introduced if he is not present? As mentioned above, a person can be present even in absence, if something of themselves is put into the void of physical absence. In the case of the ascended Christ, he has asked the Father to send the third Person of the Trinity, the Holy

Spirit, to take his place in the world, clearly a personal presence. The context for this manifestation of divine presence is the church. In it God has instituted the sacraments, in particular baptism and the Eucharist. Each of these comes with the promise of Christ's Spirit-mediated presence, which in turn generates the most essential field of divine-human presence available to humanity. He has also established the church as a multi-hypostatic unity, his own body, in which the faithful and their guests participate in a human-human field of presence under the guidance of the Spirit. The church, as the context of invitation, will have to be established, preserved, and defended against such changes or situations that would limit or even eliminate its role as the host of divine presence. This is the task of contextualization.

### *b. A Context Shaped by the Personhood-engaging Gifts of Ecclesial Tradition (Chapter 3)*

When I first began to think about contextualization, I was puzzled by the fact that most of its practitioners spent little time reflecting on the nature of context. It seemed as though they simply assumed that everyone knew what a context was, that it did not need to be defined. As a result, attention was focused on a host of things that separated people and tended to make the transfer of information difficult. In one case it was primarily linguistic differences, and contextualization became an exercise in dynamic equivalence. In another case religious dissimilarities were paramount, and the process took on the character of the comparative religious studies sustained by dialogue. Still others dealt with social or cultural variance and looked for points of entry, redemptive analogies, cultural places in which the biblical message could reside. But as I saw it, all of these models were concerned with disparate aspects of the human situation, one of the many nested layers that define every culture—each with different implications for the task of contextualization. What was missing, I thought, was a single, universal framework which applied to all people. So I suggested we consider the idea of a universal set of semantic fields which defined a kind of internal template possessed by each individual. It was at this level of template matching that effective contextualization could be achieved.[93] I was not suggesting that the other elements were unimportant; obviously language barriers have to be overcome if communication is to take place. However, driven by the conviction that one Savior was to be introduced to all peoples, I knew there had to be some point of universal, divine-human correspondence if the gospel was going to be understood.

I now believe that that point of correspondence is the universal fact of human personhood. If God exists as person and if he has replicated his own personal image in humanity, then personhood must be the divine-human link and its conditions part of what defines the core context in which an introduction to the divine person of Christ can be given and received. The other aspect of this context is its definition as church, the privileged place of divine self-manifestation in the world today. Contextualization will come into play as we seek to develop an invitational context that engages the conditions of personhood in keeping with its definition as church. It will have to direct the invitation at both the finitude and the infinitude of human beings by being, accepting, mediating both divine and human presence. It will have to invite by acknowledging and respecting the human capacity for belief, adjudicating between differing beliefs, and articulating Christian belief as means to reestablishing a conceptual framework supportive of Christian truth. Contextualization will also have to redefine, redirect, and activate forms of self-actualization that favor relationship, and establish, evaluate, and make active second-order beliefs that provide the moral setting for communion. To these ends, the church has been given a series of tools that secure, preserve, and defend the base missionary context. These gifts of tradition, such as Holy Scripture, engage the conditions of personhood and define the context in which we issue the invitation.

### c. *A Context that Enables Conditions that Facilitate Communion (Chapter 4)*

Another task of contextualization is to develop the core context in such a way as to facilitate communion, both divine-human and human-

93 Hesselgrave and Rommen, *Contextualization*, 165–68.

human. This will involve three distinct fields of presence. First, the field of divine-human communion in which the witness is brought to spiritual maturity. This can only be accomplished within a life of repentance, spiritual discipline, participation in the sacraments, and direct knowledge of God. This is the first step on the way to fully realized personhood and the ability to be completely present. It leads to self-transcendence that allows a commitment to both God and the other which is characterized by love and freedom. So a vital aspect of the process of contextualization is the spiritualization of the one mediating the invitation.

In a second field of presence, human-human communion is established between the self-transcendent witness and those who do not yet know Christ. This will be a form of service, an unmistakable expression of love, in an environment of complete freedom. But it is no small challenge. How, for example, do I challenge another person's beliefs and at the same time show myself to be a servant? Can I "require" the abandonment of self-love and still be loving, seek to redefine self-actualization, and promote freedom? But these are exactly the kinds of things contextualization will have to achieve.

Assuming the first two states of communion, a third is likely to develop, namely a field of divine-human presence into which the invitee enters. Part of the task of contextualization will be to facilitate that move, to help recognize when this is happening; that is, to help the newly reborn to negotiate his or her own life of intimacy with God.

### *d. A Context that Reaches Extra-ecclesial Fields of Human Presence (Chapter 5)*

In spite of sin-truncated personhood, human beings do make themselves present to one another and do make moves toward communion. Normally this happens in circumstances of social interaction which I have been calling fields of presence. These fields are generated in various venues or localities and are used temporarily for specific forms of interpersonal engagement. It could be a restaurant, a classroom, a factory; a family, a church; and it might involve the use of printed media, photographs, video, telephone, or even computer-mediated communication (CMC). It is into these places that the core context extends the presence of Christ via its witnesses. Because of its recent popularity CMC has become one of the newest and least explored of these fields. It is also a rather puzzling "place" since it seems to allow presence-in-absence. As such it begs special attention.

Chapter 2

# The Place of Divine Presence

If God desires to personally engage the world in Christ, it seems reasonable to ask where and how Christ is present in the world today.[94] After his ascension his physical, visual presence was removed from the active realm of our experience. Nevertheless we do speak of his continued presence in the Holy Spirit and in the sacraments of the church. How, then, can this mode of presence be concretized to the point where a personal introduction can make sense? How can this presence-in-absence become the basis for an ongoing relationship? It is to these questions of divine presence that I now turn.

## 1. Church as the Place of Divine Presence

If, as I have said, all of creation exists in God, then all of created space is in some sense sacred, occupied by God's presence. There is no part of it that does not reflect the divine will and prototype and, as such, it can all serve as a place of worship, prayers, and Christian fellowship.

However, the close link or correspondence that exists between the divine and the created order would seem to allow for a more direct or concentrated presence of God. Indeed we do notice in the Scriptures that, in addition to this general presence of God, there are specific manifestations of the Divine Person, which create especially sacred spaces and which occur under temporally and spatially limited circumstances. These are often repeated, lending the divine presence a degree of permanence or predictability.

94 Of course there have been many reports of visions that Christ has granted his followers. But these do not represent the general mode of his presence today.

> Inasmuch as the Absolute is God for the world and man, the Absolute takes upon itself the kenosis of empirical phenomenal being; God does not destroy but fulfills the foundations of creatureliness, spatiality, and temporality, which were called into being by Him Himself; and therefore He connected Himself with spatiality and temporality by a voluntary act of love and condescension, in order to come close to man: space and time exist for God too. This does not mean that space and time set a limit to His omnipotence, i.e., to His freedom; it does not mean that they are included in the absolute Essence of God; rather, it means that, insofar as God is present in the world and in man (more precisely, simply in man, for the world is Man, the anthropocosmos), He lives in space and time; and places and times are not a matter of indifference in this Being of God's. In other words, God is not present everywhere; and when He is present, He is present not by His omnipotence, but by His grace-bestowing power, and there are holy, God-chosen places as well as places forsaken by God.[95]

The burning bush mentioned in Exodus 3:2–6 speaks of a space around the bush that is sacred, thus the need for Moses to remove his shoes. The space is sacred because of the special presence of God, not the setting, the architecture, the lighting, etc. Moses' experience on the mountain while receiving the law must have been similar. Note the physical effects of the divine presence—thunder, lightning, darkness (Ex 20:18–21). These phenomena are, of course, repeated in the lives of the saints and the prophets, through whom God spoke (Isa 6), and are also associated with God's persistent presence in the Ark of the Covenant (Deut 10; Josh 3).

The same thing can be said of the tabernacle and the temple, each of which had a most holy place where God was said to meet with the priests (Ex 30:36). This space was to be carefully honored, and adorned with

95 Sergius Bulgakov, *Relics and Miracles: Two Theological Essays*, trans. Boris Jakim (Grand Rapids: Eerdmans, 2011), 15.

oils, implements, the Ark of the Covenant, an altar, vestments, etc., all of which were said to be holy by virtue of their proximity to the "dwelling" place of God. Simply touching the holy oil of the tabernacle could make both objects and persons holy (Ex 30:29). So the temple was the focal point of God's manifestation to the Old Testament community; here the lamb was slain, atonement made; here the community met God. Notice how often God is referred to as *being* in the sanctuary (Ps 68:24; 73:17; 77:13; 150:1).

There is also the most obvious manifestation of God in the Incarnation, Emmanuel, God with us. Again I observe that it is only because God is "repeated" in human beings by the divine image that the Incarnation is even conceivable. Whatever else it was, the Incarnation was a tangible, palpable person-to-person manifestation of divine being at a specific time and in a specific place.

But thinking now about our postpaschal, post-Ascension, new-covenant situation, we are bound to ask if there is a place (or places) where God manifests himself in this special way today. While his descent at Pentecost has made the Holy Spirit generally available to all, providing each individual with the potential of unmediated contact with Christ, it also gave birth to the church, in which the particular presence of Christ is made available. Here we have a known, regular, and predictable place of divine manifestation. So today the focus of God's special presence is embedded in the layers of spatial and temporal dimensions that make up the church, the body of Christ, the temple of the Spirit.

The Ascension of Christ was the only way in which his continued personal presence in the world could be guaranteed, and in which the benefits of his Incarnation, death, and resurrection could be made available to all human beings (John 16:7). Just as the Father had sent the Son, so now the Son asks the Father to send *another* Comforter, who will dwell in the faithful and will abide with them forever (John 14:16,17). This other Comforter is the third person of the tri-hypostatic unity of divine being (John 14:26). Just as the Father and the Son mutually indwell one another, so too the Holy Spirit indwells the other persons of the Trinity. The Son reveals the Father, and the Holy Spirit rests on the Son, each indwelling the other. Thus the words of one are the words of the others; the presence of one is the presence of the other two. So, for example:

"we" (the whole Divine Person) will come to them and make our home within them (John 14:23). Yet this divine presence is in particular the presence of Christ ("*I*" will come to you"; John 14:18,20), who promises to manifest himself to the faithful (John 14:21). This is also indicated in the phrase "another Comforter." The Holy Spirit is sent to continue the work of Christ the Comforter, to give witness to the Son and not himself. It is interesting to note that the Holy Spirit is the one member of the Godhead that we do not know in his own person. He was not sent to add anything to what Christ had accomplished, but rather to affirm, authenticate, make available the personal presence of Christ, and he does that within the household of God—that building, that holy temple, which is "the dwelling place of God in the Spirit" (Eph 2:22).

Jesus did indicate that these promises were conditioned upon believers keeping the commandments and so loving Christ (John 14:15,16; 15:10). Chief among those commandments is the one to love one another (John 15:1), and that we do so as a witness to the world (John 13:34,35). These commandments, of course, are not taught, learned, or kept in individualized isolation. It is the Holy Spirit who, in the context of the temple, reminds (John 14:26) and builds us together to be a dwelling place for himself (Eph 2:20–22). It is this mutuality of love that presupposes a community of love (i.e., the church), and at least one of this love's objectives enabling the world to recognize the presence of Christ in it. So without implying that the presence of the Holy Spirit is limited to the canonical boundaries of the church,[96] we can say that the witness of the Spirit to Christ's continued presence (John 16:14) is clearly located in the church. What was new at Pentecost was the creation of the church as the context of Christ's presence, enabled by the gifts of the Spirit, giving witness to the whole world. This is the body of Christ, the work of the Spirit, ground zero for the Christian witness to the world.

96 A favorite prayer in the Eastern Church is addressed to the Holy Spirit, who is said to be everywhere: "O Heavenly King, the Comforter, the Spirit of Truth, who art everywhere present and fillest all things. Treasury of Blessings and Giver of Life: come and abide in us and cleanse us from every impurity, and save our souls, O Good One." *Orthodox Daily Prayers,* (South Canaan, PA: St. Tikhon's Seminary Press, 1982), 5.

## 2. Sacrament as Concretization of the Field of Divine Presence[97]

Christ promises to manifest himself to us if we keep his commandments. The confluence of the promise of Christ's presence in the church and its witness to the world is strikingly evident in two of those commandments, namely the commandment to make disciples of all nations by teaching and baptizing them (Matt 28:19) and the commandment to celebrate the Eucharist ("*do* this in remembrance of me ...," 1 Cor 11:24,25 NIV). In each one, there is a promise of Christ's presence ("I am with you always, even unto the end of the age," and "this is my body"), and in both cases we are dealing with a sacrament. Like the other commandments, Christ's insistence upon the sacraments, that is to "do this in remembrance of me" (1 Cor 11:26) and to make disciples by baptizing (Matt 28:19), belong to and presuppose the church. When the people of God gather for the celebration of the Eucharist, they constitute the church, they are the body of Christ, in the midst of which Christ is present (Luke 24:35). When repentant sinners are baptized in faith, they are being incorporated by the ever-present Christ into his body the church. It is in this place of God's presence, the church, that the sacraments have been established as special foci of divine manifestation.

As I see it, a sacrament involves the sanctification, by the Holy Spirit, of some earthly or creaturely substance (water, wine, bread) for the revelation of divine personhood. We speak of Christ infusing water, oil, bread, and wine with his very own presence,[98] and these becoming "symbols" of divine presence. This kind of symbolism has become a problem since we have grown accustomed to making a sharp distinction between form and essence and between signifier and signified. As a result we tend to view Christian symbols, especially the sacraments, apart from the reality which they signify, as if they were, because they are symbols, less than real.

---

97 What follows is based on the Byzantine rite of the Eastern Orthodox Church. My purpose here is not to give a complete description of these rites, but rather to point out the ways in which they can be said to represent the real presence of Christ, and show how they are related to the mission of the church.

98 This idea can be expanded to include the sanctification of other things such as icons and water (as in holy water) and even on to the idea that our sacramentalism should not be limited to a set number of rites but should include the sanctification of all of creation.

Central to my understanding of symbolism is the notion of mystery. No matter what term is used (icon, symbol, type), each one is subordinated to the idea of mystery—the mystery of Christ and his saving ministry—which means both

> the very content of faith, the knowledge of the divine mystery revealed in Christ, and the saving power communicated through and in the Church. Within this theological context the symbol is the mode of the presence and action of the *mysterion*, and primarily ... of its presence and action in the liturgy, which is the privileged locus of the symbol. The symbol, then, is the very reality of that which it symbolizes. By representing, or signifying that reality, it makes it present.[99]

Through its symbols the Divine Liturgy gives us the knowledge of these saving mysteries,[100] just as, on another level of the same symbolism, the Liturgy re-represents, makes present and active, the ascension of the human soul to God and communion with him.[101]

We sometimes make use of the ideas of type and antitype or prototype to show that the symbol points us to the reality of the prototype. But our understanding goes beyond a simple pointing to an actualization, making real in the present the reality of the prototype. For example, the cross used on the Feast of the Elevation of the Precious and Life-Giving Cross is usually a wooden cross set in a bed of flowers. The symbol points to and makes real to us the reality of the cross on which our salvation was accomplished—the symbol becoming for us the reality it represents.

Alexander Schmemman suggests that we look at this in terms of *eschatological symbolism*, in which the symbol fulfills the reality it

---

99 Alexander Schmemann, *Liturgy and Tradition: Theological Reflections of Alexander Schmemann*, ed. Thomas Fisch (Crestwood, NY: St. Vladimir's Seminary Press, 2003), 122–23.This actually represents a different way of apprehending reality, a different worldview.

100 It should be noted that according to Orthodox thinking, the text of the liturgical services of the church represent definitive, dogmatic affirmations. This reflects the conviction that since the texts have been used throughout the centuries and the world, false teachings will have been noticed and expunged. Thus, sections of the Liturgy, for example, can be cited as authoritative evidence of some particular teaching.

101 Ibid., 23.

represents, the reality of the symbol fulfilled especially in the sacrament. "The essential particularity of the eschatological symbolism is the fact that in it the very distinction between sign and signified is simply ignored."[102] The whole point of the eschatological symbolism is that in it the sign and that which it signifies are one and the same thing. For example, at one point during the Liturgy the clergy and servers process and then reenter the sanctuary. This liturgical entrance is our, or rather, the church's entrance to heaven where we do not simply symbolize the presence of the angels, but we actually join them in their unceasing glorification of God.

Schmemann suggests another possibility, *epiphanal symbolism*; i.e., the symbol as an epiphany of God's holiness and presence. This is a radically different view of the relationship between signifier (A) and signified (B). It is not semantic (A means B), not representative (A represents B), not causal (A is the cause of B), but rather the whole of A expresses, communicates, reveals, manifests the reality of B, without losing its own ontological reality, without being dissolved in another *res*.[103]

So, in this way of thinking, the dichotomy of form and essence is essentially overcome and we speak of form as the likeness or the pattern of reality. We refer to baptism, for example, as the likeness and the pattern of Christ's death and resurrection. The "likeness" is at the same time the revelation of the "essence." Baptism being performed in the likeness and after the pattern of the death and resurrection therefore *is* death and resurrection. Baptism *is* what it represents, because what it represents is *true*. Again we see the epiphanic nature or function which reveals the essence, that which truly is. It is an actual dying and rising again. "It was the gift not of something resulting from these events, but of that unique and totally new possibility, truly to die with Christ, truly to be raised with Him to newness of life."[104]

Similarly we speak of the elements of the Eucharist as the likeness, the reality of Christ's body. By the operation of the Holy Spirit, the "essence" is revealed in the "form," the form-essence distinction is overcome, the elements are the very reality they symbolize. The bread and the wine *are*

---

102 Ibid., 127.

103 Alexander Schmemann, *For the Life of the World: Sacraments and Orthodoxy* (Crestwood, NY: St. Vladimir's Seminary Press, 2004), 141.

104 Alexander Schmemann, *Of Water and the Spirit* (Crestwood, NY: St. Vladimir's Seminary Press, 2003), 58.

Christ's body and blood, and these concrete materials are used by God to mediate the present reality of the Savior. Not that the elements are miraculously transformed into something else. Christ did not come to "replace 'natural' matter with some 'supernatural' and sacred matter, but to restore it and to fulfill it as the means of communion with God."[105] "The fulfillment of the Eucharist is in the communion and the transformation of man for which it is given."[106] Notice how at the breaking of bread the eyes of the disciples were opened and they knew Christ (Luke 24:30,31). So in the consecrated bread and wine we are shown the resurrection of Christ,[107] we see the true light, and receive the heavenly Spirit,[108] as well as forgiveness and eternal life.[109] To partake of this Mystery is to participate in the life of Christ, to actually know him, to be in his presence.

We need to say a bit more about the mode of this presence. Just before communion is given to the people, the priest prays, "Attend, O Lord Jesus Christ our God, from thy holy dwelling place and from the glorious throne of thy kingdom, and come to sanctify us, O thou that sittest with the Father above, and that art *invisibly* present here with us ..."[110] The invisibility of his presence raises the question of presence-in-absence. If Christ sits "above" with the Father, how can he be present with us during the Liturgy? If his presence is "invisible," how are we going to introduce anyone to him? As we saw above, the presence of person is not limited to physical presence. Presence-in-absence can be maintained if the person injects something of himself or herself into the void created by physical absence. In the Eucharist the Holy Spirit (who is with Christ as part of the personal unity of the Trinity) is put into the void created by the Ascension and mediates the presence of Christ. The gospel comes to us as the person of Christ and is perceptible as such because human beings, having been created as persons in the image of God, are predisposed to divine-human communion. We have been given the ability to sense the presence of another person, penetrate their being, even in absence. So when the Holy Spirit transfigures

---

105 Ibid., 49.
106 Ibid., 50.
107 Orthodox Church in America, *The Priest's Service Book*, 161.
108 Ibid., 162.
109 Ibid., 161.
110 Ibid. (italics added)

and sanctifies the visible and insignificant elements of communion offered by the church,

> we experience the unconfused interpenetration of created and uncreated life, of life and death, of movement and motionlessness, of mystery and rational thought, of miracle and law, of freedom and nature.
>
> In the end, one cannot tell if things invisible are more perceptible than created things.[111]

That manifestation, while itself invisible, is "seen" by the faithful, not externally but rather within them, Christ taking shape in them by the personal interpenetration, the illumination of the Holy Spirit, the communion of grace.[112] In that transfiguration, Christ is personally present and represents a reality to which the faithful can give witness.

It is clear, then, that Christ is particularly present in the sacraments. For that reason there can be no contrasting of the sacrament with the gospel, as if we expected the sacrament to do what the gospel is supposed to do. If the gospel is Christ and if Christ is present in the sacrament, then the sacrament is the gospel.

Yet there remains the question of their link to the mission of the church. In the case of the Eucharist, we can say that it is celebrated on behalf of the world. According to D. Passakos, "The Eucharist in Paul was understood not only as an icon of the *eschata*, but also as a missionary event with cosmic and social consequences. The Eucharist for him was not only the sacrament of the church but also the sacrament of the world."[113] This is expressed in several ways throughout the Liturgy, the context in which the Eucharist is set. For example, during the Service of Preparation the Lamb a cube-shaped piece of the bread (later fractured and distributed to the faithful) is cut crosswise while the priest intones

---

111 Vasileios, *Hymn of Entry: Liturgy and Life in the Orthodox Church*, Contemporary Greek Theologians 1 (Crestwood, NY: St. Vladimir's Seminary Press, 1984), 68.

112 Ibid., 76.

113 Cited by Petros Vassiliadis, *Eucharist and Witness: Orthodox Perspectives on the Unity and Mission of the Church* (Brookline, MA: Holy Cross Orthodox Press, 1998), 63, n. 13.

the words, "Sacrificed is the Lamb of God, who taketh away the sin of the world for the life and salvation of the world."[114] Near the end of the Preparation the celebrant refers to Christ as the food of the whole world:

> O God, our God who didst send forth the heavenly Bread, *the food of the whole world*, our Lord and God Jesus Christ, Savior, Redeemer, and Benefactor, blessing and sanctifying us, do thou thyself bless this offering and receive it upon thy most heavenly altar. Remember, as thou art good and the Lover of man, those who brought it and keep us uncondemned in the celebration of thy Divine Mysteries.[115]

The litanies and prayers of the Liturgy include prayers for the world, civil authorities, the sick, the suffering, the captives, and beg God for plentiful harvest, the cessation of war, protection from natural disasters, mercy, peace, and salvation. Typical of these world-encompassing prayers is the one that comes just after the anaphora:

> Remember, O Lord, the city in which we dwell, every city and country; those who in faith dwell in them. Remember O Lord, travelers by land, by sea, by air, the sick and the suffering; captives and their salvation ...[116]

The choir responds with "and all mankind" to solidify the universal intent of the prayer.

After the Great Entrance the elements of bread and wine are placed on the altar and the great Eucharistic Prayers of Thanksgiving are said. This is followed by a "remembering" of the saving works, the Cross, the grave, the Resurrection, the Ascension, the Second Coming, at which point the elements are raised in the air and presented to God "on behalf of *all* and for *all*."[117] In celebrating the Eucharist we proclaim Christ's

---

114 Orthodox Church in America, *The Priest's Service Book*, 103.
115 Ibid., 111 (italics added).
116 Ibid.
117 Ibid., 146 (italics added).

death and confess his resurrection until he comes.[118] This proclamation has as its intended recipients not just the faithful, but the whole world to which the gospel is addressed. The text of the Liturgy explicitly states that this reasonable worship is being offered for the world,[119] that some benefit will accrue to the world because the Liturgy has been celebrated. The Liturgy and the Eucharist are an announcement to the world that Christ, the ascended one, is present, is here with us, ready to engage anyone who approaches. And when at the end of the Liturgy the faithful are dismissed, it is to go into the world as witnesses of what they have actually seen and received. As Archimandrite Meletios Webber puts it, "Having been touched by God, we go out into the world to proclaim the kingdom to all nations—not with our words or actions, but by who we are, or more correctly, who we have become through the actions of the Holy Spirit."[120]

The Divine Liturgy is "undoubtedly the starting point of Christian mission, the springboard of the church's witnessing exodus to the world."[121] It is a fundamentally missionary act, celebrated on behalf of the world and providing a context in which the living Lord can be personally encountered. If that presence is, at least in part, intended to benefit nonbelievers, then the Liturgy becomes a place of missionary encounter with the immanent Savior. Mission, then, depends

> primarily on our being real witnesses to the joy and the peace of the Holy Spirit, to that new life of which we are made partakers in the Church. The Church is the sacrament of the Kingdom—not because she possesses divinely instituted acts called "sacraments," but because, first of all, she is the possibility given to man to see and to "live" it in Christ.[122]

---

118 Ibid., 205. In the Liturgy of Saint Basil the Great referencing Christ's own words as reported by Saint Paul in 1 Corinthians 11:26.

119 Ibid., 150.

120 Meletios Webber, *Bread and Water, Wine and Oil* (Chesterton, IN: Conciliar, 2007), 146.

121 Vassiliadis, *Eucharist and Witness*, 52.

122 Schmemann, *Life of the World*, 113.

Like the Eucharist,[123] the sacrament of baptism involves calling on the Holy Spirit to sanctify ordinary, earthly items—oil and water. Water is an ancient religious symbol that points to creation, to life and death, as well as cleansing and purification. Baptism begins with the preparatory rites of exorcism and the confession of faith. The prayers of exorcism by which the devil is cast out and banned from the candidate's life are an expression of the belief that evil itself is a personal presence and reality in the world. During the confession of faith the one to be baptized is repeatedly asked if they renounce the devil, if they have united themselves to Christ, and they are then required to recite the Nicene Creed. This sequence of actions speaks to the true conversion of the individual, who has now fled the world and chosen refuge in Christ. Once this is completed, the water itself is blessed. Part of the prayer of blessing reads:

> Wherefore, O King who lovest mankind, come thou now and sanctify this water, by the indwelling of the Holy Spirit. And grant unto it the grace of redemption, the blessing of Jordan. Make it the fountain of incorruption, the gift of sanctification, the remission of sins, the remedy of infirmities, the final destruction of demons, unassailable by hostile powers, filled with angelic might. Let those who would ensnare thy creature flee far from it. For we have called upon thy Name, O Lord, and it is wonderful and glorious, and awesome to adversaries.[124]

The water thus consecrated, the priest turns to bless the oil, another ancient symbol of healing and life.

> Bless also this holy oil with the power and operation and indwelling of the Holy Spirit, that it may be an anointing unto incorruption, an armor of righteousness, to the renewing of soul and body, to the averting of every assault of the devil, to the deliverance from all evil of those who

123 The similarities are so pronounced that Schmemann speaks of baptismal *anamnesis* and *epiclesis*. *Of Water and the Spirit*, 47–48.

124 Orthodox Church in America, *Baptism* (New York: Orthodox Church in America, Department of Religious Education, 1972), 50–51.

> shall be anointed with it in faith, or who are partakers thereof; unto thy glory and the glory of thine only begotten Son and of thine all-holy, and good, and life-creating Spirit, now and ever and unto ages of ages.[125]

After the blessing, the candidate is anointed with the oil on the forehead in the name of the Father, the Son, and the Holy Spirit; on the breast and shoulders unto the healing of soul and body; on the ears unto the hearing of the faith; on the hands which God has made and fashioned; and on the feet that he or she may walk in the way of his commandments. Immediately after the anointing the candidate is immersed in the water three times in the name of the Father, the Son, and the Holy Spirit. In the Byzantine rite this is then followed by chrismation, another anointing with a special oil, chrism, by which the newly baptized person is sealed with the gift of the Holy Spirit (Eph 1:13; 4:30).

From this brief description of the baptismal rite, it is obvious that the presence of the divine tri-hypostatic person is assumed and assured by the descent and operation of the Holy Spirit. It is in the context of this real presence that the candidate knows Christ and actually dies and rises with him, and is fully transformed, redeemed. The water and the oil, while not magically transformed into something extranatural, are restored to their original state and are used by God to work the transformation. The water is *shown* to be "the water of redemption, the water of sanctification," in which the Lord manifests himself and grants that the one baptized is transformed.[126]

Baptism's connection to the mission of the church is, of course, indisputable. It is the one means by which we make disciples, inaugurating them into life in Christ and the church. If this sacrament is applied according to the instructions of our Lord, with faith, and in keeping with the practice of the early church,[127] it brings with it the potential for the real conversion of unbelievers. It represents a first step on the journey of faith. It is here that the sinner meets the Savior and is changed into a citizen of the kingdom of heaven, a member of the body of Christ. There is no way around this sacrament; it is essential to the mission of the church; without it there can be no fulfillment of the Great Commission.

125 Ibid., 53–54.

126 Ibid., 52.

127 This, of course, raises the question of tradition, to which I will turn in the next chapter.

## 3. Implications for the Process of Contextualization

If contextualization is a process whereby we seek to establish the core missionary context in the presence of the Divine Person, and if that divine presence manifests itself in the sacraments, what does this mean for the process? There are at least three implications that grow out of this perspective: (1) the process begins with the church, (2) it is the Holy Spirit who mediates Christ's presence, and (3) to participate in this process the faithful have to be spiritually sound.

### *a. We Must Start with the Church*

The church is the place from which mission emanates and to which it gravitates. On the one hand, the church is the point of departure for its own mission in the world. Here the faithful behold the resurrection, meet Christ, and are thus emboldened for the task. It is here that they are filled with the Holy Spirit's enabling power. And it is here that their confidence is bolstered by divine presence. Moreover, believers know that the Divine Liturgy is being done on behalf of the world and for its salvation. At the end of the Liturgy the faithful are dismissed into the world to be witnesses of what they have seen. Thus the church, the body of Christ, radiates light and hope into the darkness of a fallen world. On the other hand, the church is the place to which all mission gravitates. Here there is the healing environment of a people unified in love. Here are living examples of divinely transfigured (fully personal) persons permeated by and partaking in the Divine Person. Here the nonbeliever can see firsthand the effects of this interpenetration, this communion. In addition, this is the place where the one seeking God can find him present. The church, then, is a focal point of missionary activity, the enlivened faithful going out and bringing the seekers in to meet Christ for themselves. All this being the case, a fully functioning, canonical church[128] gathering to celebrate the Eucharist is the most effective instrument of missionary outreach.

---

128 This raises the difficult question of what the church is and where it is to be found. The Fathers of the ecumenical councils, guided by the Holy Spirit, established a framework for answering this question by incorporating into the Creed four attributes of the One, Holy, Catholic, and Apostolic Church.

The centrality of the church indicates that mission involves a two-staged invitation. While in the world the faithful will invite individuals to come and see the glory of God, the presence of Christ in the Divine Liturgy. While in the church the faithful will call invitees to act on what they have seen and unite themselves to Christ in faith.

The extra-ecclesial invitation to "come and see" will, of course, have to be appropriate and understandable in each given field of presence. In contemporary North America, discussions of religion are generally discouraged in the name of tolerance and individual preferences. Mass invitations are impersonal and are largely ignored. So it will most likely come down to an intimate, person-to-person invitation of someone to whom we have become fully present (more on this in chapter 4). The invitation should also prepare the individual for their visit to the church by letting them know what they will see and hear. This will be especially true of the Eastern Church since its form of worship will be different from that which most invitees will have seen. In this way they will avoid being distracted by external differences and be able to concentrate on what is central, the presence of Christ. They will also need to be put at ease, encouraged to participate, and assured that they simply cannot do anything wrong.

The ecclesial invitation is, on the one hand, given by Christ himself who, when lifted up, draws all people to himself. In John 12:23 Jesus is referring to his being lifted up on the Cross, and that is exactly what is being actualized during the Eucharist, from which place Christ continues to draw. I do not mean to suggest that every nonbeliever present will respond. Some may even be repulsed. Nevertheless, Christ is actually present in the Eucharist, and given the nature of his love for humankind, that presence is itself an invitation. On the other hand, the invitation can be issued by the faithful from within other parts of the Liturgy, during the sermon, after the dismissal, or even during the ensuing fellowship. Again, this is a simple straightforward person-to-person appeal to unite oneself to Christ, which is itself rooted in the confident assumption of that presence. It requires no clever presentation, no slick arguments, no modern packaging, but rather a compassionate appeal to act on what has been seen. At the end of one recent Liturgy, I said, "You have been here today to seek and worship the living God. You have, no doubt, sensed his presence among us. We who know him would be honored to introduce you to him. Please talk to me, or stay after and talk to others, but by all means get to know him." Afterwards, a number of people did stay and converse with our faithful, and we had a chance to introduce them to Christ.

### *b. The Holy Spirit Mediates the Presence of Christ*

It is the Holy Spirit who mediates Christ's presence, personally and directly, no matter the language or culture. What then are the differences in language, music, imagery, and the like? We will get to those issues in the next chapter. For now we must simply acknowledge that our task is to remain faithful in the celebration of the Liturgy and Eucharist and that there is nothing else we can do to conjure up the presence of Christ. No amount of singing, swaying, or swooning is going to bring Christ into our midst. Trying to drum up Christ's presence, to see him externally, will only lead to a "delusive emotionalism" that is alien to the church.[129]

> By contrast the quiet celebration of the Liturgy gives guidance for a correct Orthodox attitude and provides an air of devout contrition. Joy does not laugh aloud and wound those who are sorrowful, nor does pain cast gloom and disillusionment over the weak. There reigns everywhere the devout contrition which secretly and inexhaustibly comforts everyone, making them joyful and uniting them as brothers. Human emotionalism is one thing and the devout contrition of the Liturgy is quite another.[130]

What then of the extraordinary events reported in the book of Acts? Was not the early mission of the church accompanied by unusual and miraculous happenings (Acts 10:44)? Indeed, but those appearances were made necessary by the initial absence of the church in the regions into which the gospel was being introduced. These forays into enemy territory

---

129 Vasileios, *Hymn of Entry*, 77.

130 Ibid.

required special support since the church had not yet been planted, since the sacraments were not yet being administered. Once the church was in place it became the place of divine manifestation. Today the church has been planted in almost every segment of populated earth.[131] Now we are to rely on the presence of the church, the celebration of the Divine Liturgy, the sacraments with their promise of divine presence.

We might also ask if the presence of God in the sacraments is something that a nonbeliever can even perceive. Given the personal nature of both God and human beings, their predisposition for communion, it seems apparent that even a nonbeliever has the prerequisites necessary for the perception of the Divine Person. We know, of course, that sin has broken that communion and blinded their eyes, making it difficult to see what they have rejected. Nevertheless we have the promise that the Holy Spirit will open their eyes and convict them of their own sinfulness (John 16:8,9). Again we see that it is the Holy Spirit and not our contrivances that facilitates awareness and mediates Christ's presence.

Additionally, the form of the sacraments, as it has come down to us through the church, does not need to be changed or altered. We may need to think of liturgical renewal in cases where the contemporary practice has already changed the shape of worship in order to bring it back into line with tradition. But there is nothing to be gained by trying to adjust the sacraments themselves to fit the contemporary moment. It is the Holy Spirit who gives the sacraments their efficacy, not our attempts to make them relevant. In fact, changing the form and/or the content will only lead to their being deprived of their symbolic realism. For example, to change or eliminate the earthly elements of bread, wine, water, and oil, as in the case of waterless online baptisms,[132] can only cause a rupture of the sign/signifier union achieved by the sacraments and displace the

---

131 There are, of course, many unreached peoples.

132 After giving instructions on the waterless online baptism, one site asks, "So is an online baptism as valid as a real-life one? Our non-theological answer is that the symbolism makes a reasonable case to consider an online baptism as valid as a real-life immersion of your physical body. However, we feel it is best to treat the online baptism as a chance to profess your faith to fellow believers online so that they may celebrate the conversion experience with you. Then also plan a baptism in water in real life." http://www.infinitechurch.com/baptism.htm. Are there, then, two baptisms? One with and one without water?

reality they are designed to represent. If the sacrament is thus deprived of divine presence, its missionary potential is lost.

### c. *All Things Being Equal*

All things being equal and ideal, a person outside the faith who comes into the church during the Divine Liturgy will sense the personal presence of God and the invitation to relationship, both in the sacrament itself and in the transformed lives of the faithful. However, not all things are equal and ideal. If we can, as a minimum, assume the presence of real, personal faith on the part of the faithful, they still face a number of pitfalls that can hamper the mission of the church. Their ability to participate in the Holy Spirit's mediation of Christ's presence depends, in part, on the spiritual health of the faithful.

The most obvious obstacle is continuing and persistent sin. We know that the actions of one member affect all the members of the body of Christ (1 Cor 12:26). It is reasonable to think that such sinfulness could diminish the light of the Liturgy, that this person will not see the true light. How will they be able introduce Christ if they themselves have not seen him? It is not so much a question of Christ not being present, but rather the broken communion, the lack of interpenetration, between the sinner and Christ and therefore between the sinning member and the other members. The witness of the church is weaker in direct proportion to the lack of transformation in the lives of its members. Seen this way, the essential foundation of Christian witness is the spiritual health of its members and not their ability to adapt, reformulate, repackage the message. If we want to introduce Christ to the world, we will have to begin with the things Christ has asked us to do—love him, love one another, and keep the commandments. It is the radical nature of life lived in Christ and not our similarity to the world that will announce the good news of a genuine alternative in Christ.

Empty ritualism is another danger for Christians, especially in highly liturgical settings. Week after week the same Liturgy is celebrated, large portions of it are passively memorized allowing the mind to disengage. If this happens, the mind wanders, attention to the Liturgy is lost, and the perception of Christ's presence fades. Again this is not to say that

Christ is not present, but rather that an individual has substituted mere repetition of ritual for the conscious participation in the Liturgy. Without that dynamic, deliberate attention to the Liturgy and the Eucharist, the ability to sense God's presence is dulled, and the individual is unfit for witness, neither confident, having seen nothing, nor willing, having been touched by nothing. This is not a necessary outcome of the liturgical nature of the church's services. This kind of routinization is, of course, also experienced in nonliturgical groups, who, in spite of their denials, do have set patterns that are partially memorized. The problem here is a lack of discipline, an individualistic withdrawal from the other faithful, and the gradual loss of the ability to perceive the presence of Christ. Without personal communion of the participants, the Liturgy, any liturgy, becomes empty and void of life.

Another difficulty is that of nonparticipation. Dom Dix has pointed out that the celebration of the Eucharist is one of the most ancient givens of Christian worship.[133] He goes so far as to say that the very reason the early Christians gathered at all was to celebrated communion and that all of the faithful partook of the sacrament. Yet in some ecclesial settings the holiness and the awesomeness of the sacraments has sometimes been used as an excuse for not participating. This attitude is centered on the supposed unpreparedness and unworthiness of the individual and leads to a reluctance to take communion. In many cases this is just a case of sinful laziness, not being willing to spiritually prepare for communion by saying the precommunion prayers, fasting, and participating in the sacrament of penance. In other cases it is acceptance of the long-established convention of taking communion only once a year. This came about because there was a time when entire populations were included in the church and many never took communion. The church responded by saying that, in order not to excommunicate themselves, they would have to take it at least once a year. This once-a-year ruling then became the standard of practice for many. These practices are, of course, based on misunderstandings of the sacrament, primarily a failure to see that the Eucharist is given for the forgiveness of sin and that it restores communion with Christ. Consider the words of John Cassian:

---

133 Dom Gregory Dix, *The Shape of the Liturgy* (Westminster, England: Dacre, 1945).

> We must not avoid communion because we deem ourselves to be sinful. We must approach it more often for the healing of the soul and the purification of the spirit, but with such humility and faith that considering ourselves unworthy … we would desire even more the medicine for our wounds. Otherwise it is impossible to receive communion once a year, as certain people do … considering the sanctification of the heavenly Mysteries as available only to saints. It is better to think that by giving us grace, the sacrament makes us pure and holy. Such people manifest more pride than humility … for when they receive, they think of themselves as worthy. It is much better if, in humility of heart, knowing that we are never worthy of the Holy Mysteries we would receive them every Sunday for the healing of our diseases, rather than, blinded by pride, think that after one year we become worthy of receiving them.[134]

In addition to the harm done to the individual, nonparticipation does great damage to the unity of the body. In the early church, "communion of all the faithful at every Divine Liturgy was a self-evident norm … The Eucharist was both defined and experienced as the Sacrament of the Church, the Sacrament of the assembly, the Sacrament of unity."[135] If the church is the gathering of the faithful in order to celebrate the Eucharist and if some present choose not to participate, what happens to unity? What happens to its witness? With this in mind Vassiliadis calls for

> the restoration of the *catholic* participation in the eschatological table of the kingdom. This means reception of communion by *all* (not just frequent communion), with no juridical or legalistic preconditions (such as worthiness or strict preparation of the individual faithful), i.e., without any subordination of the sacrament par

---

134 Cited byAlexander Schmemann, *Great Lent: Journey to Pascha*, rev. ed. (Crestwood, NY: St. Vladimir's Seminary Press, 1974), 116.

135 Ibid., 113.

> excellence of the church to other sacraments (repentance, priesthood, etc., which are certainly of lesser importance from the point of view of Orthodox theology).[136]

In spite of the shortcomings of its members, the church can still be referred to as holy, as a place of divine presence, and thus as a witness in the world. The church exists by virtue of the Incarnation, by which the possibility of the sanctification of human beings was established. Those who are members of the body of Christ are in communion with him and are made holy by the union with him. This is not to say that the church knows no sin or does no wrong. Quite to the contrary, "the church tolerates sinners, shelters them, instructs them, that they may be awakened and aroused to attention and spiritual recovery and transformation; but they do not hinder the church from being holy… Actually, she is the theanthropic workshop of human sanctification and, through man, of the sanctification of the rest of creation."[137] Holiness is an essential and immutable attribute of the church, but it is not a function of its members, but rather it is a function of the sanctifying grace of Christ.

At a recent conference a brother from eastern Europe suggested that since the situation on the ground was not all that encouraging (that is, in spite of the beautiful Liturgy many did not attend church), my ecclesio-sacramental approach was rather romantic or perhaps he meant idealistic. I cannot argue with the fact that things are not always as they should be, yet I willingly accept the label of being a romantic, since I believe that we need to constantly point to the realities that can and should be realized. The sinfulness of the church's members simply indicates that the process of sanctification is not complete. The church is a work in progress, and given the fallen state of the world and its manifold temptations, we need all the help we can get. Of course the key is communion with Christ. Here is where the sacraments of the church provide decisive help. Given that baptism and chrismation provide the initiation into the body, then the Eucharist serves to maintain the ongoing, vital communion with Christ. Every time the faithful partake of the very body and blood of our Lord, they refresh

136 Vassiliadis, *Eucharist and Witness*, 58.

137 Saint Justin Popovich, "The Attributes of the Church," Orthodox Christian Information Center. http://orthodoxinfo.com/general/attributes.aspx.

and renew their communion with him. This then is the first stage of contextualization, whereby we facilitate an invitation to Christ by faith and active participation in the very place where the Holy Spirit mediates the presence of Christ; i.e., the church.

## Chapter 3

# The Core Context of Mission

When thinking of contextualization, it is quite natural to ask what we mean by context. Put differently, with what context do we have to align our efforts to introduce the person of Christ? Does this involve translating some content across linguistic or cultural boundaries? Is it some apologetic defense in the face of other philosophical or religious frameworks? Are we to embed our invitation in a particular set of social, individual, or perhaps institutional structures? Does it mean coordinating our presentation with prevailing art forms and media? Well, if, as I have insisted, the gospel is in reality a person and not merely information about that person, then none of the aforementioned activities, important as they might be, define the core context of missionary outreach. If God exists as person, and if he has replicated his own personal image in humanity, and if he desires communion with those beings, then the engagement has to take place between persons at the level of personhood. In other words, this core context of invitation will be defined by the two persons being introduced—Christ and the invitee.[138] In the case of human beings, we are faced with the challenge of both their numbers and their apparent diversity. How can we conceive of a context that would apply equally to each one? One way to do this would be to think in terms of the integral human, multi-hypostatic humanity possessed of a single characteristic—personhood, which can be expressed in terms of four universal conditions. Every human person has (a) dual, finite/infinite being, (b) the faculty of belief, (c) the ability to act (agency), and (d) second-order beliefs (morality). So one axis of the core invitational context is personhood.

---

138 I will take up the role of the third person, the inviter, in chapter 4.

The other axis of the base context would have to be defined by the presence of the other person involved—Christ. Here we face the problem of his presence-in-absence, and so we turn to the privileged place of Christ's presence in the world today, the church (Eph 2:22). This is where those who have "come to see" are offered an opportunity to get to know Christ. It is here that their personhood is engaged, and it is here that they will negotiate intimacy with Christ, come to love him, to obey his commandments, to commune with him. As already noted, the church is established when the faithful come together to celebrate the Eucharist. While this minimalist definition is true and helpful, it does not tell us much about how that gathering is to be constituted, how everything given in Christ passes over into the reality of ecclesial life, and how that life is to be preserved from generation to generation. Fortunately God, in his infinite wisdom, has given the church a number of practical tools which define and limit the church, thus protecting and preserving this inheritance. These good and perfect gifts come down from the Father of lights (Jas 1:17,18) and include (1) the Holy Scriptures, (2) apostolic succession, (3) liturgical structures, (4) councils (dogma and canons), (5) hagiography, and (6) iconography. I know that there are many other gifts given to the church. These, however, are the ones that are generally associated with the idea of tradition in the Eastern Church. I am also aware that some of my readers will not accept all of these as gifts. Yet discussing them as follows will help to demonstrate how the base missionary context takes shape, and it may be possible to transpose them into another ecclesial key. Taken together these gifts constitute the tradition of the church, authoritatively given by Christ, definitively passed on to the apostles (Eph 2:20), preserved and developed in stability under the guidance of the Holy Spirit. These gifts of tradition provide a universal yet dynamic reality within which the people of God can live,[139] and in which Christ is present. The elements of this ecclesial axis reflect and engage the conditions of the axis of personhood, and together they form the base context; that is, the set of facts and circumstances that surround the primary missional event, the incitation. This context can be mapped as follows:

---

139 Saint Irenaeus, *Letter to the Ephesians*, ch. 17, cited in George Bebis, *The Mind of the Fathers* (Brookline, MA: Holy Cross Orthodox Press, 1994), 10.

| | Finite/Infinite | Belief | Agency | Morality |
|---|---|---|---|---|
| | Provide expression for both the finitude and the infinitude of human beings. | Acknowledge capacity for belief, adjudicate between differing beliefs, and guide probability structures. | Redefine, redirect, and activate forms of self-actualization. | Establish, evaluate, make active second-order beliefs that provide a setting for communion. |
| ***Holy Scripture*** | Infinite word in finite form | Truth affirmed and interpreted | Instructions for life in Christ | Foundations established |
| ***Apostolic Succession*** | Divinely established, finite structure | Didactic continuity | Assistance and accountability | Structures of support |
| ***Liturgical Structures*** | Finite foretaste of infinite | Truth presented, proven, preserved | Participation in truth | Transformation |
| ***Councils*** | Divine guidance of the finite | Truth in words | Standards of behavior | Presuppositions |
| ***Hagiography*** | Realized deification | Personal continuity | Transcendentalized agency | Examples |
| ***Iconography*** | Windows onto heaven | Truth actualized | Accountability | Examples |

It is within these parameters and with these tools that the invitation to life in Christ can be meaningfully issued. However, this core context does not come into existence on its own; it needs to be actively, and with the Lord's help, built and preserved (Ps 127:1). On the ecclesial side, each one of the gifts of tradition has to be faithfully executed, consistently used, obediently adhered to. On the side of personhood, the faithful must continually invite others to enter this context and meet Christ. The task of contextualization, then, is not to adapt a message to some context, but rather establish a stable context within which the person of Christ can be introduced. In other words, it is to match, within the boundaries set by tradition, the ecclesial axis with the conditions of human personhood and thus provide a context for the invitation and the negotiation of divine-human intimacy. In what follows I will seek to show how, according to the wisdom of God, each gift effectively engages the conditions of personhood. That established, I will explore ways in which each gift can be used to create one aspect of the core invitational context.

## 1. Holy Scripture

Although we moderns have become somewhat suspicious of historical documents, the first and perhaps most obvious mechanism for defining the base missionary context is the written record of the early church, the Holy Scriptures. Being witnesses of Christ's life and teaching, the apostles sought to pass on the things that had been given to them. Some of this was done in written form. Saint Luke, for example, sets out to write an orderly, eyewitness account of Christ's life and teaching (Luke 1:2,3). Thus his Gospel contains some of the very words of our Lord. Saint John gives written testimony of the things he has seen. Although not everything that Christ did and taught could take the form of a written record (John 21:24,25), Saint Paul admonishes the Galatians to remain faithful to the gospel which they had received (Gal 1:8,9). He presents his teaching on the Eucharist to the Corinthians as that which he had received from Christ and had also delivered to them (1 Cor 11:23). And knowing that the Thessalonians had accepted the word of God from him, he urges them to hold fast to the traditions they had received—whether by word or by epistle (2 Thess 2:15). Obviously the authors of the New Testament documents understood that it was their responsibility to pass on what they had been given. "During the apostolic years we have already a set of certain doctrines, creeds, liturgical practices, which originated from our Lord himself and which the apostles felt obliged to expound, present, interpret and preserve"[140]—in unwritten and especially written form as their own living experience, a narrative to be read against the larger context of the life of the whole church.

### a. *Infinite Word in Finite, Accessible Form*

These written records, later affirmed by the whole church set into a canon,[141] had two distinct advantages for the believers. On the one hand,

140 Ibid., 7.

141 This interpretational concern is not limited to Eastern scholars. Linbeck, for example, in his desire to recover the classical hermenutic (a conensus-and-community-

they represented the very word of God addressed to humanity. This was obviously and particularly the case with the sayings of Jesus contained in the Gospels.[142] But it was soon recognized, for example, by Saint John of Damascus, that the Holy Spirit had superintended the writing process in such a way as to render the entire canon of Scripture divine word. As he put it, "Faith comes by hearing. For hearing the divine Scriptures we believe in the teaching of the Holy Spirit."[143] On the other hand, the written form of Scripture preserved the word of God in a form accessible to all. In this way the unique development of the Scriptures engages the human person in both her infinity (divine word) and in her finiteness (human language). There is little wonder when observing that throughout the ages people have heard the word of God in the Scriptures. When speaking of the rules that govern monastic life, one author insisted:

---

building pattern of biblical interpretation) asks to what extent "the Bible can be profitably read in our day as a canonically and narrationally unified and internally glossed (that is, self-referential and self-interpreting) whole centered on Jesus Christ, and telling the story of the dealings of the Triune God with his people and his world in ways which are typologically (though not, so at least the Reformers would say, allegorically) applicable to the present." George A. Lindbeck, *The Church in a Postliberal Age: Radical Traditions*, ed. James J. Buckley (Grand Rapids: Eerdmans, 2003), 203.

142 This also applies to the Old Testament, of which the New Testament is considered the fulfillment. This has led in the East to typological, allegorical interpretation of the Old Testament. "This entire approach, of course, appears to be totally at odds with modern methods of interpretation based on 'historical' or 'narrative' criticism. The consensus among Orthodox exegetes, however, is that a proper typological approach can complement in a very fruitful way the more conventional scientific approaches. The relation between type and antitype is not susceptible to 'proof' in the usual sense of the term. It can only be attested or witnessed to on the basis of *ecclesial experience*." John Breck, "Orthodox Principles of Biblical Interpretation," *St. Vladimir's Theological Quarterly* 40, no. 1–2 (1996): 92. See also Mary Ford, "Towards the Restoration of Allegory: Christology, Epistemology and Narrative Structure," *St. Vladimir's Theological Quarterly* 34, no. 2–3 (1990): 161–95.

143 Interestingly, Saint John of Damascus relates information on the dormition of the Theotokos, admitting that it is not referred to in Scripture, but received from ancient and true tradition. John of Damascus, "Homily 1 on the Dormition of the Theotokos," Monachos.net, http://www.monachos.net/content/patristics/patristictexts/680-john-damascus-homily-1-dormition. And Saint Basil the Great mentions a whole series of liturgical practices that were handed down by tradition but are not contained in the Scriptures. Saint Basil, ch. 27 in "The Book of Saint Basil on the Spirit," in *Basil: Letters and Select Works*, vol. 8 of *A Select Library of the Nicene and Post-Nicene Fathers of the Christian Church*, 2nd series, ed. Philip Schaff and Henry Wace (Grand Rapids: Eerdmans, 1975), http://www.ccel.org/ccel/schaff/npnf208.vii.xxviii.html.

> All the ancient monks considered their real rule, in the sense of the ultimate determinant of their lives, to be not some product of human effort but the Word of God himself as contained in the Scriptures. Monasticism was simply a form of the Christian life, and hence it drew its inspiration from divine revelation.[144]

Human beings, having divinity repeated in them, resonate with infinity and have an innate longing for the eternal. This often finds expression in a search for the transcendent by means that cannot satisfy. Still it is the vain hope of many that all manner of human contrivance, from art to cultic practices,[145] will lead them to an integration with the divine. Yet those things, anchored in finitude, do not, cannot satisfy the eternal longing. But the Holy Scriptures, rooted in the infinite, effectively bridge the divide. They are filled with divine power (Heb 4:12) and thus engage this basic condition of human personhood by speaking directly to that longing. Think of how the reading of a Psalm quiets the fears of the troubled soul. Notice how the words of Scripture convict, console, move, and direct, doing what no other words can do, for these words are the infinite voice of God spoken into the temporal and spatial context of God's own creatures.

### *b. Truth Affirmed and Interpreted by the Church*

Being the word of God, the Holy Scriptures also engage human persons in their ability to hold cognitive content to be true. In fact, this is the very basic demand that the Scriptures make on the reader, meeting that constitutional need to believe something by telling us what can be believed, informing and building plausibility structures, and enabling us to adjudicate between conflicting claims. What becomes difficult at times is the fact that the human capacity for belief often distorts and misinterprets that truth. This has been especially true of heretics who have promoted all manner of false teaching based on their "perverse interpretations

144 Placid Spearritt. "Benedict," in Cheslyn Jones, Geoffrey Wainwright, and Edward Yarnold, *The Study of Spirituality* (New York: Oxford University Press, 1986), 151.

145 Note the recent rise in the interest in spirituality. Downey speaks of "spirituality sprawl." Michael Downey, *Understanding Christian Spirituality* (New York: Paulist, 1997).

and deceitful expositions,"[146] insisting that they have biblical warrant for their claims. Of course these claims could be countered on the basis of Scripture itself, but what was readily apparent was that the heretics were interpreting the Scriptures outside the framework of the tradition in which it was given. This is the tradition "which originates from the apostles, and which is preserved by means of the succession of presbyters in the Churches,"[147] that enabled the early believers to distinguish between true and false interpretations.

> It is within the power of all, therefore, in every church, who may wish to see the truth, to contemplate clearly the Tradition of the apostles manifested throughout the whole world; and we are in a position to reckon up those who were by the apostles instituted bishops in the Churches, and to demonstrate the succession of these men to our own times; those who neither taught nor knew anything like what these heretics rave about.[148]

> Since therefore we have such proofs, it is not necessary to seek the truth among others which it is easy to obtain from the Church since the apostles, like a rich man deposits his money in a bank, lodged in her hands most copiously all things pertaining to the truth.[149]

So the Scriptures speak to the human faculty of belief by relieving the tension that is caused by having to choose what to believe, by showing us what should be believed, and by doing so within an ecclesial context that preserves its true meaning, the Word helps the individual avoid false "truths" and bring order and stability to their plausibility structures. As such, Scripture is an invaluable asset against the contemporary cacophony of truth claims.

---

146 Saint Irenaeus, "Against Heresies," in *Ante-Nicene Fathers*, vol. 1, ed. Alexander Roberts and James Donaldson (Peabody, MA: Hendrikson, 1995), book 1, ch. 3, 6.

147 Ibid., book 3, ch. 2, 2.

148 Ibid., book 3, ch. 3, 1.

149 Ibid., book 3, ch. 4, 1.

### c. *Instructions for Life in Christ*

This consistency of interpretation is, of course, extremely important since the Scriptures are to be used as a means of empowering and inspiring right human self-actualization. Scripture contains the instructions needed to live life in Christ. The record of Jesus' Sermon on the Mount (Matt 5–7), for example, provides practical instructions on how the individual can transcend her own boundaries and, in love and freedom, make the move toward communion with others by loving, serving, forgiving them (Matt 5:44; 6:1–4,14), and with God through purity, nonhypocritical prayer, and obedience (Matt 5:8; 6:5–13; 7:24). All of these instructions appeal to the human freedom of will and capacity for self-actualization by helping to guide that action with normative instruction in an accessible form.

### d. *Foundation for Morality*

The Scriptures go beyond a simple appeal to agency and direct the reader to second-order beliefs and desires by teaching that it is proper and right to think, speak, and act in certain ways. It is a "blessed" thing to make peace (Matt 5:9) and even to allow oneself to be persecuted for Christ's sake (Matt 5:10). The rightness of peacemaking and suffering for Christ are, of course, based on the first-order belief that what Christ says is true. But this is followed by the second-order belief that it is right to act in that way. Similarly, Jesus engages this condition of personhood when he declares, "You have heard that it was said … but I say to you," unmistakably guiding the listener to a belief about the belief that certain things are right or wrong (Matt 5:21,22,27,28,31,32), thus providing a foundation for morality, for the rightness of certain behavior.

### e. *Building the Core Context with Scripture*

The Holy Scriptures, then, engage the human person on every front of personhood and thus help define the base context of missions. Building that core context does not involve adapting Scripture to a particular context, as has so often been assumed, but rather it means using the Scriptures to bridge the finite/infinite gap by accepting and asserting its divine authority in the face of all competing claims. It means allowing the content of the Word to establish what is believable and become the primary informant of our plausibility structures. It means using Scripture to establish the patterns of our behavior (the commandments) and the principles of our morality.[150] For all this to happen, the missionary will have to (1) make that text available and accessible, (2) defend the correct interpretation of that text, and (3) teach its content.

***i.*** Making the text available begins with translating it into the language of those seeking communion with God.

This has always been one of the church's first priorities as it has expanded across linguistic and cultural boundaries. One of the most famous examples is the work done by Saints Cyril and Methodius, ninth-century missionaries to the Slavs, who not only translated the Scriptures but had to first reduce the local language to writing by inventing an alphabet. Similarly, the eighteenth-century Russian mission to Alaska began with the translation of the Scriptures into the local languages. This practice has been continued by translators of the modern age as evidenced by the great work of the Wycliffe translators, the various Bible societies, and people like Eugene Nida, Kurt Aland, Eberhard Nestle, and others. Contributing to the core context, the Orthodox Churches

---

150 There are, of course, many today who would disregard the authority of Scripture and dismiss it as a source of moral principle. James Nash, for example, argues "against every appeal to scriptural authority as a justification in moral argument. It is a cultic ritual that deserves a quick end for the sake of Christian ethical integrity. The pursuit of biblical warrants has contributed to Christian moral distortion and confusion on a host of issues, from racial and gender equality to war and the death penalty, from homosexuality to sexuality per se, from population policies to ecclesiastical polities. It also has hindered the development of Christian ecological commitments." James A. Nash, "The Bible vs. Biodiversity: The Case against Moral Argument from Scripture," *Journal for the Study of Religion, Nature and Culture* 3, no. 2 (2009): 227–28. Others reject Nash's approach as an outdated reading of Scripture which is now replaced by an understanding of Scripture as canon which "functions not in the precise literal-propositional terms in which Nash, like his literalist adversaries, tends to read Scripture, but as a culture-shaping, character-forming genre which forms part of the larger set of processes and rituals that together construct moral communities of the kind Christians inhabit. Story and narrative in this perspective take on a paradigmatic hermenéutical significance, such that the particular narratives of Scripture are to be read in the context of a larger narrative history." Michael S. Northcott, "Loving Scripture and Nature," *Journal for the Study of Religion, Nature and Culture* 3, no. 2 (2009): 251.

in North America have also published new translations.[151] This is part of the work of contextualization.

***ii.*** The work of defending and interpreting the text takes place within the context of the ecclesial community in which and for which it was developed.[152]

> The *Church* is the proper locus for the *interpretation* as well as the proclamation and celebration of the Word of God. Exegesis is a function of the worshiping, witnessing community of faith. While personal interpretations of Scripture are welcome and encouraged, those interpretations forfeit their claim to authority if they sever their connection with the ecclesial Body and its Tradition. This does not mean that the exegete's conclusions are predetermined by the doctrinal stance of the Church. Nevertheless, Orthodox exegetes accept as integral to their calling the obligation to submit their reflections to the *phronema ekklesias*, the 'mind of the Church.' This implies that they will conform their interpretative work to the doctrinal and moral teachings of the Church, that they will assume their exegetical labors as a *diakonia* or service to the Church, and that they will carry them out in the interests of the Church and its mission within the world.[153]

151 The Orthodox Study Bible provides, among other things, a new translation of the Septuagint, which is the Old Testament text preferred by the East.

152 "Orthodox hermeneutics takes as a point of departure the affirmation of 2 Timothy 3:26, 'All Scripture is inspired by God.' That inspirational work involves a *synergy*, a cooperative effort between the Spirit and the human instrument who receives divine revelation and translates it into the gospel proclamation. As the inspired author composes his work, he draws upon elements of tradition, both oral and written. The Gospel or Epistle he produces, therefore, is given both shape and content by holy tradition. Indeed, tradition is the matrix in which the Scriptures are conceived and from which they are brought forth. Tradition, however, is the 'living memory of the Church' (Fr. Sergius Bulgakov). It is the Church, in other words, that produces the canonical Scriptures." Breck, "Biblical Interpretation," 77–78.

153 Ibid., 88.

In spite of the best practices and standards, interpreters are sometimes swayed by their own personal persuasions when choosing how to translate a particular word or phrase. Take, for example, the difficulties associated with the translation of the Greek word ιλαστηριον. Should it be rendered "expiation" or "propitiation," and what difference does it make? Obviously the issue is complex and cannot be resolved solely on the basis of linguistic considerations.[154] However, it is interesting to note that English translations such as the ESV and the NKJV choose to render the Greek as "propitiation" (Rom 3:25; Heb 2:17; 1 John 2:2; 4:10), while a recent Orthodox translation renders it as "expiation" in all four cases.[155] One thing that may be influencing the choice of term is the underlying soteriology of the translators. In the East ιλαστηριον is taken to be an expression of God's mercy toward the sinner in removing sin,[156] rather than the common Western idea that it is an appeasement of the offended justice or wrath of God. So as we use Scripture to build the core context, we will have to be sure that our interpretation of it is in line with the mind of the church, which in this case favors expiation.

The same thing applies, for example, to the larger context of the exact nature of human sinfulness. There is little question that we are correct in referring to Adam's rebellion as the original sin. It is also correct to say that his disobedience brought sin and corruption to all humanity. However, the term "original sin" is often associated with a Roman Catholic or Protestant notion of total depravity. By that they mean that not only Adam but also every other human being has lost the image of God. As a result, man is utterly incapable of turning back to God, because the loss of the image brought with it a loss of human free will.

---

154 Note the various definitions given in William Arndt et al., *A Greek-English Lexicon of the New Testament and Other Early Christian Literature: A Translation and Adaptation of the Fourth Revised and Augmented Edition of Walter Bauer's* Griechisch-Deutsches Wörterbuch zu den Schriften des Neuen Testaments und der Übrigen Urchristlichen Literatur, 2nd ed. (Chicago: University of Chicago Press, 1979), 376.

155 *The Orthodox New Testament*, vol. 2 (Buena Vista, CO: Holy Apostles Convent, 2000).

156 Florovsky, quoting Saint Gregory the Theologian, writes, "The Cross is made necessary by human nature, not by Divinity … 'We are purified by the eternal Spirit who purges the earlier damage in us which we received from the flesh, and we are also purified by our blood (for I call the blood which Christ my God has shed our own), which expiates our original weaknesses and redeems the world.'" Johanna Manley, *The Bible and the Holy Fathers for Orthodox: Daily Scripture Readings and Commentary for Orthodox Christians* (Menlo Park, CA: Monastery Books, 1990), 171–72.

This teaching can be traced back to Augustine who, according to Eastern thought, misinterpreted part of Romans 5:12. In the New King James Version the verse reads as follows: "Therefore, just as through one man sin entered the world, and death through sin, and thus death spread to all men, because all sinned." The difficulty grows out of the last clause of the verse. The Greek text has ἐφ' ᾧ πάντες ἥμαρτον, which should be translated "in that all sinned."[157] However, Augustine was using the Vulgate, which translates the same clause as *eo quod omnes peccaverunt*. That translates into English as "in whom all sinned." What Augustine inferred from this reading is that "all men were mysteriously present in Adam[158] and "participated in his sin."[159] If each and every one of Adam's descendants has directly participated in Adam's sin, then each one is as culpable as he is; that is, they share in his personal guilt by virtue of being his offspring. "This means that every person, before any independent and willful act of his own is a generic inheritor of Adam's personal sin and guilt."[160] For Augustine, then, every individual comes into the world totally depraved and bereft of the image of God.

The Orthodox interpretation of Romans 5:12 is very different from Augustine's. Reading "in that all sinned," it becomes apparent that what humanity inherited from Adam was death and corruption, not culpability and total depravity.

---

157 "The Latin version of ἐφ' ᾧ πάντες ἥμαρτον in Rom 5:12 is *eo quod omnes peccaverunt*. The masculine *quo* must refer to 'one man,' mentioned earlier in the sentence: 'all have sinned *in Adam*.' The Greek does not allow for such a meaning, and admits two grammatical possibilities: ἁ ιφ ἐφ' ᾧ is neuter and means 'because,' the sentence defines death as the punishment for individual sins of any human (not 'original' sin); (b) if it is masculine, it refers to 'death' (*qanatoj*), so that death—as cosmic, personal reality—becomes the cause of individual human sins. It is in that sense that the text was read by Theodoret and Theodore, as well as by many other Greek authors including Chrysostom, Cyril of Alexandria, Maximus the Confessor, and later Byzantine theologians." John Meyendorff, *Rome, Constantinople, Moscow: Historical and Theological Studies* (Crestwood, NY: St. Vladimir's Seminary Press, 1996), 162–63. See also John Meyendorff, *Byzantine Theology: Historical Trends and Doctrinal Themes* (New York: Forham University Press, 1979), 143–46.

158 In its attempt to explain our "presence" in Adam's sin, Western theology has spawned numerous theories; e.g., the Calvinist idea of the federal headship of Adam. Millard J. Erickson, *Christian Theology*, 2nd ed. (Grand Rapids: Baker Book House, 1998), 631–36.

159 Symeon Rodger, "The Soteriology of Anselm of Canterbury: An Orthodox Perspective," *Greek Orthodox Theological Review* 34, no. 1 (1989): 31.

160 Jordan Bajis, *Common Ground: An Introduction to Eastern Christianity for the American Christian*, 2nd ed. (Minneapolis: Light & Life, 1996), 231–32.

> In the patristic view, sin is attributable only to the person-hypostasis, for the person is the irreducible subject of the nature he hypostasizes and that nature has no independent existence. Thus it is impossible to assert that all sinned in Adam and are somehow guilty even prior to their first volitive act.[161]

In Adam human nature was corrupted and subject to death. But each person remained free and therefore responsible (i.e., culpable) for his own actions. Thus guilt is a result of individual sin and is not inherited from Adam. The teaching of Romans 5:12 is that Adam sinned, corrupting our shared nature with death, and each one of us has sinned. "Original sin was not just an erroneous choice, not just an option for the wrong direction, but rather a refusal to ascend toward God, a desertion from the service of God."[162] So there "is indeed a consensus in Greek patristic and Byzantine tradition in identifying the inheritance of the Fall as an inheritance essentially of mortality."[163]

As these illustrations show, the translation and subsequent interpretation of the Holy Scriptures is not a matter that can be left to the whims of the individual translator or interpreter but has to be done within the community of the church and evaluated against the standard of its traditions. It is the church, not the individual, that normatively interprets the word of God, even as that interpretation takes place during the process of translation. In this way the faithful are both illumined by the truth of Scripture and protected from error.

***iii.*** Teaching the truth is, of course, the ultimate goal of this stage of contextualization.

No effort or culturally appropriate methodology should be spared in encouraging those seeking communion with God to study the Scriptures. Of Saint John Chrysostom, Philip Schaff writes, "There is no topic on which he dwells more frequently and earnestly than on the duty of

161 Rodger, "Soteriology of Anselm," 31–32.

162 Georges Florovsky, *Creation and Redemption*, Collected Works of Georges Florovsky, vol. 3 (Belmont, MA: Nordland, 1976), 85.

163 Meyendorff, *Byzantine Theology*, 145.

every Christian man and woman to study the Bible."[164] Again it must be emphasized that this study takes place within the context of tradition; that is, that the interpretations of Scripture being taught be in accord with those of the mind of the church. In other words, the study is not to be based on the private interpretations, opinions, or the personal impressions of those teaching and studying. The often-heard words "to *me* this text means ..." must be absent in the face of what the text actually means.

The privileged place for this teaching are the services of the church and in particular the Divine Liturgy. Its didactic potency is due, in large part, to the biblical texts that inform much of its text. Fr. John Breck refers to this as the

> "doxological" aspect of the Church's ongoing work of interpretation. Such interpretation occurs through both preaching and singing, since both the sermon and the words of liturgical hymns comment on the text of Scripture and serve to convey its essential meaning to God's people. In the context of the liturgy, then, the Word of God is preached and celebrated for the edification and spiritual nurture of those gathered in the church assembly. At the same time, that life-giving Word is *actualized* in the experience of the people, who, if they truly have ears to hear, respond to it with joy and thanksgiving. Thereby they complete their *leitourgia*, their "liturgical service," by offering both the Word and themselves back to God as a sacrifice of praise. Through this interaction between preaching and liturgical hymnography, proclamation of the divine Word creates a living communion between the believer and the triune God, from whom that eternal, life-giving Word comes forth.[165]

---

164 Philip Schaff, ch. 13 in "Prolegomena," in *Saint Chrysostom: On the Priesthood; Ascetic Treatises; Select Homilies and Letters; Homilies On the Statues*, vol. 9 of *A Select Library of the Nicene and Post-Nicene Fathers of the Christian Church*, ed. Philip Schaff (Grand Rapids: Eerdmans, 1975). http://www.ccel.org/ccel/schaff/npnf109.iii.xiii.html. See Saint Chrysostom, "Homily 2," in *Saint Chrysostom: On the Priesthood; Ascetic Treatises; Select Homilies and Letters; Homilies on the Statues*, vol. 9 of *A Select Library of the Nicene and Post-Nicene Fathers of the Christian Church*, ed. Philip Schaff (Grand Rapids: Eerdmans, 1975), http://www.ccel.org/ccel/schaff/npnf109.xv.iv.html.

165 Breck, "Biblical Interpretation," 79.

Take, as examples, the first three antiphons (hymns) of the Liturgy. The first is the text of Psalm 102 (103), the second is taken from Psalm 145 (146), and the third is made up of the Beatitudes from Matthew 5:3–12. Every aspect of the Liturgy is rooted in the biblical text.[166] As the faithful sing the service week after week, they gradually come to memorize large portions of the Bible. In addition to the underlying text, the Liturgy also has a special place for the reading of the Epistle and the Gospel of the day, which are selected from the lectionary of daily readings. The reading of the Gospel is generally followed by a homily, which provides yet another opportunity to teach the Word.

Outside the services, the lectionary provides daily exposure to the Scriptures, which are to be read with morning and evening prayers. In some cases these daily readings are sent out through an online forum which provides an opportunity for teaching and discussion. Individual study groups also bring people together around the Word. What is important in all of this is that the church is the context for the interpretation and the study of the Holy Scriptures. When practiced within the context of the church, the participants are held accountable to the teachings of the church and avoid the dangers inherent in allowing a simple exchange of opinions to determine the meaning of the text. By translating, exegeting, teaching, and celebrating the Holy Scriptures, the church is establishing one aspect of the core context in which God himself is encountered.

## 2. Apostolic Succession

Another mechanism given to the church to aid the development of the core missionary context is apostolic succession. This involves the ongoing line of bishops who are the successors of the apostles. Confirming the New Testament pattern (Eph 2:20; 2 Tim 2:2), Clement of Alexandria states that "the Lord after his resurrection imparted knowledge to James the Just and to John and Peter, and they imparted it to the rest of the apostles, and the rest of the apostles to the seventy."[167] That this practice

166 Cf. Constantine Nasr, *The Bible in the Liturgy* (Oklahoma City: Theosis, 1988).

167 Eusebius Pamphilius, ch. 1 in "Church History," in *Eusebius Pamphilus: Church History; Life of Constantine; Oration in Praise of Constantine*. Vol. 1 of *A Select Library of the Nicene and Post-Nicene Fathers of the Christian Church*, 2nd series, ed. Philip Schaff and Henry Wace (Grand Rapids: Eerdmans, 1975), http://www.ccel.org/ccel/schaff/npnf201.iii.vii.ii.html.

was adopted by the early church is evident in the writings of Irenaeus of Lyons who insists:

> It is within the power of all, therefore, in every Church, who may wish to see the truth, to contemplate clearly the tradition of the apostles manifested throughout the whole world; and we are in a position to reckon up those who were by the apostles instituted bishops in the Churches, and [to demonstrate] the succession of these men to our own times.[168]

Because apostolic succession was the norm, Eusebius of Caesarea begins his *Ecclesial History* by announcing "that it is his purpose 'to hand down a written account of the successions of the holy Apostles … and of the number of those who were illustrious guides and leaders in especially prominent Dioceses.'"[169] This practice was also formalized in the Nicene Creed, which confesses "one holy Catholic and Apostolic Church," and which, as part of the official teaching of the church, has been continued throughout the centuries down to our own day. It is not my intention to offer a defense of this ancient practice.[170] Rather I want to show how this gift, this continuity of ecclesial office, benefits the faithful, how it engages the conditions of human personhood and helps establish part of the base context for the mission of the church.[171]

---

168 Saint Irenaeus, "Against Heresies (Book 3, Chapter 3)," trans. Alexander Roberts and William Rambaut, in *Ante-Nicene Fathers*, vol. 1, ed. Alexander Roberts, James Donaldson, and A. Cleveland Coxe (Buffalo, NY: Christian Literature Publishing, 1885), revised and edited for New Advent by Kevin Knight, http://www.newadvent.org/fathers/0103303.htm.

169 Thomas Halton, *The Church*. Message of the Fathers of the Church, edited by Thomas Halton, Vol. 4, (Wilmington Deleware: Michael Glazier, 1985.),98 "It is my purpose to write an account of the successions of the holy apostles, as well as of the times which have elapsed from the days of our Saviour to our own; and to relate the many important events which are said to have occurred in the history of the Church; and to mention those who have governed and presided over the Church in the most prominent parishes, and those who in each generation have proclaimed the divine word either orally or in writing." EH 1.1.1. He even mentions the list of apostolic succession of the bishops and notes that in each city "things are as the law, the prophets, and the Lord preach." EH 6.8.

170 For that, see for example: Francis A. Sullivan, *From Apostles to Bishops: The Development of the Episcopacy in the Early Church* (Mahwah; NY: Newman, 2001).

171 It should be noted that it is not only the Eastern and Roman Churches that seek to maintain the idea of apostolic succession. The Lutheran theologian Pannenberg

## a. A Divinely Established Finite Structure

This gift of tradition provides the church with a hierarchical structure that is initiated by divinity and implemented by humanity. As such it synergistically bridges the gap between the divine and the created order. Notice how the early Fathers affirm that finite/infinite connection by equating the bishops with the presence of Christ. Ignatius of Antioch admonishes the faithful in Smyrna to "follow the bishop, even as Jesus Christ does the Father … Wherever the bishop shall appear, there let the multitude [of the people] also be; even as, wherever Jesus Christ is, there is the Catholic Church."[172] And writing to the Ephesians, "For even Jesus Christ, our inseparable life, is the [manifested] will of the Father; as also bishops, settled everywhere to the utmost bounds [of the earth], are so by the will of Jesus Christ."[173]

So for every new region into which the church expanded, new bishops were appointed, who in turn ordained priests to represent them in the local

---

responds to the Catholic idea that the Reformation churches lost the succession of bishops by insisting that "Luther maintained the idea of episcopal succession of office. He also wrote in his 1531 *Commentary on Galatians* that to the end of the world this was the *generalis post Apostólos vocatio in orbe terrarum*, to which he added *neque est mutanda* (*WA* 40/1, 59, 23f). The apostles had called their disciples to be their successors, as Paul called Timothy and Titus. These, in turn, called bishops as their own successors, and that has been continued into our own time. According to Luther's judgment, this structure was not to be changed. That did not rule out the possibility that in times of need— when there is no bishop who can supply the communities with preachers of the gospel—another way would have to be found, as Luther wrote in 1523: 'The example of Titus and Timothy does not apply here, rather one has to call someone out of the community, and God determines whether he is confirmed by Titus or not' (*WA* 11, 414, 30ff). According to Luther, however, this is not the normal means of investing an individual with an office in the church—the normative mode remains ordination in episcopal succession. That is a mark of the unity of the church in the teaching of the apostles and must be preserved." Wolfhart Pannenberg, "Ecumenical Tasks in Relationship to the Roman Catholic Church," *Pro Ecclesia* 15, no. 2 (2006): 168.

172 Ignatius of Antioch, "The Epistle of Ignatius to the Smyrnaeans," trans. Alexander Roberts and James Donaldson, in *Ante-Nicene Fathers*, vol. 1, ed. Alexander Roberts, James Donaldson, and A. Cleveland Coxe (Buffalo, NY: Christian Literature Publishing, 1885), revised and edited for New Advent by Kevin Knight, http://www.newadvent.org/fathers/0109.htm.

173 Ignatius of Antioch, "The Epistle of Ignatius to the Ephesians," trans. Alexander Roberts and James Donaldson, in *Ante-Nicene Fathers*, vol. 1, ed. Alexander Roberts, James Donaldson, and A. Cleveland Coxe (Buffalo, NY: Christian Literature Publishing, 1885), revised and edited for New Advent by Kevin Knight, http://www.newadvent.org/fathers/0104.htm.

parishes. This succession of bishops gives the church a living link back to that divine-human union, the Incarnation itself. As a result, something of infinity resides in the structure of the church providing for a stability that protects from the perpetual advances of power-hungry men and that is immune to the pressures of nationalism and to the social and political pressures that have, for example, caused some Christian organizations to reshape themselves in the image of prevailing political structures.[174] But the succession of episcopal office established by Christ, because its origin is divine, engages the dual nature of human personhood, anchors it in the infinite, while at the same time allowing for temporal and spatial expression.

> Through countryside and city [the apostles] preached, and they appointed their earliest converts, testing them by the Spirit, to be the bishops and deacons of future believers. Nor was this a novelty, for bishops and deacons had been written about a long time earlier … Our apostles knew through our Lord Jesus Christ that there would be strife for the office of bishop. For this reason, therefore, having received perfect foreknowledge, they appointed those who have already been mentioned and afterwards added the further provision that, if they should die, other approved men should succeed to their ministry.[175]

By engaging both the infinite and the finite aspects of human personhood, apostolic succession also creates a form of unity of teaching and practice that would otherwise not be possible. Both Irenaeus and Tertullian recognize this practical benefit.

> The Church, though dispersed through the whole world, even to the ends of the earth, has received from the

---

174 This is not to say that the church has not, at times, been greatly damaged by the power hungry and nationalism. Yet because of its divine origin the church has survived all such setbacks. See for example: Donald Fairbairn, "Orthodoxy and Nationalism," in *Eastern Orthodoxy through Western Eyes* (Louisville: Westminster John Knox Press, 2002), 143–51.

175 Pope Clement I, "Letter to the Corinthians," 42:4–5, 44:1–3 (AD 80), in "Apostolic Succession," ed. Robert H. Brom, Catholic Answers, 2004, http://www.catholic.com/library/Apostolic_Succession.asp.

> apostles and their disciples … this preaching and this faith … as if occupying but one house, carefully preserves it … and she proclaims them, and teaches them, and hands them down, with perfect harmony, as if she possessed only one mouth.[176]

> The churches, although they are so many and so great, comprise but the one primitive Church, [founded] by the apostles, from which they all [spring] … All are primitive, and all are apostolic, while they are all proved to be one in unity.[177]

### b. *Didactic Continuity*

One of the most striking things about apostolic succession is that the role of the bishops was not primarily administrative, but rather to preserve apostolic teaching.[178] This is already seen in the New Testament with Saint Paul telling Timothy that the things he had heard should be passed on to faithful men who would be able to teach others as well (2 Tim 2:2). Note that this passage refers to three generations of apostolic succession—Paul's, Timothy's, and those that Timothy would teach.[179]

---

176 Saint Irenaeus, "Against Heresies (Book 1, Chapter 10)," trans. Alexander Roberts and William Rambaut, in *Ante-Nicene Fathers*, vol. 1, ed. Alexander Roberts, James Donaldson, and A. Cleveland Coxe (Buffalo, NY: Christian Literature Publishing, 1885), revised and edited for New Advent by Kevin Knight, http://www.newadvent.org/fathers/0103110.htm.

177 Tertullian, "Demurrer against the Heretics," 20, (AD 200), in "Apostolic Succession," ed. Robert H. Brom, Catholic Answers, 2004, http://www.catholic.com/library/Apostolic_Succession.asp.

178 This too is an idea accepted by the Reformation. As Pannenberg notes, "The Reformation understood the office of bishop as well as that of the pastor or presbyter as a ministry of preaching (*CA*, 28, 5). That the content of the office of bishop in the Augsburg Confession is considered identical with that of the presbyter or pastors, as it is expressed in the phrase *episcopi seu pastores* (*CA*, 28, 30.53), is, nevertheless, in keeping with the prevailing opinion of medieval canon law, as made known by the *Decretum Gratiani* (*Deer. Grat.* I D 95 c 5): The office of bishop and the office of pastor are in essence one and the same office, to be distinguished only by the extent of the bishop's jurisdiction and his right to ordain." Pannenberg, "Ecumenical Tasks," 168.

179 Cf. Robert H. Brom, ed., "Apostolic Succession," Catholic Answers, 2004, http://www.catholic.com/library/Apostolic_Succession.asp.

> Where in practice was [the] apostolic testimony or tradition to be found? ... The most obvious answer was that the apostles had committed it orally to the Church, where it had been handed down from generation to generation ... Unlike the alleged secret tradition of the Gnostics, it was entirely public and open, having been entrusted by the apostles to their successors, and by these in turn to those who followed them, and was visible in the Church for all who cared to look for it.[180]

In the early church the rise of heretics made the question of true doctrine an existential concern. The heretics, it seemed, were very adept at twisting the Scriptures to fit their own teachings. Thus some standard was needed against which to measure competing claims. There had to be some way of determining how those Scriptures should be interpreted. That, it seems, is what Tertullian had in mind when, ignoring the defective exegesis of one heretic, he asked, who their bishop was.[181] Which was the same thing as asking if the teaching was apostolic. Similarly, Saint Athenasius urges the faithful to look carefully at that very tradition, teaching, and faith of the Catholic Church from the very beginning, which the Lord gave, the apostles preached, and the Fathers preserved.[182] This

> identity of the oral tradition with the original revelation is guaranteed by the unbroken succession of Bishops in the great sees going back lineally to the apostles ... An additional safeguard is supplied by the Holy Spirit, for the

180 J. N. D. Kelly, *Early Christian Doctrines*, 4th ed. (London: Black, 1968), 37.

181 "But if there be any [heresies] which are bold enough to plant [their origin] in the midst of the apostolic age, that they may thereby seem to have been handed down by the apostles, because they existed in the time of the apostles, we can say: Let them produce the original records of their churches; let them unfold the roll of their Bishops, running down in due succession from the beginning in such a manner that [their first] bishop shall be able to show for his ordainer and predecessor some one of the apostles or of apostolic men—a man, moreover, who continued steadfast with the apostles. For this is the manner in which the apostolic churches transmit their registers: as the church of Smyrna, which records that Polycarp was placed therein by John; as also the church of Rome, which makes Clement to have been ordained in like manner by Peter." Tertullian, *Prescription Against Heretics*, 32. http://www.newadvent.org/fathers/0311.htm.

182 Saint Athenasius, *First Letter to Serapion*, as quoted in George Bebis, *The Mind of the Fathers*, 17.

> message committed was to the Church, and the Church is the home of the Spirit. Indeed, the Church's bishops are … Spirit-endowed men who have been vouchsafed "an infallible charism of truth."[183]

We see then that this mechanism of preservation, this gift of tradition, engages the human faculty of belief, not only by showing what is to be believed (i.e., how the Scriptures are to be interpreted), but also by adjudicating between the competing claims of false teachers. The bishops are the church's chief exegetes and its primary defenders of the truth. Tracing their lineage back to apostolic times, they set the didactic parameters of the contemporary core context of missions.

### c. *Accountability*

Initially this God-given structure might seem to be at odds with human freedom to self-actualize. I suppose that in one way it does limit that freedom simply by holding the faithful to apostolic teaching and practice. By eliminating individualism in the church, the faithful are protected from heresy and held accountable for their own beliefs and piety. It is the bishops' responsibility to set boundaries and regulate the affairs of the church in accordance with apostolic tradition. Thus the faithful are not free to believe and do anything they choose to do. But they are able to live life in Christ freed from the burden of possible violations of the truth or divergence from proper practice. Secure in what they believe, affirmed in their practice, they can freely express their faith without fear of error. Should they wander from the true faith, the love and strength of their bishop will bring them back to the right way. Thus the very constraints implied in apostolic succession serve to secure a true freedom of faith in Christ.

### d. *Structures of Support*

Finally, the succession of bishops engages the human faculty and need for moral foundations. Another contribution made by the bishops is an

183 Kelly, *Early Christian Doctrines*, 37.

active, unified, and authoritative engagement with the moral and social issues of the day. This is often done by the Synod of Bishops who, in keeping twith their responsibility to teach, issue guidance for the church. For example, one of the pressing concerns of contemporary culture is that of the sanctity of life. How should we as Christians face the challenges of the raging debate over abortion? It is not uncommon for believers, faced with an overwhelming amount of conflicting information, to disengage, to give up and try to ignore the problem. Here the bishops come to our aid. By way of example, the Holy Synod of Bishops of the Orthodox Church in America issued the following affirmations:

> Abortion is condemned as a form of murder.
>
> The teaching of the Orthodox Church is well expressed by canon 91 of the Sixth Ecumenical Council. Those who give drugs for procuring abortion, and those who receive poisons to kill the fetus, are subjected to the penalty for murder.
>
> The willful aborting of unborn children, as an act of murder, is contrary to the will of God. The unborn child is human life with potential, and not potential human life. The Church recognizes the existence of certain extreme cases in which difficult moral decisions must be made in view of saving human life, and fully sympathizes with those who must make such decisions. Such an extreme circumstance is the definitely diagnosed danger to the life of the mother at childbirth. The mother must decide whether to lay down her own life for that of her unborn child. Whatever the decisions of human legislatures and courts, the Church cannot accept the willful destruction of an unborn child at any stage of its development as anything other than the destruction of life.[184]

184 The Holy Synod of Bishops, "Encyclical Letter of the Holy Synod of Bishops of the Orthodox Church in America on Marriage," Orthodox Church in America, http://oca.org/holy-synod/encyclicals/on-marriage.

These affirmations were disseminated to all the parishes and are reaffirmed annually on the Sanctity of Life Sunday in January.[185] It is this kind of practical guidance that helps the faithful formulate second-order beliefs, beliefs about the rightness of certain actions.

### e. *Building the Core Context with the Bishops*

Apostolic succession is a divinely imposed, humanly implementable ecclesial structure, which helps define an essential part of the base missionary context. Since this structure engages all four conditions of human personhood by providing normative frameworks, the construction of this aspect of the core context is not an expression of creative freedom, but rather one of obedience. The task is not to adapt these structures or allow them to be informed by the prevailing social imaginary, but rather to preserve the divinely given arrangement in the face of competing models. For example, ideas of individual freedom should not be allowed to transform the church into some kind of democracy. That would only serve to break the divine-human link, it would transform authoritative teaching into personal opinion,[186] and provide little in the way of accountability and guidance. Obedience and submission is called for, and in the missionary situation that involves establishing, working within, and honoring the structures set by apostolic succession.

**i.** In the case of initial outreach into an area not currently under the jurisdiction of a canonical bishop, the evangelists and church planters will be authorized for ministry and sent by a neighboring bishop.

Once the work has begun and there are converts to care for, a new bishop for that region can be appointed. This pattern can be seen at work in the history of the Russian Orthodox Mission to Alaska.

By 1650 Russian adventurers had already begun the exploration of the Bering Sea.[187] During the next fifty years Siberian frontiersmen

---

185 Metropolitan Jonah, "Sanctity of Life Sunday 2009," January 18, 2009, Orthodox Church in America, http://oca.org/holy-synod/statements/metropolitan-jonah/jonah-2009-0118.

186 The Eastern Church welcomes and encourages individual thought and opinion. In the theological realm such thoughts are referred to as *theologumena*. However, these opinions must be subjected to or tested by the mind of the church to see if they conform to the teachings that have been handed down.

187 The earliest settlement was established in 1648 by "the Russian explorer Simeon

occasionally crossed the straits to trade with native Americans. Once the Alaskan coast had been mapped by Vitus Bering (1728, 1741), regular navigation across the straits became possible, and Russian traders and trappers began to make annual or biannual trading expeditions to the Aleutian Archipelago in search of valuable furs.

One of the most interesting aspects of these early encounters is the way in which these traders adapted to local culture and at the same time initiated the gradual evangelization of the indigenous people. The frontiersmen, mostly bachelors, learned the tribal languages, studied native customs and "married local women who provided their Siberian husbands with the same clothing, tools, and food they would have given native Alaskan spouses." So thorough was the acculturation of the Russians that the British explorer James Cook, who visited the Aleutian Islands in 1793, "could not distinguish the Slavs from the native Alaskans." But the Russian frontiersmen had also brought with them their own religious traditions. These Orthodox laymen brought the Orthodox faith to North America, "baptized their own native wives and children, and even constructed the first chapels."[188] And so the first "missionaries" planted the seed of Orthodoxy into the North American culture without imposing their own. In other words, the first converts in North America became Orthodox Christians without first having to become Russian.

By the end of the eighteenth-century, Russian businessmen had established a trading colony on Kodiak Island and asked that a priest be sent to care for the spiritual needs of the community. Then Metropolitan Gabriel responded by commissioning an entire team of missionaries from the Valaam monastery in Finland. They arrived in Alaska on September 24, 1794. Not long after, Fr. Joasaph reported on their initial success.

> I have, praise God, baptized more that seven thousand Americans, and celebrated more than two thousand weddings. We have built a church and, if time allows, we shall build another, and two portable ones, but a fifth is

---

Dezhnev who sailed from the Arctic Ocean, around the Chukotka Peninsula, and founded the post of Anadyr on the Bering Sea, facing Alaska in 1648." Mark Stokoe and Leonid Kishkovsky, "Orthodox Christians in North America (1794–1994)," Orthodox Church in America, http://oca.org/history-archives/orthodox-christians-na/chapter-1.

188 Ibid.

> needed. We live comfortably, they love us and we them. They are a kind people, but poor. They take baptism so much to heart that they smash and burn all the magic charms given them by the shamans.[189]

In the decades that followed, the church sent more missionaries "to the many tribes of its eastern territories, devising alphabets for the native languages, translating the Scriptures and service books, and training native clergy."[190] Among those missionaries was Fr. John Veniaminov who, after missionary work on the island of Unalaska, was ordained as the bishop of the newly established Diocese of Kamchatka and the Kurile and Aleutian Islands. Bishop Innocent took up residence in Sitka and

> for the next eighteen years he supervised the remarkable expansion of the mission into the interior and northern coastal regions of Alaska. In Sitka he launched a major building campaign that produced the Mission House and its Annunciation Chapel … St. Michael's Cathedral was consecrated in 1848 in the presence of nearly fifty clergy of the Alaska mission. This dramatic rise in the number of clergy was due above all to another of Bishop Innocent's projects, a seminary where native and creole, or mixed-race, candidates for ordination studied not only theology but also native languages (Aleutian, Eskimo, and Tlingit), medicine, and Latin.[191]

Another more recent example of this basic pattern can be seen from the dramatic revival of the Church of Albania. Almost exterminated by an aggressively atheistic state, the fall of communism brought a new opportunity. In this case, since there had been a church in Albania, albeit nearly extinct and without a bishop, the ecumenical patriarch appointed a bishop, Archbishop Anastasios, to oversee a renewal of missionary work in Albania. Under his direction a number of missionaries from several

---

189 Cited in John H. Erickson, *Orthodox Christians in America: A Short History* (New York: Oxford University Press, 2008), 23–24.

190 Ibid., 27.

191 Ibid., 29.

countries worked to proclaim the gospel, plant new churches, rebuild those destroyed, train local clergy at a newly organized seminary, and initiate the rebirth of an ancient church.[192]

**ii.** The two previous examples illustrate the way in which ecclesial continuity can be established and maintained as the church reaches out into new areas or is reestablished in areas from which it was driven, and how that continuity facilitates the overall mission.

In the case of mission work in areas already under the oversight of a bishop, all such efforts are to be conducted with his blessing. This pattern is well illustrated by the legacy left by Archbishop Dmitri of the OCA's Diocese of the South.[193] The diocese was established in 1978 out of the Southern Missionary District with about sixteen parishes, and under Archbishop Dmitri's leadership it has now grown to over seventy.[194] The planting of our mission in Raleigh, North Carolina, is typical of missionary outreach under the constant guidance of a bishop.

Early in September 2000 a group of about twenty Orthodox faithful in the Raleigh area of North Carolina asked their bishop for permission to start a new parish. Archbishop Dmitri granted his blessing, approved the parish's name (Holy Transfiguration), and assigned a priest. Such an assignment does not entail "employment" by the local mission whereby the priest would work at the behest of mission and be subject to their individual whims. Rather the appointment creates a direct link of responsibility between the priest and the bishop, whom he represents, to whom he has pledged obedience, and to whom he is alone responsible. Through the end of October 2000 they met for weekend services at a local Holiday Inn. After an intensive search, space in a light industrial complex was found, rented, and transformed into a place of worship. At the same time, the national church (OCA) and Diocese of the South awarded Holy Transfiguration a three-year church planting grant. By the beginning of 2001 the mission was "up and running."

192 Luke Veronis, *Go Forth: Stories of Mission and Resurrection in Albania* (Ben Lomond: Conciliar, 2009).

193 For a brief history of the diocese, see B. Peter Robichau, "From District to Diocese: An Examination of the Founding and Missionary Methods of the OCA Diocese of the South," masters thesis (St. Vladimir's Orthodox Theological Seminary, 2010).

194 Ibid., 65, n. 3.

After only a year (January 2002) the facilities had become too small. Additional space was gained by renting an adjacent unit. By January 2004 the mission successfully assumed full financial responsibility when the church planting grant came to an end. Financially independent and still growing, the parish offered a full cycle of services with an average attendance of about seventy at Sunday Liturgy.

By the beginning of 2005, larger facilities were again needed. The obvious next step was to locate and purchase property for a new church building, but in spite of considerable effort no affordable property could be found. However, a church building for rent was located and rented. The new facility provided more space in the nave, an adequate fellowship hall with a kitchen, more classrooms, and offices. In June 2006 they signed the lease for the new building and started necessary renovations. On July 15, 2006, they began church services at their new location.

On August 27, 2009, the process of purchasing the church and property was completed. Right from the beginning, then, the church was present in the person of the bishop, as a foundation for the base context of evangelism.[195]

These applications of apostolic structure show how a base missionary context, defined in part by ecclesial continuity, is something that both the faithful and the missionaries need. Fledgling churches are often a small minority of the local population and are easily overwhelmed by that feeling of smallness. However, knowing that they are part of something that is larger, not only geographically but also historically, gives them courage and the stability to persevere, a courage which is not tied to the statistics of the immediate situation, but is rooted in the register of bishops that can be traced back to the apostles.

## 3. Liturgical Structures

As indicated above, human persons are temporal beings caught up in the process of "becoming"; that is, reaching the fullness of their destiny in God. This temporality causes them to be acutely aware of the passing of time and the great rhythms of life—the seasons, the stages of life, even

195 Holy Transfiguration Orthodox Church, "Information," http://holyTransfiguration-oca.org/information.htm.

daily routines. In fact these basic patterns are so important that we bemoan their absence with words and phrases like "chaos," "hectic," and "out of control." We have a built-in need for ordered time, yet we always seem to be running out of time, are rarely on time, and are constantly scraping to save time.[196] It is here that the church's gift of liturgical structures comes to our aid. This *officium divinum* is a life-encompassing pattern, a sacred rhythm, a finely textured hierarchy that is superimposed on the flat chaos of secular time, effectively sanctifying all of time. This structure is not defined solely by the various offices, but by the totality of the way in which they are set into a liturgy of time, what has been called the Ordo.[197] This liturgy of time is tied to three great cycles: the daily, weekly, and yearly. The daily cycle is made up of five services or offices: Vespers, Compline, Nocturnes, Matins, and the hours (first, third, sixth, ninth, and the interhours). The weekly cycle does not have its own offices, except for the Sunday celebration of the Eucharist, but inserts hymnographic material into the daily offices according to the day of the week using one of the eight liturgical tones or melodies.[198] The yearly cycle is dominated by Nativity with its weeks of Advent, Easter with its preparatory weeks of Lent, and Pentecost. Other feasts such as Theophany are interspersed throughout the year giving it its basic pattern and predictable order. In this way every phase of life is included in the rhythm of sacred time.[199] This is not the place to describe the details of these offices.[200] However, I do want to show how this Ordo meets basic human needs by engaging each of the four conditions of personhood.

---

196 As to the futility of that idea, see Michael Ende, *Momo* (New York: Penguin Books, 1986).

197 Alexander Schmemann, *Introduction to Liturgical Theology*, 4th ed. (Crestwood, NY: St. Vladimir's Seminary Press, 2003), 41–45.

198 The daily themes are as follows: Saturday, All Saints; Sunday, Christ's Resurrection; Monday, Bodiless Powers (Angels, Archangels); Tuesday, Prophets (esp. Saint John the Forerunner); Wednesday, Cross (Judas' Betrayal); Thursday, Holy Apostles and Hierarchs (esp. Saint Nicholas); Friday, Cross and Crucifixion.

199 This included the great cycle of birth and death (and everything in between), for which the church has liturgical acts and prayers. St. Tikhon's Monastery, trans., *The Great Book of Needs: Expanded and Supplemented*, 4 vols. (South Canaan, PA: St. Tikhon's Seminary Press, 1998).

200 For that, see Demetrius Wysochansky, *Divine Office: Horologion, Octoechos, Triodion, Menaion* (Stamford, CT: Ukrainian Catholic Eparchy of Stamford, 2003); Hugh Wybrew, *Orthodox Feasts of Jesus Christ and the Virgin Mary: Liturgical Texts with Commentary* (Crestwood, NY: St. Vladimir's Seminary Press, 2000).

### a. *Finite Foretaste of Infinite*

The finite/infinite nature of human being is most obviously engaged by the Divine Liturgy and Eucharist. While there are times when this liturgy is not celebrated, it is not limited to any one element of the three cycles. It is celebrated on all the feast days of the yearly cycle, any day of the week, and not just in the morning, but occasionally in the afternoon, evening, or even the night. It has a temporal independence that marks another kind of time—the time of God's kingdom, of the *eschaton*. The Divine Liturgy begins with the exclamation, "Blessed is the kingdom of the Father, and of the Son, and of the Holy Spirit." With this appeal to the kingdom, all ordinary time is suspended, and we enter into sacred time and are given a foretaste of the kingdom.

> The new element in Christianity is not its conception of time or the world living in time, but in the fact that the event which … constituted the "center' of time and which defined its meaning has already begun … The Eucharist is therefore the manifestation of the Church as the new aeon; it is participation in the Kingdom as *parousia*, as the presence of the Resurrected and Resurrecting Lord … This is a conquest of time not in the sense of rendering it empty and valueless, but rather in the sense of creating the possibility of being made partakers of or participants in the "coming aeon" … while still living in "this world."[201]

For the hour and a half of the Liturgy we are no longer bound by ordinary time but are granted a moment of eternity. Time, then, must be hierarchical. There is the ordinary, cyclical time of our lives that passes irrevocably moment by moment. But there is also the time of eternity, of which we get a sense during the Divine Liturgy.

---

201 Alexander Schmemann, *Introduction to Liturgical Theology*, 3rd ed. (Crestwood, NY: St. Vladimir's Seminary Press, 1986), 71–73.

### *b. Truth Presented, Proven, Preserved*

The human faculty of belief is engaged by it being connected with the rhythm of God's mighty acts. The yearly cycle, in particular, is an ongoing reminder of all that God has done for us. It is the story of salvation repeatedly told, beginning with Christ's birth, including his death and resurrection, his ascension, and ending with the coming of the Holy Spirit. Throughout the centuries that story has been tested and found to be complete and true, so much so that the liturgical texts of the church are themselves sources of biblical and theological truth. Time itself becomes the teacher, never letting us forget where we are in this grand narrative, calling us to belief. The liturgy of time gives us the opportunity to regularly reaffirm what we believe, even as that belief tends to fade with the passing of ordinary time.

### *c. Participation in the Truth*

The liturgical cycle also provides an environment for human agency, self-actualization. In order for the Ordo to be effective, the faithful have to participate. This can mean anything from attending a Sunday Liturgy, to taking time off for a feast-day service, or to organizing one's personal calendar around the festal cycle. Since the very nature of liturgy is primarily sacrifice to God rather than benefit derived, the faithfuls' action during the service has to be that of deliberate engagement. Not only attending to the text, but singing the hymns, praying the prayers, reciting the Creed, making the sign of the cross, venerating the icons. Without that active participation the truth of the Liturgy passes us by, the gradations of the hierarchy of time are lost, belief is weakened, and participation in the divine limited. But it is precisely the opportunity to do those things, and to do them without fear of error or distortion, that the liturgical framework provides. It counters the chaos of secular time and draws us into the peaceful, pulsing, living rhythm of eternity.

### *d. Transformation*

That, of course, will change us; not simply through content that is truth, but also through the rightness of order itself. The Ordo establishes second-order beliefs about time and its use. Most of us accept the imposition of temporal orders rather uncritically. For example, when our society flattens the hierarchy of time, decides that there was no such thing as sacred time, and begins treating Sunday as any other work day, how do we respond? Many have simply capitulated and gone over to doing anything from shopping, to carpentry, to playing football on Sundays. In other words, we have lost a sense of what we should believe about time. Participating in the liturgical life of the church would sort that out. I don't think it is possible to actively participate in these structures and to, for example, take one's vacation over Easter. Participation leads to transformation and to a morality of time informed not by the secular but by the sacred layers of time and liturgy.

### *e. Building the Core Context with Liturgy*

Since these liturgical structures speak to the fundamental needs of human personhood, they must also be considered part of the base context of missions, part of what God is offering to the world. To abandon what we have received in favor of personal preference would be to violate the nature of the worship that the Ordo entails. The term "liturgy" has several layers of meaning. Etymology shows that it is a form of service, an offering, a sacrifice. What is important here is the idea that worship is centered on God and not the worshiper. It is not about some benefit derived, but rather is about a sacrifice offered, service rendered, hard work (Rom 11:33–36; 12:1,2). If that is true, then the individual taste of the worshiper is irrelevant. Any alteration of the Ordo based on personal preference, age, contemporary standards of music, modern technologies, is immediately disqualified. The listener's aesthetic sensibilities are not the issue. In other words, there is no need to adapt, short of translating the texts and resolving the occasional musical issue. The Liturgy is not to be revised in order to make it more appealing to a specific population. Rather, that population is to be taught how to participate in the Ordo. It is and is to remain an alternative to the world around us. It is to remain identifiable as ecclesial activity and not an imitation of everything else that society offers in its place. The Ordo is not to be recast in the image of any particular culture.

Nevertheless, culture does have some effect on the Liturgy. That has certainly been true throughout the history of liturgical development. For example, when in the early 1800s missionaries to Alaska discovered that their translations of Scripture and service books could not be chanted using the traditional eight tones, they developed a new set of eight tones that complemented the local languages.[202] As a result, Alaskan liturgical chant is distinct from its Greek or Russian cousins, and yet it is still clearly the Liturgy, because the changes were fitted into the traditional structure of the Liturgy. In other words, there can be liturgical development, new petitions, new prayers, new hymns, but nothing that violates the fundamental structure of the service and, above all, nothing that is introduced by individuals outside the context of the Synod of Bishops. What this process of liturgical development looks like can be seen from the history of the Liturgy of the Presanctified Gifts.

Today the church makes use of three liturgies—the Liturgy of Saint John Chrysostom, the Liturgy of Saint Basil the Great, and the Liturgy of the Presanctified by Saint Gregory Dialogos. As the name indicates, the elements offered during this service are presanctified; i.e., consecrated during a previous liturgy. This Liturgy is celebrated during Lent on those days when the ordinary Liturgy is not celebrated.

The Liturgy of the Presanctified Gifts probably has its roots in various offices celebrated in Jerusalem and Antioch.[203] It was probably transferred from Antioch to Constantinople, some time during the sixth century, where it underwent further liturgical development, receiving its final shape sometime after the eleventh century. It is first mentioned in an anonymous work, the *Paschalion* (616), where we are told:

> In the fourth year of Emperor Heraclius (614), under Patriarch Sergius of Constantinople, beginning with the first week of Lent, the people, following the Psalm "Let my prayer ascend to You" and the celebrant's invocation

202 For texts and mp3 examples, see All Saints of North America, "Alaskan Orthodox Texts," http://www.asna.ca/alaska/.

203 The oldest text of the Presanctified Liturgy as it is celebrated today is found in the *Codex Barberini* (eighth century). The oldest description of the Presanctified Liturgy is provided in a short work: Saint Theodore, "Explicatio Divinae Liturgiae Praesanctificatorum," in *Patrologia Graeco-Latina*, vol. 90 (Turnhout, Belgium: Brepolis), cols. 1687–90.

> "Through the gift of Christ," while the Presanctified Gifts were being carried to the altar, started to sing "Now the Powers of heaven." This hymn is sung not only during Lent, but every time the Presanctified Gifts are celebrated.[204]

From this source we can conclude that: (1) at the beginning of the seventh century the Liturgy of the Presanctified Gifts was well developed and celebrated in Constantinople, (2) during Lent of 614, a new hymn "Now the Powers of Heaven" was introduced, and (3) at that time this Liturgy was celebrated not only during Lent but also on some other occasions.[205]

According to Gabriele Winkler, the modern Byzantine Liturgy of the Presanctified Gifts is composed of four parts: (1) the present-day Vespers, which was developed between the eleventh and thirteenth centuries and replaced the original Evening Service at Constantinople, (2) the Antiochian Ninth Hour service used during the great fast with special Old Testament readings, (3) the original kernel of the Antiochian Vesper which included the rite of illumination and the censing at Psalm 103, and (4) the Antiochian communion service.[206]

The next stage of development probably took place between 511 and 518, when the Liturgy of the Presanctified Gifts was introduced by Patriarch Severus. The regularly celebrated Liturgy was considered to be a joyous celebration.[207] Lent, by contrast, was a time of repentance, thus the celebration of the Divine Liturgy during the Lenten period was

---

204 Anonymous, "Chronicon Paschale," in *Patrologia Graeco-Latina*, vol. 92 (Turnhout, Belgium: Brepolis), col. 989.

205 Canon 52 of the Council of Trullo (692) states, "On all days of the holy fast of Lent, except on the Sabbath, the Lord's day and the holy day of the Annunciation, the Liturgy of the Presanctified is to be said." More recent legislation limited its celebration to the Wednesdays and Fridays of Lent, and to Monday, Tuesday and Wednesday of Holy Week. A. Mikita, *Typykon* (1901), 174, quoted in Byzantine Leaflet Series 21 (Pittsburgh: Byzantine Seminary Press, 1981).

206 Gabriele Winkler, "Der Geschichtlich Hintergrund der Presanctienvesper," *Origens Christianus* 56 (1975): 185–206.

207 A Syrian commentator and contemporary of Saint John Chrysostom, Theodore of Mopsuestia (d. 426), in his recently (1933) discovered *Catecheses* writes, "To participate in the Mysteries (Liturgy) is to commemorate the death of the Lord, which procures for us the resurrection and the joy of immortality." Theodore of Mopsuestia, *Catecheses* 15, 7.

limited to Saturdays and Sundays.[208] In order to give to the faithful an opportunity to receive Holy Communion during the week, the Liturgy of the Presanctified Gifts was celebrated on the other Lenten days. At the time of Patriarch Severus of Antioch, the Eucharist part of the service took place at the conclusion of the Evening Office, which was made up of (1) the lighting of the lamps, (2) the reading of Psalm 103, and (3) the litanies.

Sometime before the seventh century the Old Testament Readings, Vespers, and the actual Communion were combined into a single service and adopted in Constantinople.[209] This may have been during the time of Justinian and probably before the council in 536. It was here in Constantinople that the Liturgy of the Presanctified Gifts received further development[210] and its final form.[211]

From this brief review it can be seen that the process of liturgical development is a slow, almost reluctant one; that it is regulated by bishops and councils; that it is not an adaptation of extra-ecclesial trends; and that the changes serve to focus the faithfuls' attention more fully on Christ, not to pander to their ever-changing tastes. So in the case of the liturgical aspect of the core context, contextualization is more about preservation than innovation. Or to put it another way, it is about implementing the services as they have been developed by the church. Doing that gives us the confidence of ecclesial continuity as well as protection against the errors of individual preferences. As the development and preservation of the Presanctified Liturgy shows, this process also provides us with

> one of the great masterpieces of Orthodox piety and liturgical creativity. It reveals the central Christian doctrine and experience in its form and content, namely that our life must be spent in prayer and fasting in order that we might enter into communion with Christ Who

---

208 As legislated by canon 49 of the Synod of Laodicea (ca. 365): "In Lent it is not lawful to offer the Bread (Holy Eucharist), except on the Sabbath and the Lord's Day alone." Byzantine Leaflet Series 21 (Pittsburgh: Byzantine Seminary Press, 1981).

209 Anonymous, "Chronicon Paschale."

210 For example, the hymn "Now the Powers of Heaven" is of Constantinopolitan origin.

211 Thomas Hopko, *The Liturgy of the Presanctified Gifts* (New York: Orthodox Church in America, 1978).

> comes at the end, as "a thief in the night." It tells us that all of our life, and not only the time of Great Lent, or one day of the Fast, is completed with the Presence of the Victorious Christ who is risen from the dead. It witnesses to the fact that Christ will come at the end of the ages to judge the living and the dead, and to establish God's Kingdom "of which there will be no end." It tells us that we must be ready for his arrival, and to be found watching and serving; in order to be worthy to "enter into the joy of the Lord."[212]

Worship is not primarily an act of the intellect, but rather an experience in which the totality of human personhood participates in the divine. Its form and content are divinely given and are to be preserved and developed within the church. The liturgical life of the church is part of the core context that the process of contextualization helps to establish. It is part of that stable and reliable place where the individual confronts the resurrected and ascended Christ.

## 4. Councils

Another gift of tradition is the church council. These gatherings of the church were often precipitated by some crisis or challenge to the integrity of the church's teaching. Under the guidance of the Holy Spirit their findings take the form of dogmatic statements (designed to articulate teaching), creeds, as well as canons (laws intended to regulate practical affairs of the church). As such they address the fundamental conditions of personhood and help define the base missionary context.

### *a. Infinite Guidance of the Finite*

The origins of the council are found in the earliest days of the church. In Acts 15 we are told about the dispute concerning the conditions for receiving converts into the church. In order to resolve the issue the apostles and elders came together in Jerusalem to consider the matter.

212 Ibid., 4–5.

After considerable debate several prominent voices were heard—Peter, Barnabas, Paul, and James. Finally an agreement was reached and put into writing. What is significant about this method of conflict resolution is that it was not only the result of careful human deliberation but also of the Holy Spirit's direct involvement. In their letter, the apostles, elders, and brethren declared that their findings seemed good to them and to the Holy Spirit (Acts 15:28).

This pattern was taken up by a series of local councils and became a standard procedure for the church. As early as 175 a council of bishops and laymen was called to deal with the Montanism. In 190 Pope Leo convened a council in order to resolve the dispute over how to calculate the date of Easter. With time this conciliar approach proved its worth and there were councils in Carthage (256–257), Antioch (264–268), Elvira (ca. 306), and Ancyra (314). Some have suggested that this pattern may have reflected Roman senatorial deliberations.[213] Yet in the church there was, in addition to the contributions of the bishops, the ever-present leading of the Holy Spirit, and it is that divine involvement that sets the church council apart. A council's decisions were not considered binding or authoritative by virtue of any external circumstance such as a convocation by an emperor, a certain number of bishops, or even their unanimity. What allowed the bishops to expect universal acceptance of the conciliar pronouncements was the work of the Holy Spirit. After the first ecumenical council in Nicaea, Constantine justified his appeal for obedience with that very argument.

> That which has commended itself to the judgement of three hundred bishops cannot be other than the judgement of God; seeing that the Holy Spirit dwelling in the minds of persons of such character and dignity has effectually enlightened them respecting Divine will.[214]

The councils, then, with their finite/infinite dynamic, engage the dual nature of not only those who participated in the councils but also

---

213 Leo Donald Davis, *The First Seven Ecumenical Councils (325–787): Their History and Theology* (Collegeville, MN: Liturgical Press, 1990), 22–23.

214 Ibid., 69.

of those who submit themselves to the conciliar outcomes as expressions of the very will of God.[215]

## *b. Belief and the Development of Dogma*

The primary outcome of the ecumenical councils was, of course, their dogmatic affirmations, these coming down to us in the form of the Creed and other pronouncements. For example, during the first ecumenical council at Nicaea in 325 the primary issue was the nature of the relationship between the Father and the Son. Arius had been teaching that the Son was not of the same essence. As he understood it, the Son was begotten; i.e., created and therefore not eternal and therefore not of the same essence or nature as the Father. The Fathers of the council rejected that teaching, insisting that "begotten" does not mean the same thing as created. They affirmed that the uncreated nature of the Son was the same nature as the Father. They were both of one divine nature.

> What the Council of Nicaea was doing through its creedal statements with its use of *homoousios* was enunciating a judgement about reality as revealed in the Scriptures: what is said of the Father is also said of the Son, except that the Son is Son and not Father; therefore, the Son is of the same substance as the Father but not the same person as the Father.[216]

During the second ecumenical council at Constantinople in 381, the council continued the discussion of the first council by dealing with the third Person of the Trinity, the Holy Spirit. The Fathers amended the Creed and affirmed the full divinity of the Holy Spirit who proceeds from the Father, as the Son is begotten of the Father.[217] At Ephesus in 431 the third ecumenical council rejected the teaching of Nestorius by affirming the

---

215 This is particularly true of the seven ecumenical councils which received the approval of the church universal.

216 Ibid., 71.

217 This is the only truly "ecumenical Creed," established by the Council of Nicaea, edited and completed by the Council of Constantinople. This Creed—the Symbol of Faith—is the universally accepted summary of all the important Christian doctrines, and is used for catechism and for worship.

presence of two natures but only one person in Christ. Chalcedon in 451 took up the Monophysite heresy and once again affirmed the teaching of the two distinct natures and the one person in Christ. The fifth ecumenical council held at Constantinople in 553 advanced the church's ability to express the doctrine of Christ by developing more adequate terminology. As did their predecessors, they affirmed the two natures and then added the idea that these two were joined hypostatically, to form one person in which there was no dilution or distortion of the two natures. The sixth ecumenical council at Constantinople in 681 continued the work done by previous councils by taking up yet another aspect of Christology by rejecting the Monothelites, who taught that the union of two natures in Christ lead not only to one person but also to one will. That is, the human will was merged into divine will. This was rejected because the will is considered a part of each nature that is not changed in any way by the union. In 787 the seventh ecumenical council at Nicaea considered the issue of icons. It was, of course, not a question of artistic expression, but rather a profoundly theological issue again related to Christology. The production and veneration of icons was accepted on the basis of the Fathers' understanding of the Incarnation. Christ incarnate, being the Icon of God himself, was thus seen as the theological basis of the use of icons in the church.

The councils, then, were about defining the teaching, the dogma of the church. The concept of dogma had a long history of meaning, ranging from the decree of an emperor (Luke 2:1; Acts 17:7) to the opinions of various schools of philosophy. This was somewhat problematic since the idea of an opinion runs counter to the assumed, normative, prescriptive nature of doctrine. But Eusebius of Caesarea in his *Church History* speaks of an ecclesiastical decree (5:23.3) and the decisions of the synod (6:43.2) in such a way as to yield the idea of dogma as official, binding pronouncements of the church.[218] Dogma, then, are the result of a process whereby the truth made known by God's own revelation and passed down by the apostles is (re)formulated by councils, synods, and individual theologians. A complete system of dogma was compiled

218 Eusebius Pamphilius, "Church History," in *Life of Constantine, Oration in Praise of Constantine*, Vol. 1 of *A Select Library of the Nicene and Post-Nicene Fathers of the Christian Church*, 2nd series, edited by Philip Schaff and Henry Wace. Grand Rapids: Eerdmans, 1975. http://www.ccel.org/ccel/schaff/npnf201.iii.x.xxiv.html.

in the eighth century by Saint John of Damascus under the title *Exact Exposition of the Orthodox Faith*, in which he summed up the whole of the theological thought of the Eastern Fathers and teachers of the church up to the eighth century.[219]

These dogma, these explanations of the truths of the faith, are themselves an instrument of preserving the base missionary context, since they give precision to the expression of the truths of Christian teaching, create a unified language of dogmatic pronouncement, systematically relate specific truths to the testimony of sacred Scripture as well as the other gifts of tradition, develop for them arguments based on reason, formulate them for use in missions, and are valid elements of teaching the one true faith, "that which has been believed, always and in all places."[220]

What this brief summary indicates is that the councils sought to "attend to what the Scriptures assert as true" and to "reduce that multitude of true statements to the one judgment which is the foundation of all the rest." In other words, they were paving "the way for the development of dogma," by "appealing to the intellects of Christians for their assent to this judgment as the foundation of further religious belief and experience."[221] In other words, the dogmatic assertions of the councils engage the human ability to hold cognitive content as true by defining exactly what that content is.[222]

---

219 Saint John of Damascus, in "An Exact Exposition of the Orthodox Faith," in *Hilary of Poitiers; John of Damascus*, vol. 9 of *A Select Library of the Nicene and Post-Nicene Fathers of the Christian Church*, 2nd series, ed. Philip Schaff and Henry Wace (Grand Rapids: Eerdmans, 1975), http://www.ccel.org/ccel/schaff/ npnf209.iii.

220 Vincent of Lerins, " Commonitorium," trans. C. A. Heurtley, in *Nicene and Post-Nicene Fathers*, 2nd series, vol. 11, ed. Philip Schaff and Henry Wace (Buffalo, NY: Christian Literature Publishing, 1894), revised and edited for New Advent by Kevin Knight, http://www.newadvent.org/fathers/3506.htm.

221 Davis, *First Seven Ecumenical Councils*, 71.

222 In light of the ongoing task of preserving tradition, the councils convened in the East after the separation between East and West Christianity are also important in terms of establishing the faith and enunciating its content. Such are the important councils of 1341 and 1351, which established the Orthodox Christian doctrine concerning divine grace, the divine energies of God, and the "uncreated light," according to the doctrine of Saint Gregory Palamas. Councils convened during the seventeenth century to establish the Orthodox doctrine vis-à-vis the Protestant teachings, like the councils of Jassi (1662) and Jerusalem (1672). The documents produced by these councils, along with other documents such as "confessions of faith" by Orthodox prelates and teachers (Saint Photios, Michael Cerularius, Mark of Ephesus, Gennadios of Constantinople, Jeremiah II of Constantinople, Metrophanes Kritopoulos, Peter Moghila, etc.), are given the name of

## *c. Standards of Behavior*

Another outcome of the councils were the canons which, while they don't have the same enduring quality as the dogmatic assertions of the creeds, sought to apply faith and moral principles to concrete, local, and historical situations, such as church order, baptisms, ordinations, church government, and the obligations of the church hierarchy and clergy and of every Christian. As such they are examples of the practical application and ongoing rearticulation of tradition to meet the ever-changing needs of the church. Like dogma the canons are a distillation of the principles of Scripture as they apply to human behavior. A good example of this is the canonical perspectives on divorce and remarriage.

The basic principle expressed in the canons is that "at the beginning" (Matt 19:4) God created human beings as male and female. The couple was to coexist

> precisely so that they, in creaturely form, might reflect and participate in the uncreated life of God the Trinity, a life of perfect openness, of personal communion, of complete sharing, mutual interiority and mutual indwelling.
>
> Even after the Fall, after man and woman exchange being for having, true personhood for self-absorbed and self-sufficient individualism, marriage remains their most immediate possibility for transcending autonomous natural necessity through self-giving love.[223]

So "at the beginning" situates marriage in creation but also points to the kingdom, affirming that "perfect and *perpetual* monogamy is the norm of marriage," transcending even the necessity of death.[224] For that reason remarriage was frowned upon. "He who rids himself of his first wife, even if she be dead, is an adulterer."[225] According to Gregory

---

"Symbolic Books" of the Orthodox Church.

223 John H. Erickson, *The Challenge of Our Past: Studies in Orthodox Canon Law and Church History* (Crestwood, NY: St. Vladimir's Seminary Press, 1991), 40.

224 Ibid., 41.

225 Second-century apologist Athanagoras, quoted in ibid.

Naziansus, "A first marriage is in full conformity with the law, a second is tolerated by indulgence, a third is noxious."[226] An individual involved in multiple marriages was considered a serial bigamist. Nevertheless, based on Matthew 19:8,9, divorce was allowed in the case of adultery. Even though marriage cannot be destroyed by death, adultery, which is its antithesis, can and does destroy it. As a result, following adultery, divorce was not only possible, it was required. However, if a monogamous marriage was dissolved by adultery, the norm for Christians remained divorce without remarriage.[227]

### *d. Foundations Established*

These canons, then, speak to the human faculty of self-actualization by limiting freedom, not according to some static and rigid catalogue of rules, but by an application of biblical principles. At the same time, they establish the foundations for second-order beliefs or the "rightness" of certain behaviors. For example, if marriage is not held in high regard, then according to the seventh canon of Neocaesarea it would be morally reprehensible for a priest to attend the banquet of a couple entering a second marriage. "A presbyter shall not be a guest at the nuptials of persons contracting a second marriage; for since the digamist is worthy of penance [no Communion for a year], what kind of presbyter shall he be, who, by being present at the feast, sanctioned the marriage?"[228]

### *e. On Building the Core Context with the Help of the Councils*

The works of the councils, speaking as they do to each one of the basic conditions of personhood, provide part of what defines the base context of mission. On the one hand, they offer the timeless, nonnegotiable dogmatic assertions, which state clearly what it is that Christians believe. On the other hand, they provided dynamic precedence of how that teaching is to be applied to the immediate needs of the church and society.

Like the Scriptures themselves, the conciliar affirmations do not need to be adapted since they are themselves part of what determines

226 Quoted in ibid., 42.
227 Ibid., 42–45.
228 Quoted in ibid., 47.

the context. However, like all other text/language-based content, they do have to be translated into the various languages that will enable that definition of context. Part of the missionary task, then, will be to provide translations of the Creed, catechisms, and dogmatic summaries. The Creed will set the dogmatic baseline and will have already been translated as part of the work on the service books. Having been explained and given its proper place in the liturgical cycle of services, the Creed will function as doctrinal bedrock for both the seekers and the faithful, a constant reminder of what is to be believed. But simply memorizing and repeating the Creed does not by itself create a broad enough foundation for those coming into the faith. That is why the church formally receives the seekers as catechumens and provides them with anywhere from three months to thee years of instruction intended to firmly situate them in the dogmatic context of the church. In many cases this is done using a catechism,[229] which will have had to be translated. It is only after such instruction that the creedal summary of doctrine will have its intended effect.

Related to this, there has been considerable recent interest in the idea of "doing theology cross-culturally." In most cases the assumption has been that a local context or situation needed to be used as an interpretive filter for Christian doctrine. Those filters could be anything from politico-economic conditions, revolution, gender, non-Christian religious ideas, to prevailing social structures. What has often taken place is that the dogma of the church have been modified to fit the "context" in which they find themselves. For example, in a chapter entitled "Christian Theology in the Context of Buddhism," Lynn A. de Silva suggests that Christian theology has to be reformulated with reference to the traditions of Asia. He writes:

> We possess an imported theology, which in the context of Sri Lanka … has extremely little relevance. There are deep insights in Buddhism, which could enrich Christian thought, but the Christians are afraid of contact with Buddhism. In contrast one determines that

229 An interesting example of a catechism is a work entitled *The Living God*. It was compiled by Orthodox Christians in France and translated into English. Organized around the twelve major feasts of the church year, it provides a systematic introduction to the faith. *Living God: Catechism for the Christian Faith* (Crestwood, NY: St. Vladimir's Seminary Press, 1988).

> Buddhism in all its fields of expansion has adapted itself to each culture.[230]

Then to illustrate he shows how Buddhism had redefined and reinterpreted basic vocabulary, some taken over from other religions, such as *karma*, *nirvana*, and *pancasila*. Because, in his opinion, no such adaptation (*Anpassung*) has yet taken place in Christianity, Christian dogmatic terminology needs to be reconstituted (*neu darstellen*) in keeping with Theravada-Buddhist thought. That is, "it should begin where Buddhism also begins,"[231] with the Buddhist understanding of the basic characteristics of human existence: *annica*, that everything is passing away; *dukkha*, that nothing has lasting substance; and *anatta*, non-self, no-self.[232] While the first two terms can be tangentially related to the biblical teaching of the temporality and spatiality of creation, they do not seem to incorporate the idea of becoming; that is, of the appointed *telos* of creation. Nevertheless, there does seem to be some, albeit narrow, commonality. However, as the author points out, the third term is rather difficult since, in direct contrast to Christian thought, it implies the mortality of the soul[233] and a denial of divine-human correspondence in the image of God[234] in human beings.[235] Faced with this discontinuity, de Silva opts for abandoning the Christian concept and thus illustrates the danger of subjecting Christian dogma to the content-altering authority of another context. While I have no doubt that insights from other cultures and religions can be used to illumine aspects of Christian doctrine, I am convinced that the dogmatic assertions delivered to us by the councils,

---

230 Lynn A. de Silva, *Mit Buddha und Christus auf dem Weg*, vol. 24 of *Theologie der Dritten Welt* (Freiburg, Germany: Herder, 1998), 123 (my translation).

231 Ibid., 127.

232 Ibid., 124.

233 "Mit *anatta* dürfte es allerdings schwieriger sein, denn der Begriff einer unsterblichen Seele ist im christlichen Denken tief verwurzelt. Wie man jedoch heutzutage weiß, ist dieser Begriff nicht genuin christlich, sondern als Fremdgut aus der griechischen Philosopie in das Christentum eingedrungen. Die neueren Studien in Biologie, Psychologie und Physiologie stimmen darin überein, die Lehre von der Unsterblichkeit der Seele als unglaubwürdig zu verwerfen." Ibid., 127.

234 Redefined as the mere possibility of a relationship between the divine and the human. Ibid., 133.

235 "Dieser menschliche Geist meint nie einen göttlichen Funken im Menschen. Als eine natürliche Dimension des Menschen, die in sich über keinerlei göttliche Qualität verfügt." Ibid.

under the guidance of the Holy Spirit, remain normative cross-culturally, establishing the context rather than being adapted; that is, absorbed into another context. In this case, the Creed itself provides a hedge against doctrinal redefinition. It sets clear limits on just how far we can go when seeking to relate Christian thought to other contexts. According to the Creed, Christ "shall come again with glory to judge the quick and the dead," and his "kingdom shall have no end." What is clearly implied is, as Epiphanius put it, that we believe in "the resurrection of the dead, and the just judgment of souls and bodies, and in the Kingdom of heaven and in life everlasting."[236] Since it is the dogmatic assertions of the councils that, in this case, establish part of the base missionary context, this is the terminology of Christian dogma that interprets, reformulates, redefines the vocabulary of other religious contexts and not the other way around.

By comparison, whereas the dogmatic affirmations of the church are timeless, its canons are very much rooted in the times and places they were formulated. For that reason they play a dynamic rather than static role in helping to set the base context. Take, for example, the issue of divorce and remarriage mentioned above. Many of the church's canons on marriage were formulated during the Byzantine era, which was characterized by the ideal of harmony between church and state. One expression of this mutual openness is the nomocanon, "which conveniently arranged civil *nomoi* and ecclesial *kanones* by topic."[237] This harmonizing of civil and church law led to an understanding of marriage as "a union of a man and a woman, a sharing of the whole life, a participation in divine and human laws."[238] Although the church was initially more interested in the character of the marriage than the wedding ceremony itself, the idea of an ecclesiastical blessing did develop and was by the tenth century a requirement for a legal marriage.[239] This Byzantine marriage law survived the fall of the empire and has been widely used in Orthodox countries.

---

236 The Second Ecumenical Council, "The Holy Creed Which the 150 Holy Fathers Set Forth, Which Is Consonant with the Holy and Great Synod of Nice," in *The Seven Ecumenical Councils*, vol. 14 of *A Select Library of the Nicene and Post-Nicene Fathers of the Christian Church*, 2nd series, ed. Philip Schaff and Henry Wace Grand Rapids: Eerdmans, 1975), http://www.ccel.org/ccel/schaff/npnf214.ix.iii.html.

237 Erickson, *Challenge of Our Past*, 46.

238 Roman jurist Modestinus, quoted in ibid.

239 Emperor Leo VI's Novella 89 reads, "We order that marriage be confirmed by evidence of sacred blessing." Quoted in ibid., 47.

However, that harmony has not survived into the modern North American context. So today the church must face problems that were not anticipated by the nomocanonic system as well as those which no longer function.

> Confronted with this new situation, the Church faces many temptations. Instead of communicating its own deepest insights about marriage to the world of today, it could end up woodenly maintaining all the external forms and requirements of a bygone age, whether civil or ecclesiastical, and in the very process capitulate to an understanding of marriage quite at odds with Christian teaching.[240]

How can the church continue to live within the tradition of the conciliar canons and at the same time redefine the base context for a new era? One example is the "Encyclical Letter of the Holy Synod of Bishops of the Orthodox Church in America on Marriage." In it they try to balance the contemporary situation with the canonical tradition of the church.

> We find it imperative to address you on an issue of crucial importance for the Christian life. An increasingly secularized world tends more and more to neglect the traditional biblical understanding of marriage and family. Misunderstanding freedom and proclaiming the progress of a humanity supposedly too mature, sophisticated and scientific to follow Christ's Gospel, many have abandoned its moral demands. The consequences are plain for all to see: the family is disintegrating, legalized abortion is killing millions of unborn children, corrupt sexual behavior is rampant. The moral foundations of society are collapsing.
>
> We, the bishops of the Orthodox Church in America, therefore proclaim anew to you, the flock entrusted to our care, the great and holy vision of marriage that is gloriously preserved and manifested in the doctrine, liturgy and canonical tradition of the Church …

---

240 Ibid., 48.

> Marriage is the most perfect realization of love between a man and a woman: two become one. Love unites in such a way that two lives become one life in perfect harmony. This love, sanctified by God, is the great source of the happiness which is sought in marriage, and in it lies a power that transforms both those who love and those who are loved. Because of this transforming power of love, all the difficulties and defects in family life can be overcome. True love never ceases, whether in this world or in the age to come …
>
> The perfect marriage can only be one, single and unique. The prototype of marriage, the unity between Christ and His Church, excludes multiple marriages: Christ has only one Church; the Church has no other Christ. Even death cannot break the bond of perfect love. Therefore, the Church does not advocate second or third marriages, even for widows or widowers; rather, they are tolerated as condescension to human frailty and weakness, while fourth marriages are totally forbidden.[241]

Operating within the tradition of the church, sensitive to the conditions of the contemporary moment, the bishops seek to set the context for Christian life, without the dry and dusty sterility of rigid traditionalism, holding the line against the encroaching secularism with a compassion that helps heal the wounds of the abused and dispossessed.

## 5. Hagiography

As we have already seen, didactic continuity (apostolic succession) is an important aspect of defining the base context of missions. Another form of continuity, a spiritual continuity, is provided by the church's teaching on the communion of the saints or by its hagiography. As with the other ecclesial gifts, this one clearly engages the conditions of human

241 The Holy Synod of Bishops, "Encyclical Letter of the Holy Synod of Bishops of the Orthodox Church in America on Marriage," Orthodox Church in America, http://oca.org/holy-synod/encyclicals/on-marriage.

personhood. It brings together the infinite and the finite as realized deification. It addresses belief by revealing truth in person, it supports agency through its interaction with the transcendent world. And it undergirds morality with countless examples.

## *a. Realized Deification*

Deification is a process whereby human beings created in the image and likeness of God are gradually conformed to that divine likeness. It is, so to speak, the goal of all human becoming. Because God alone possesses holiness (moral perfection) as an attribute of his nature, the only way contingent beings can become holy is by participation in the holiness of God; that is, to become "partakers of the divine nature" (2 Pet 1:4). The possibility of such participation (*theosis*)[242] is restored in the Incarnation. By taking on human nature without abandoning divinity, Christ brought about the regeneration of the "image" and its elevation toward the archetype. Consider the words of Saint Gregory Palamas:

> God's Son became man to show to what heights He would raise us; to keep us from self-exaltation through thinking that we ourselves have secured the revocation of our fall; to join together, as a true mediator, and as Himself being both divine and human, the sundered aspects of our nature ...; to make men sons of God and participators in divine immortality ...; to show how human nature was created in the image of God above all other created things, for it is so kindred to God that it can form a single hypostasis with Him ...; to unite what is separated by nature, mankind and God, since He became a mediator both human and divine by nature.[243]

---

242 Interest in *theosis* is not limited to the Eastern Church. Cf. Keating, *Deification and Grace*; Roger E. Olson, "Deification in Contemporary Theology," *Theology Today* 64, no. 2 (2007): 186–200.

243 Saint Palamas Holy Saturday sermon, quoted in Georgios I. Mantzarides, *The Deification of Man: St. Gregory Palamas and the Orthodox Tradition*, Contemporary Greek Theologians (Crestwood, NY: St. Vladimir's Seminary Press, 1984), 26–27.

This communion becomes a concrete reality only by the mediation of the Holy Spirit.[244] "The Spirit of God residing in the spirit of human beings makes them participants of God's grace."[245] Listen again to Saint Palamas:

> As the beam of the eye, uniting with the sun's rays, becomes actual light and thus sees sensible things, so the intellect, becomes "one spirit with the Lord," clearly perceives spiritual realities.[246]

Mantzarides goes on to say that

> the Spirit of God accomplishes man's deification by means of the energy and grace natural to Him, and not by created means or through his own essence … The Energy of the Holy Spirit … brings man into union with God … The grace of the Holy Spirit penetrates the soul of man … Those of the faithful who participate in the grace of the Spirit achieve within themselves a lasting regenerative quality and are rendered spiritual or holy.[247]

This grace is thought of in terms of the concrete manifestation of the divine Spirit by means of divine energy. Thus, in a created being this energy or grace constitutes the very existence of the spiritual/holy person, upon whom it bestows true life.[248] Human beings become holy or "sainted" by virtue of the gift (charisma) given by God to man, through the grace of the Holy Spirit, manifested in the divine energy of the Holy Spirit.

While participation in the divine nature is a gift of God's grace, the believer's involvement is crucial. The believer must actively engage those concrete means of deification offered by God in the church, and in particular the sacraments. In baptism the grace of God confers two benefits, the regeneration of that which is "in the image" and the possibility

---

244 Ibid., 34.
245 Ibid.
246 Saint Palamas Holy Saturday sermon, quoted in ibid.
247 Ibid., 37.
248 Ibid., 37.

of realizing that which is "after the likeness."[249] The Eucharist brings about the advance toward the "likeness" and full union with Christ.

> In partaking of the sacrament … man is united with the divinizing flesh of Christ and shares in eternal and incorruptible life.
>
> When the believer is united in this manner with Christ, he is transformed into a temple for the Trinitarian divinity.[250]

Another way to participate in divine nature is to imitate Christ's submission to the will of God. This involves the moral, ethical life of the believer; it entails keeping the commandments, as well as ascetic practice and dispassion (more in chapter 4). At its core asceticism is the living out and transcending of the afflictions of the Fall in the hope of the Resurrection. It offers us the possibility of experiencing death in this world as life in the Lord. Fasting, hardship, silence, mourning, and in general all deprivations and afflictions of the spiritual are useful aids to overcoming the passions, which prevent us from ascending to godlikeness. While our own efforts do not in and of themselves create holiness, they do create a context in which the divine grace can flow unhindered. The same thing can be said of prayer. While it is not sufficient to bring about union with God, it might be seen as a conduit of divinizing grace, a spiritual means by which man is elevated toward God. "This is the nature of prayer: it raises man from earth to heaven and, surpassing every celestial name, eminence, and dignity, it presents him to God who is above all things."[251]

Given this approach to personal holiness (deification) we see that all Christians could be called saints. This was done in the early church with reference to those who had been baptized in the name of the Holy Trinity, had received the seal of the Spirit in chrismation, and frequently participated in the Eucharist (Eph 1:1; 2 Cor 1:11). It should be equally clear that there have been some believers who have realized a greater degree of holiness than others. These are the canonized saints of the church. Saint Maximus the Confessor writes that the saints are those who

249 Ibid., 46.
250 Ibid., 51–56.
251 Ibid., 89.

have actually reached deification, have avoided unnatural development of the soul. By turning and looking always towards God, they have achieved total unity with God through the Holy Spirit.

## *b. Truth in Person*

This realized deification of the saints can also be thought of in terms of the truth having been actualized in their persons. As truth personified, they engage our ability to believe and help adjudicate between various claims to truth, uncovering the truth, showing us through their lives what can be believed. The ways in which they do this are revealed in the appellations that are used in conjunction with their names. Some are called *apostles*, because they were the first ones to spread the message of the Incarnation of the word of God and of salvation through Christ. In many cases these apostles uncovered and challenged the lies of pagan religions and practices. A good example of this is found in the work of Saints Cyril and Methodius. Sent to the Muslims, they challenged their attackers on the teaching of the Trinity.

Others are called *prophets*, because they predicted and prophesied the coming of the Messiah. Here we venerate Isaiah, David, and the other prophets for giving us the truth about Christ, enabling us to identify him and believe in him.

Some are *martyrs*, for sacrificing their lives and fearlessly confessing Jesus Christ as the Son of God and the Savior of mankind. There are, of course, countless examples of Christians who have given their lives for the faith. These are found not only among the early Christians but our own more recent history. A good example is Saint John Kochurov, born in 1871, a man of excellent education having graduated from the Theological Academy in Moscow; internationally traveled, having served the church in America and Alaska; a man known for his teaching abilities and personal piety. He is a saint martyred for the faith in 1917, the first of the New Russian Martyrs.

Still others are referred to as *confessors*. These are Fathers and hierarchs of the church, who excelled in explaining and in defending, by word and deed, the Christian faith. Then there are *monastics*, who lived in the desert and dedicated themselves to spiritual exercise (*askesis*), reaching, as far as possible, perfection in Christ. In the tradition of the monastic saints of old, such as Saint Macarius the Great and Saint Pachomius the Great, who lived in genuine piety and absolute obedience to God, they pleased him and have therefore been "sanctified" both in soul and body, and subsequently glorified in this world.

And finally the *just*, those who lived in the world, leading exemplary lives as clergy or laity with their families, becoming examples for imitation in society. On the tradition of Saint Philaret the Almsgiver, Saint John the Almsgiver, etc., they sacrificed for others in spite of danger, constantly giving to and working to help the needy.

In addition to this, many of the saints were given special "grace" or "favor" to perform *miracles*—either before or after their deaths—healing in the tradition of Saint Martin of Tours, Saint Nicholas of Myra in Lycia, and others. Their physical bodies are sanctified, becoming incorrupt, even fragrant,[252] and in some cases working miracles. Others had special *insight* (clairvoyance), readers of hearts, who could identify and name people never seen before; hear and answer people's thoughts before they expressed them; and foretell the future, including the time of their own death.

## c. *Transcendentalized Agency*

The church's understanding of the saints also facilitates personal agency by making us aware of the transcendent world and that the effects of our self-actualizations are not limited to the temporal/spatial realm but have implications for eternity. When the saints die, they do not simply slip out of existence. Rather, they continue to exist in Christ, conscious, aware of our world, and able to interact with it.

This reality is clearly spoken of in the Scriptures. The transfiguration of our Lord (Matt 17:1–9; Mark 9:2–10; Luke 9:28–36) shows that the

---

252 As when Saints Cyril and Methodius discovered the relics of Saint Clement. "Hearing that the remains of Pope Clement were in the sea, Constantine prayed: 'I believe in God and put my hope in Saint Clement, that I might find him and bring him up out of the sea.' Stirring up the archbishop along with all the clergy and the faithful, they went by ship to a certain place. Then, when the sea was completely calm, they began to dig, while singing hymns. Soon a fragrance arose, like that of incense, and afterward they found the sacred relics of Clement. Then they carried the relics into town, amidst great reverence and the praises of all the citizens." (Saint Clement was martyred around 100—an anchor tied around his neck and cast into the sea). Franz Grivec, *Kontantin und Method: Lehrer der Slaven* (Wiesbaden: Harrassowitz, 1960), 47–52.

faithful departed continue to live, in this case in the persons of Moses and Elijah who appear and speak with Jesus there. In Luke 20:37,38 the spirits of those who have died are aware of what is taking place both in heaven and on earth: "But even Moses showed in the burning bush passage that the dead are raised, when he called the Lord 'the God of Abraham, the God of Isaac, and the God of Jacob.' For He is not the God of the dead but of the living, for all live to Him" (NKJV). Luke 16:19–31 relates the parable of the rich man and Lazarus in which Jesus relates a conversation/negotiation after death. In Luke 23:43 Jesus promises the thief on the cross, "Today you will be with Me in Paradise" (NKJV), implying a conscious continuation of life, awareness after death. Saint Paul expresses similar sentiments. On several occasions he expresses his conviction that he will be alive with Christ after his death. "For I am hard-pressed between the two, having a desire to depart and be with Christ, which is far better" (Phil 1:23 NKJV). To the Corinthians he writes, "We are confident, yes, well pleased rather to be absent from the body and to be present with the Lord" (2 Cor 5:8 NKJV). Hebrews 12:1 exhorts, "Therefore we also, since we are surrounded by so great a cloud of witnesses [including the Old Testament heroes of faith listed in chapter 11], let us lay aside every weight, and the sin which so easily ensnares us" (NKJV).

These "witnesses" are the saints from all ages, both known and unknown, canonized and uncanonized. Certainly they would not have been called "witnesses" if they were unconscious of their surroundings. Hebrews 12:22–24 reads:

> But you have come to Mount Zion and to the city of the living God, the heavenly Jerusalem, to an innumerable company of angels, to the general assembly and church of the firstborn who are registered in heaven, to God the Judge of all, to the spirits of just men made perfect, to Jesus the Mediator of the new covenant, and to the blood of sprinkling that speaks better things than that of Abel. (NKJV)

The text refers to those believers who have died and are with Christ, having become part of the "church triumphant." What is interesting for our discussion is that they are, though still waiting for the Second Coming, living consciously with Christ. This passage indicates that in the church's worship, here and now, we are in the presence of angels, God the Father, Jesus, and "the spirits of just men made perfect," active and aware. Finally the book of Revelation (4:4,10,11; 5:8–10,13; 6:9–11; 7:9–12) shows the saints in heaven, before the Great Tribulation, actively worshiping, casting their crowns to the King of Glory, singing his praises, and speaking to him.

This biblical data is corroborated by the (re)appearance of Christians after their deaths. One early example is found in "The Martyrdom of Ignatius." This is an eyewitness account concerning Saint Ignatius, the third bishop of Antioch, who was thrown to the lions by the Romans in about AD 110. The writer of this account relates:

> Having ourselves been eye-witnesses of these things [his martyrdom], and having spent the whole night in tears within the house, and having entreated the Lord, with bended knees and much prayer … it came to pass, on our falling into a brief slumber, that some of us saw the blessed Ignatius suddenly standing by us and embracing us, while others beheld him again praying for us, and others still saw him dropping with sweat, as if he had just come from his great labor, and standing by the Lord. When, therefore, we had with great joy witnessed these things, and had compared our several visions together, we sang praise to God.[253]

A more contemporary example of this kind of event comes from the twentieth century. Saint Nektarios, bishop of Pentapolis, Egypt, and founder of the Holy Trinity Convent on the Greek island of Aegina, died on November 9, 1920, in a hospital in Athens. Since then he has appeared many times, either in dreams or visions, as he continues his ministry to

---

253 Ch. 7 of "The Martyrdom of Ignatius," in *The Apostolic Fathers; Justin Martyr; Irenaeus*, vol. 1 of *Ante-Nicene Fathers*, ed. Alexander Roberts, James Donaldson, and A. Cleveland Coxe (Buffalo, NY: Christian Literature Publishing, 1885), http://www.ccel.org/ccel/schaff/anf01.v.xxv.vii.html.

his earthly flock, giving spiritual counsel, and being an instrument of God's healing power. As Saint Nektarios' biographer relates:

> It has become well known that many Greek Orthodox Christians who were incurably ill, suffering, and close to death, have seen a live old monk wearing a cap appear to them. It does not matter who they are, or from where they are, for many times he has been seen in far away countries other than Greece. He always smiles softly and consoles them, assuring them that they will regain health, and not to fear, for God will not abandon them. He simply reminds them to have patience and faith. "And who are you, old man?" many ask in a moment of astonishment. "I am the former Bishop of Pentapolis, Nektarios of Aegina," the monk replies, and then vanishes.[254]

It is this lively awareness of the transcendent world and its inhabitants that constantly remind the faithful of their own destiny and the importance of their present behavior (Luke 16:19-31). The desire to keep the awareness of the afterlife active has led to two practices sanctioned by the church, the veneration of and the intercession through the saints. Once an individual has been declared a saint, icons are made, hymns are written, and at least one day of the year is designated as a feast day for that saint. Of course, it is important to emphasize that

> the hymns, the icons, the feast-days are all important aspects of the veneration of the saint, indicating profound respect and love for the person, but in no way do these things mean that the person is being *worshipped*. Worship, of course, is due only to God. And indeed, all the veneration expressed to a saint is entirely based upon that person's closeness to Christ. Every saint has become holy only through the mercy and grace of God; it is He who is glorified when we honor His holy ones.[255]

254 Sotos Chondropoulos, *Saint Nectarias: A Saint for Our Times* (Brookline, MA: Holy Cross Orthodox Press, 1989), 277.

255 David C. Ford, *Prayer and the Departed Saints* (Chesterton, IN: Conciliar, 1994),

Intercession through the saints is simply asking the departed saints for their prayers in the same way we ask our fellow Christians on earth to intercede for us. Since the departed remain alive in Christ, why should they cease to express their love and concern for us through prayer? The practice is based on passages like Revelation 5:8, where the four living creatures and the twenty-four elders fell down before the Lamb, each with bowls full of incense, which are the prayers of the saints. It is prefigured in the New Testament: Saint Paul asks the Christians to pray for him (Rom 15:30,31; Eph 6:19; Col 4:3; 1 Thess 5:25). It has been consistently defended by the Fathers of the church.

> In one of his letters, St. Basil explicitly writes that he accepts the intercession of the apostles, prophets and martyrs, and he seeks their prayers to God (Letter 360). Then, speaking about the Forty Martyrs who suffered martyrdom for Christ, he emphasizes that "they are common friends of the human race, strong ambassadors and collaborators in fervent prayers" (Chapter 8). St. Gregory of Nyssa asks St. Theodore the Martyr "to fervently pray to our Common King, our God, for the country and the people" (*Encomium to Martyr Theodore*). The same language is used by St. Gregory the Theologian in his encomium to St. Cyprian St. John Chrysostom says that we should seek the intercession and the fervent prayers of the saints, because they have special "boldness" (*parresia*), before God (Gen. 44:2 and *Encomium to Julian, Iuventinus and Maximinus*, 3).[256]

This kind of prayer is not meant to be a substitute for the prayer of the living nor is it to mask the fact that there is only one Mediator between God and his creatures. The saints can never answer prayers in their own strength, they can only appeal to Christ on our behalf. Thus, "to imagine

---

http://www.holy-trinity-church.org/index.php?option=com_content&task=view&id=70&Itemid=131&limit=1&limitstart=1.

256 George Bebis, "The Saints of the Orthodox Church," Greek Orthodox Archdiocese of America, http://goarch.org/resources/saints.

that prayer to the saints means that they can grant our requests apart from Christ is a totally unacceptable idea."[257]

### d. Examples

Finally, the church's teaching on the saints provides a foundation for morality by giving us examples of how we should live. As Christians we want to grow in the likeness of Christ, to have that likeness shine in us. For this to occur, we look to the saints to see that likeness, for real, practical examples of how to live. Consider Saint Basil's analogy:

> Just as painters, in working from models, constantly gaze at their exemplar and thus strive to transfer the expression of the original to their own artistry, so too he who is eager to make himself perfect in all kinds of virtue must gaze upon the Lives of the Saints as upon statues, so to speak, that move and act, and must make their excellence his own by imitation.[258]

### e. Building the Core Context with the Help of the Saints

One of the ways in which this gift can be used to help establish the base missionary context is seen in the practice of taking on the name of a patron saint. Many Orthodox Christians have what we call "church names" which are often given at baptism. To facilitate this choosing, the Lives of the Saints have to be taught as part of the base context of mission. They have to be presented as individuals who encountered Christ and who can transmit to us something of that encounter. This building of awareness takes place during the regular cycle of services. At the end

---

257 "But as to their ability to hear our requests for their prayers, we ought not to limit the powers of spiritual perception of those who are now so intimately linked with God. If we on earth experience the help of the Holy Spirit praying in us and through us (Romans 8:26,27), how much more must the Spirit's help be present in the saints in heaven? And we should remember that in heaven, in the spiritual realm, there are none of the limitations of time, space, or physical mortality which so restrict us as we live on earth." D. Ford, *Prayer*. http://www.holy-trinity-church.org/index.php?option=com_content&task=view&id=70&Itemid=131&limit=1&limitstart=1

258 Quoted in Constantine Cavarnos, *Holiness: Man's Supreme Destiny* (Belmont, MA: Institute For Byzantine and Modern Greek Studies, 2001), 35.

of each service the dismissal (benediction) includes reference to the saint(s) of the day. In some places the Lives of the Saints[259] are read after Vespers on Saturday evenings. The daily calendar includes information on the saints commemorated on each day.[260] Against this backdrop of information, individual believers choose as their own the name of a saint. This identification creates a personal bond based not only on information, but on a desire to emulate the life of the saint, and it obviously engages all the conditions of personhood. In my case, I kept my own name, since there is a Saint Edward.[261]

Edward the Martyr was born between 957 and 962, the elder son of King Edgar the Peacemaker. Edgar, born in 943, had become king of Mercia and Northumbria about 957, then king of England as a whole in 959, and finally king of all Britain in 973. Edgar's legacy left the pre-Norman English kingdom at its apex and the monasteries at their spiritual best.

Following Edgar's untimely death in July 975, Edward was crowned king of England in late 975 at an age of between 13 and 18. Edward was much loved by the common subjects of his kingdom and is recorded to have been a young man of virtue, devotion, and holiness, generous to the poor and a champion of the faith, and a lover first of God and the church. He continued the policy of his father Edgar in supporting and protecting the monasteries from the violently aggressive noblemen who coveted the land.

At the time of King Edgar's death in 975, his Queen Elfrida, along with her allies, had argued that her own son, Ethelred the Unready, should have the throne. Elfrida, allied with noblemen who opposed the continued patronage of the monastics by King Edward, sought to usurp his throne for Ethelred.

Thus it was that after hunting near Wareham on March 18, 978, King Edward arrived at the castle and was greeted by Queen Elfrida while her accomplices ambushed and assassinated him with a dagger. Buried at the nearby church at Wareham, he was immediately regarded a martyr by

---

259 Nikolaj Velimirovic, *The Prologue from Ochrid*, 4 vols. (Birmingham, England: Lazarica, 1985). This set provides information on many Orthodox saints.

260 See for example: Orthodox Church in America, "Lives of the Saints," http://oca.org/fslives.asp.

261 Nektarios Serfes, "The Life of [Saint] Edward the Martyr, King of England," Spiritual Nourishment for the Soul, http://www.serfes.org/lives/stedward.htm.

the English people, distraught at the murder of their beloved and devout young king. One year after burial at the church he was disinterred to commence a proper royal funeral, whereupon his body was found to be incorrupt, a circumstance seen in the Orthodox Church as a sign of sainthood. Moreover, beginning the night of his death, there had been reported numerous miracles associated with his remains.

In 1008 Edward was formally pronounced a saint by the English church. In the sixteenth century Henry VIII dissolved the English monasteries, and many holy places were destroyed. The remains of Saint Edward were hidden underground to escape desecration. He lay hidden and largely forgotten until 1931 when an archaeological excavation of the Abbey site uncovered them. Since 1984 the relics of Saint Edward the Martyr, King of England, are housed and venerated in the Orthodox Church of Saint Edward the Martyr at Brookwood in Surrey County.

Four commemorations are provided for Saint Edward in the church calendar. His principal feast day is celebrated on March 18 (the date of his martyrdom in 978); the uncovering of his relics, on February 13 (at the Wareham church in 979 or 980, when they were found incorrupt); the elevation of his relics, on June 20 (to a saint's place of honor, in 1001); and the translation of his relics (back to the Orthodox Church, in 1984, at Brookwood), on September 3rd.

The facts of Saint Edward's life and character have become part of the context of ecclesial continuity, within which my own negotiation of intimacy with Christ has taken place. My communion with the saint has inspired me to strive for a life of virtue and has sustained my own, sometimes weak, commitment to the church and its faithful.

## 6. Iconography

One of the most well-known gifts of Eastern tradition is the icon, the holy image. Just by entering an Eastern Church the visitor is confronted with a whole universe of images. There is the image of Christ (Pantocrator) painted onto the domed ceiling. Mary (the Panagia), arms open in welcome, greets one from the apse. The icon screen (iconostasis), bearing images of Christ, Mary, the Forerunner, angels, and feasts, serves as a portal between heaven (the sanctuary) and earth (the nave). The walls of the nave are host to numerous saints and biblical scenes. Before anyone sets foot in the temple, it is already populated by Christ and his saints. The same thing is true in the homes of the faithful where icons establish prayer corners and occupy most of the rooms in the house.

Like the other ecclesial gifts, the icons directly engage the conditions of human personhood and thus define a part of the base context for mission. In so doing this gift also speaks to the contemporary fascination with images and in particular the way in which many of the imaginal habits and techniques of the secular world are being deployed in churches. Engaging the person and providing a model for the use of image in the church, the ancient veneration of icons offers a corrective for the uncritical use of visual media.

### *a. Windows onto Heaven*

First, it is clear that the icon addresses the dual nature of human beings by bridging the gap between the infinite world and the world of creation. In other words, the icon is situated within the economy of divine salvation. The term economy refers to the management of resources to some profitable end, such as the ways in which God has arranged for the salvation of humankind. We speak of the inner-trinitarian movements of God as immanent and hidden to us. The visible aspects of God's interface with the world we call his economic side, and it provides relative (visible relative to the invisible) knowledge of God. Thus economy is a "fulfillment and historical unveiling of the divine plan," a "temporal unfolding of God's design, through which his substance is distributed and revealed and saves us," an exteriorization of God's providential plan.[262] The ideas of *image* (the invisible) and *icon* (the visible) are central aspects of this divine economy and can be seen in creation, Incarnation, and Transfiguration.[263]

Human beings, having been created in the image of God, represent an iconographic analogy of the divine. The Fathers understood this analogy in terms of human participation in divine beauty. By creating human

---

262 Marie-José Mondzain, *Image, Icon, Economy: The Byzantine Origins of the Contemporary Imaginary*, Cultural Memory in the Present (Stanford, CA: Stanford University Press, 2005), 26.

263 "The essence of the image is not its visibility; it is its economy, and that alone, that is visible in its iconicity." Ibid., 82.

beings according to his image, he has communicated, economically made visible in human being, something of his own goodness, freedom, wisdom, justice, love, and immortality. For that reason, the human being is not simply a representation of God, but is rather a symbol in which the signifier is what it signifies, an icon, a mirror reflecting, really but relatively, the divine nature. Symbolization does not entail consubstantiality, since the icon can never become its own prototype. However, it does involve economic participation in the prototype.

Sadly, this economic image of God in human being, this icon, has been tarnished by sin. Not lost altogether, in which case human being would cease, but darkened so as to only imperfectly reflect the divine nature. That intended beauty or glory was restored through the Incarnation. In Christ a second act of creation is realized, the image of God hidden and obscured by sin is repainted. In taking on human form the Son brought into the created world the image of the Father in such a way as to perfectly unite the divine and the human, the image and the icon. As Jesus himself tells us: "He who has seen Me has seen the Father" (John 14:9 NKJV). Saint Paul calls him the image (Col 1:15; Heb 1:2), the icon of the invisible Father. This, then, is the gift of the Incarnation, a renewed possibility of seeing God, a possibility preserved not only in human being but in the holy images. For as Saint John of Damascus put it, "I venture to draw an image of the invisible God, not as invisible, but as having become visible for our sakes through flesh and blood."[264]

Finally, the Transfiguration of Christ's material body indicates the degree to which the human participation in the divine can make visible the divine image. The uncreated light visible on Mount Tabor was the result of a divine penetration of the material body of Christ, the direct presence and action of the divine in and through a material object. This sanctification or transfiguration of matter indicates that, through the power of indwelling divinity, created objects can serve to symbolize the divine image. In other words, an icon (which is mere paint and wood) can be penetrated by the divine and is thus positioned at the interface of

264 John of Damascus, *On Holy Images, Followed by Three Sermons on the Assumption*, trans. Mary H. Allies (London: Thomas Baker, 1898), 5. http://www.ccel.org/ccel/damascus/icons.i.iv.html.

the material and nonmaterial worlds—it serves as a door, portal, window onto the spiritual world.

This understanding of image and icon produces "the connective tissue that legitimates the pathways between disjunctive realities," the finite and the infinite.[265] In its role as visualizer of divine image, the icon itself fades from experience as the one contemplating it is drawn into the presence of God. Because the symbol is what it signifies, there is nothing between God and the believer. For that reason the icon has no need to display text, scenery, moving parts as do the fleeting images often projected in churches. Rather than drawing attention to some aspect of its visual self, or using color, lighting, movement to evoke a particular emotion, the icon engages, by the Holy Spirit, the viewer in simplistic wholeness, mediating not itself but the reality of the prototype it symbolizes.

### *b. Truth Actualized*

Second, the icon engages the human capacity to believe by actualizing truth. In doing so, the icon draws the viewer personally into the reality of that truth. An icon of Christ draws him to his person, makes his presence an immediate reality. An icon of a scriptural event draws him into the event, making it a living reality for him now. An icon of a saint reveals something of the holiness of the saint and draws him into communion with that person, making firm his resolve to live a life of holiness. This cannot be said of noniconographic images, such as films and images recreating biblical scenes. These are the product of human imagination and do not afford access to the actual events, but rather to the artificial speculation of the human mind. No wonder, then, that the church prohibited the making of "icons without sacred study fashioning them not by sacred image but by the self-willed imaginations of their own unlettered hearts."[266]

> The canonical appearance of unchanging forms in Byzantine art is based on an economic doctrine that takes charge of the circulation of different gazes involved, as

265 Mondzain, *Image, Icon, Economy*, 64.

266 Ibid., 94.

> well as the question of abstraction itself. The problems of formal resemblance, of essential similitude, of imitation ... appear as so many openings to action, so many horizons for knowledge, directions for active contemplation or efficient evangelization, while the servitude of reproduction and representation, as well as the imagining of illusory forms and the production of fictions are radically excluded.[267]

Thus everything—from the character of the iconographer, who has to endure a long apprenticeship; to the production of the icon, which is accompanied by a regimen of prayer and fasting and episcopal approval; to its use, which is initiated by a formal blessing—takes place within the context of the church. The icon falls under the authority of the church and is strictly regulated by its canons. In other words, it is not simply a question of human creativity, but rather creativity subjected to the mind of the church. The icon has been allowed in the liturgical setting; other forms of image media have not.

Because the icon resists a purely realistic, naturalistic representation, it helps counter some of modern reliance on its own ability to understand and depict the world. What the icon illumines is the truth of the world, the beauty behind the bare facts of our reality, the sanctity of the saint, helping us to recognize the unseen dimensions of life and integrating our lives with them, allowing us to rise above the corrupting influences of sin.

The icon also helps adjudicate between conflicting conceptions of the truth by demonstrating what is believable and making that a present reality. An icon of Jesus' healing of the paralytic confirms the words of the Gospel account, renders the viewer an eyewitness, and gives her the confidence to oppose the hyper-rationalistic, reductionistic trends of modern thought.

### c. *Accountability*

Third, the icon speaks to human agency by limiting our freedom to self-actualize, the right to choose. On the one hand, the icon is produced

---

267 Ibid., 70.

according to traditional guidelines that have been received from the church. These are given in the form manuals which provide detailed, step-by-step instructions on every aspect of iconography.

> Drawing the patterns; making charcoal, glue, and gesso; gessoing the icon board; building up the halos in the icon; gessoing the entire iconostasis; preparing pigments and gilding the icon and the iconostasis; preparing the sankhir (flesh color); applying the highlights and painting the garments—including how to mix pigments for different colors, the true proportions of the human body … plus a complete pattern book, with figures from the Old Testament, New Testament, etc.[268]

This being the case, it is easy to recognize an icon and distinguish it from other sacred art. The nonrealism together with the tradition-determined format show that it is not meant to appeal to our aesthetic sensibilities. Our likes and dislikes are completely irrelevant to the meaning and purpose of the icon. It has nothing to do with our evaluation of the icon, but rather its valuation of us. For this reason the icon has remained basically the same through the ages and across many cultural boundaries. It is true that the icons of each cultural region exhibit something of each people's unique character—Greek, Russian, African, Japanese—and yet they are all readily recognizable as traditional icons. In other words, it does not have to be changed every time our culture changes or invents a new technique. The icon resists the whole notion of perpetual progress in favor of the stability of revealed truth.

On the other hand, the reversed perspective of the icon shows that the icon is not primarily an appeal, of whatever kind, to the individual. When showing distance the lines and angles of the icon are the opposite of what we might expect. The icon is the center, the subject, and we are at a distance, the object, raising the question of who is looking at whom. It is not so much a question of us appreciating the icon, but rather the icon affecting us, drawing us away from ourselves into its own reality, thus resisting the self-centeredness and reflexivity of modern life. The icon

268 Ibid., 97.

helps break the cycle of modern preoccupation with self-monitoring—what do I feel, experience, think?—and allows it to be examined by Christ through the Spirit.

### *d. Examples*

Fourth, the icon engages human morality by providing living examples of holy living for us to follow. One of the interesting characteristics of an icon is that it is always personal; i.e., there are always persons depicted. None of them show impersonal landscapes or heavenscapes. In this way the icon resists the depersonalizing trends of modern life. This provides communion with those whose lives and characters we are called to emulate. This could be done through images of the Savior, biblical scenes, Old Testament prophets, New Testament apostles, as well as that great cloud of witnesses, the saints.

The personal character of the icon is closely related to the personal character of the Logos, the word of God, that it actualizes. As already indicated, the icon conforms completely to the written word of God in that it makes present the reality of the Scriptures. As such the icon can be referred to as the word in image and color. But the word of God is also the person of Christ, and it is Christ that is preeminently revealed in the icon.

The icon, then, engages the core conditions of human personhood, accesses our ability to visualize, but does so in a way that resists many of the secularizing, depersonalizing trends of modern life, while actively correcting for many of the uncritical uses of noniconographic image in the church today.

### *e. Building the Core Context with Holy Images*

I recently got a phone call from a young and energetic church planting pastor. He asked if we could get together to discuss Orthodox worship and that he would share some of what we talked about with his congregation. When he arrived he was not alone, but had brought his camera man to video the discussion. He intended to use clips from the video during his worship service. I told him that he could not record our conversation and that I thought that using those images in his worship service was inappropriate. (It was a bit of a struggle but, just short of my asking him to leave, he relented.) That, of course, led to an interesting discussion on the use of images in the church. And it is precisely here that I think the icon can both help and correct.

We have already discussed the characteristics and potential of the icon. From that it should be obvious that our modern use of images cannot do what an icon does, such as actualize the spiritual qualities of Christ or make present the reality of a biblical event.[269] So we could leave it at that and simply declare the superiority of icons over other images. However, since we are not speaking of the use of images in general, but rather of their use in the church, we can point to two fundamental characteristics that set icons apart. They are holy and they are sacred.

> What is the economy of the site that icons occupy? Between the holy of holies and the profane world, how does the economy negotiate the definition of iconic sacredness? Exempt from consecration and worthy of prostration, the icon inhabits an abstract space and becomes the connecting tissue that causes nature, grace, and reason to communicate with each other.[270]

A sacred object is one that has been set aside by institutional (ecclesial) decree for use in the church. This can be seen in the way in which everything from oil (Ex 30:25), images (Ex 25:18), and vestments (Ex 28:4) were declared sacred; that is, reserved for use in the tabernacle and the temple, "a sacredness legitimated by law and the institution."[271] Note that it was not the object's popularity (appeal to the worshipers) nor its use by the masses that determined its status, but rather a decision by the religious community (Ex 25:1–9). Clearly icons are sacred objects and video clips are not. Of course it could be argued that some local church has, in fact, set the video clip aside as sacred for use in worship, but I rather doubt that that discussion has taken place. It is more likely that it

269 Consider, for example, depictions of Old Testament events in which a variety of vegetables play the biblical characters.

270 Ibid., 118.

271 Ibid.

has simply been incorporated on the basis of its appeal and its widespread use in society, rendering it anything but a sacred object. Even if such a decision has been taken, the choice of an isolated Christian organization independent of the church cannot possibly be considered to be on a par with the declaration of an ecumenical council of the church. We see then how the guidance of the councils helps us make informed decisions in the contemporary moment and avoid mindlessly bringing the profane into the church. The icon is an instance of image that can be used in the church to create a proper context for the use of image in a world surrounded by images.

The second characteristic of an icon is its holiness. An object that is holy is unassailable by human sinfulness, because it has become the dwelling place of the Holy Spirit, "both holy and sacred in 'essence' because it is occupied by a transcendent principle that guarantees its purity."[272] As such they cannot be used for any purpose other than the one prescribed by God himself. The bread and wine of the Eucharist, the water and oil of baptism, once imbued with the Holy Spirit cannot serve any other purpose than to mediate the presence of Christ. Similarly the icon, once overshadowed by the Spirit, cannot be used for any purpose other than to actualize the presence of its own prototype. Icons can, of course, be desecrated and put to some nonimaginal use, made the objects of avarice, simple wall decorations, at which point they cease being icons. But, when used as icons, their holiness facilitates their primary purpose, which is to function as an interface between the human and the divine. While it is conceivable that any material object could be sanctified by the Holy Spirit, it is important to note that God in his wisdom has chosen only certain material objects for this special role of ecclesial holiness—the bread and the wine, the water and oil, and the icon. There is no indication that God has chosen alternative forms of image to reveal the transcendent, and it is quite clear that these alternatives, such as video clips, can be used for other, evil purposes. The anticipated video of my conversation with the church planting pastor could easily have been edited in such a way as to portray something other than I had actually said. This kind of distortion is not possible with an icon, since it is bounded by its sacred status in the church and the action of the Holy Spirit, the Spirit of Truth. The icon,

272 Ibid., 119.

then, has a status and a function which cannot be assumed by any other form of image, no matter how beautiful, no matter how appealing and popular. It is, quite simply, God's chosen instrument, a window onto the transcendent world.

These, then, are the defining elements of the core missionary context. As I have repeatedly suggested, the task of contextualization is not to adapt a message to some context, but rather to establish a context within which the invitation to a relationship with the person of Christ can be issued. Because the church is catholic and personhood is universal, this core context does not involve an imposition of something extraneous or unknown, but rather the creation of a new reality in which the invitation can be effectively and worthily given.[273]

Let us imagine a square bounded by the four conditions of human personhood—dual nature, belief, agency, morality—each corner defined by one of them. Then think of the plane created by the square being the first of the gifts of tradition, Holy Scripture. Now add the other gifts while maintaining the corners. Gradually we create a cube or a parallelepiped, the corners remaining the same. Establishing this space is the work of contextualization, and it is within the space thus created that the invitation to a relationship with the person of Christ can most effectively be given. In other words, we introduce Christ within a core mission context defined by the Scriptures, within the structures of the church, adhering to conciliar doctrines and canons, in the shadow of the saints, and with the help of the holy images.

273 I realize that throughout history Christians have used the nonecclesial power structures of the state and society to impose the church on others. Nevertheless I believe that what I have presented is the ideal path and that how the task is carried out depends largely on the spiritual state of the witnesses.

## Chapter 4

# The Conditions of Communion

The process of contextualization having now established the core context of the church moves on to the task of enabling its members to reach out to others under conditions that facilitate interpersonal communion, namely self-transcendence, self-emptying love, and complete freedom. Unfortunately the modern mind has difficulty seeing beyond the self, loving anything other than itself. So if this invitational communion is going to develop, the first thing that needs to happen is the full spiritualization of the witness. This takes place in the field of divine-human presence generated by Christ's presence in the church using the gifts of tradition. It entails a life of repentance, spiritual discipline, regular participation in the sacraments, and knowledge of God. This advanced spiritual state of the witness is a vital aspect of contextualization and a prerequisite of invitation.

The mature believer is in a position to initiate communion in a field of human-human presence by embodying its conditions; that is, by being fully present to others. The very act of inviting becomes a form of service to others, an unmistakable expression of love, given and received in complete freedom. It includes the ability to challenge another person's beliefs while at the same time showing itself to be a servant; the ability to direct attention to Christ's presence within the witness without focusing on itself; the ability to call the other to an abandonment of self-love while demonstrating a self-emptying love of other. Obviously a person who does not yet know Christ will not be able to reciprocate fully. However, the resultant, albeit nascent, communion, strengthened by the Holy Spirit, will enable the invitee to sense the presence of Christ, entertain the invitation, and act on it.

Once acted upon, the invitee enters the field of divine-human presence available in the church. Here the task of contextualization will be to enable the church to facilitate that move, to recognize when this is happening, and to help the newly reborn negotiate his or her own life of intimacy with God. It is to these three fields of personal presence and their respective states of communion that I now turn.

## 1. Spiritual State of the Inviter

In the Eastern tradition the spiritual life is often considered in terms of a progression through specific stages of development. Saint Symeon the New Theologian, for example, suggests that the spiritual life moves up the rungs of a ladder: first curtailing the passions, then practicing psalmody, persevering in prayer, and finally to perfection.[274] Another description of the spiritual life offered by Saint Maximus the Confessor envisions three steps: doing, natural contemplation, and mystical theology.[275] Taking into account the various ways in which these terms are used, Dumitru Staniloae proposes a threefold division of purification (replacing the passions with the virtues), illumination (knowledge of God through the created order), and perfection (direct knowledge of God by union with him).[276] These steps are not strictly sequential, but can become concurrent as development takes place. Staniloae's breakdown of spiritual development affords us a workable model for the necessary contextualization; that is, spiritualization of the witness.

### *a. Purification*

The first step on the path to spiritual growth involves freedom from what are called the passions and their replacement with the virtues. The spiritual

274 Saint Symeon the New Theologian, "The Three Methods of Prayer," in *The Philokalia: The Complete Text*, vol. 4, comp. Saint Nikodimos of the Holy Mountain and Saint Makarios of Corinth, trans. and ed. G. E. H. Palmer, Philip Sherrard, and Kallistos Ware (London: Faber & Faber, 1995), 73–75.

275 Saint Maximos the Confessor, "Questions to Thalassios" 55, cited by Dumitru Staniloae, *Orthodox Spirituality: A Practical Guide for the Faithful and a Definitive Manual for the Scholar* (South Canaan, PA: St. Tikhon's Seminary Press, 2002), 70.

276 Ibid., 73.

writers of the church identify seven or eight primary passions.[277] The lists vary depending on how the terms are defined, but they generally include gluttony, unchastity, avarice, anger, dejection, listlessness, self-esteem, and pride. Before considering how these passions can be overcome, it is necessary to know something of their basic characteristics, their origins, and the ways in which they affect the soul.

### *i. On the Passions*

Basic to the nature of the passions is the fact that they have the ability to disable the activity of the human will. According to Staniloae, "The passions represent the lowest level to which human nature can fall ... they represent mechanisms by which the human being is brought to a state of passivity, of slavery ... they overcome the will so that a man of the passions is ... ruled, enslaved, carried along by the passions."[278] A glutton, for example, has no control over his desire for food, just as the anger of hatred is uncontrollable. For this reason the passions seem to be irresistible.

Furthermore the passions create an unquenchable thirst, a thirst for the infinite turned in a direction that does not allow their satisfaction. This has to do with the dual nature of human beings who, while finite, are created in the image of God and thus yearn for integration with the transcendent, a center outside the self. The passions relocate that center in the world and the ego and make it impossible for it to fulfill its purpose. Seeking fulfillment in earthly things, the glutton and those addicted to avarice can never satisfy their cravings. As Saint Neilos the Ascetic puts it, impassioned nature "sends to the stomach through the deep canal dug by gluttony food prepared for it, as into a sea which can't be filled."[279]

The passions are also fundamentally irrational.[280] According to Saint Maximus the Confessor, the world, having been created by the Word (Logos), has a natural rationality, every entity having its own meaning (*logoi*).[281] The passions violate this basic rationality by altering the inner meaning of creation. For example, the normal and necessary feeling of

---

277 Cassian, "Eight Vices."

278 Staniloae, *Orthodox Spirituality*, 77.

279 Quoted in ibid., n. 3.

280 Ibid., 79.

281 Thunberg, *Microcosm and Mediator*, 72–79.

hunger morphs into the mindless passion of gluttony. The natural and needed emotion of anger is turned into irrational hatred. So the passions are associated with turning one's back on God, rejecting him as the meaning of life, the center of being, and substituting self-love, our own irrationality, causing chaos in our relationships to the world and others.

From this it becomes clear that the passions are related to God-given faculties inherent in human being. We might even say that the appearance of the sinful passions "is made possible by the existence of the natural passions."[282] These natural faculties can be called natural passions because they exercise control as a function of our nature, things like appetite, pleasure, fear, and sadness, and so on. If these things are kept within the limits that make them useful to our nature, they remain neutral. However, outside those limits they can become good or evil. According to Saint Maximus:

> The natural passions become good in those who struggle when, wisely unfastening them from the things of the flesh, use them to gain heavenly things. For example, they can change appetite into the movement of a spiritual ongoing for divine things; pleasure into pure joy for the cooperation of the mind with divine gifts; fear into care to evade future misfortune due to sin; and sadness into corrective repentance for present evil.[283]

But these natural passions can also be turned into something evil when the mind loses control or succumbs to the desire for pleasure. This weakening of the mind is what gives rise to the unnatural passions or the vices. Saint Anthony writes:

> Things that are done according to nature aren't sins, but those done by choice; it is not a sin to eat, so that the body will be properly maintained in life without any evil thought, but it is to eat without gratitude and improperly without restraint; neither is it a sin to look with chastity,

---

282 Staniloae, *Orthodox Spirituality*, 84.
283 Quoted in ibid., 85.

> but it is a sin to look with envy, pride and desire, it is not a sin to listen quietly but it is with anger. It is not a sin to let the tongue be unrestrained in thanksgiving and prayer, but it is to speak evil; to not let your hands do acts of mercy, but to commit murder and theft.[284]

The effects of these evil passions cause disorder and corruption, fragmentation of human being, which eventually leads to spiritual death in a never-ending and never-satisfied striving for fulfillment. In order to understand how this works we need to look briefly at the basic faculties of the soul. Existing as one essence the soul, nevertheless, has three distinct faculties: mind, will (desire), emotions (incisive).[285]

Desire and emotions are said to be born of the interaction between the soul and the body. As long as the mind (soul) is in communion with God, it has true knowledge and is able to control the use of the will and the emotions. If that connection is lost or ignored, the knowledge of and love of God fades and is replaced by self-love,[286] control is passed to the physical senses which drive the will and the emotions, triggering the passions. Saint Maximus puts it this way:

> The more a man lives by the senses, concerned only with the knowledge of the visible, the more he amasses around him the ignorance of God, the more he is engrossed in the tasting by the senses of known materials; and the more he consumes them, the more the passionate love of self is inflamed within him, started by this taste. And the more he cultivates the passionate love of himself, the more he invents other ways of pleasure, as the fruit and the goal of self-love. And because pleasure always has pain as its

---

284 Quoted in ibid., 92.

285 Saint Hesychios the Priest, "On Watchfulness and Holiness," in *The Philokalia: The Complete Text*, vol. 1, comp. Saint Nikodimos of the Holy Mountain and Saint Makarios of Corinth, trans. and ed. G. E. H. Palmer, Philip Sherrard, and Kallistos Ware (London: Faber & Faber, 1983), 184.

286 "Guard yourself from that mother of all vices, self-love." Saint Maximos the Confessor, "Four Hundred Texts on Love," in *The Philokalia: The Complete Text*, vol. 2, comp. Saint Nikodimos of the Holy Mountain and Saint Makarios of Corinth, trans. and ed. G. E. H. Palmer, Philip Sherrard, and Kallistos Ware (London: Faber & Faber, 1984), 75.

> successor, he pounces with all his strength on pleasure because of the passionate love for himself ... And forcing himself to avoid pain for the same love, he causes the birth of innumerable ruin-producing passions. Thus, if he pampers the love of self by pleasure he gives birth to gluttony, pride, vainglory, conceit, love of money.[287]

Saint Hesychios suggests that at first there is no sin because we have not acted on the provocation.[288] But when we allow the thought to join or be coupled with the mind and we begin to play with the thought, we are eventually led to an assent, an agreement to do evil, and finally to the concrete act itself.[289] This repeats itself in the sinful life and leads to a passionate state which is characterized by worry and fear, whereby the individual is thrown back and forth between pleasure and pain, out of control, given over to the passions.

Obviously a person passionate in this sense will never be able to develop the divine-human communion needed to know Christ. Nor will he be able to transcend the self, be kenotically present to another person, and issue an invitation to Christ. The first step, then, in the contextualization of the witness is to purify him of all the passions, to replace those things that darken the love for God with the spiritual clarity of the virtues and the love of God, for "the person who loves God cannot help loving every man as himself."[290]

### *ii. On the Virtues*

Purification of the soul is not aimed at restoring some neutral state of soul, but rather at replacing the passions with their corresponding virtues. Over the years there have been a number of "methods" suggested for this transformation. The one offered by Maximus the Confessor strikes me as particularly practical.

---

287 Quoted in Staniloae, *Orthodox Spirituality*, 101–02.

288 Hesychios, "On Watchfulness and Holiness," 170.

289 "The provocation comes first, then our coupling with it, or the mingling of our thoughts with those of the wicked demons. Third comes our assent to the provocation, with both sets of intermingling thoughts contriving how to commit the sin in practice. Fourth comes the concrete action—that is, the sin itself." Ibid.

290 "If we detect any trace of hatred in our hearts against any man whatsoever for committing any fault, we are utterly estranged from love for God, since love for God absolutely precludes us from hating any man." Maximos, "Texts on Love," 54.

> Love is a holy state of the soul, disposing it to value knowledge of God above all created things. We cannot attain lasting possession of such love while we are still attached to anything worldly. Dispassion engenders love, hope in God engenders dispassion, and patience and forbearance engender hope in God, these in turn are the product of complete self-control, which itself springs from fear of God. Fear of God is the result of faith in God.[291]

So the steps to overcoming a passionate life include faith, the fear of God, self-control, patience, hope, dispassion, and love.[292] I will supplement this list from other sources as we go along.

"*Faith* is the virtue for starting our journey (italics added)."[293] However, in the passionate person faith is either nonexistent or very weak. So before anything else takes place we may have to reintroduce the person to Christ and facilitate a relationship between them. In the case of a weakened faith, the Fathers recommend what they call the remembrance of Christ, a calling to mind, a rediscovery of love, through the simple prayer of the publican (Luke 18:13). Since the passions constantly war against that faith, the remembrance needs to be continual. This can often be achieved by repeating the "Jesus Prayer."[294] The basic idea is that the prayer is to be repeated constantly until it becomes second nature to us. This use of the Jesus Prayer frees the inner man from every external impulse. The constant and deliberate recollection of Christ's all-holy name allows the Holy Spirit to embrace our souls. Or to put it another way, "The divine image, found in the Name of Jesus, is impressed upon the heart by means of constant remembrance brought about by uninterrupted prayer."[295]

---

291 Ibid., 53.

292 Staniloae takes the same approach, citing Maximus. Staniloae, *Orthodox Spirituality*, 123.

293 Ibid., 128.

294 This is a short prayer developed by the early Desert Fathers which reads "Lord Jesus Christ have mercy on me a sinner." Cf. "A Discourse on Abba Philimon" in *The Philokalia: The Complete Text*, vol. 2, comp. Saint Nikodimos of the Holy Mountain and Saint Makarios of Corinth, trans. and ed. G. E. H. Palmer, Philip Sherrard, and Kallistos Ware (London: Faber & Faber, 1984), 347.

295 Christoforos Stavropoulos, *Partakers of Divine Nature* (Minneapolis: Light & Life, 1976), 77.

As faith matures it takes on the form of a *fear of God*. There are two basic forms of this fear. One is the fear of his punishments, the other is a fear of being without his blessings.[296] The first fear is born of faith and is a fear of sin and the impending judgment of God. This kind of fear is characteristic of beginners. Some of the Fathers recommend the thought of death as a means for the purification from the passions. But the true Orthodox believer is not afraid of death, so this has to be focused on the judgment that follows death. This other fear, born of a love for God, is the fear of a broken relationship, disrupted communion, and the associated blessings of God. This is a powerful deterrent in the life of a mature believer who immediately senses the break caused by sin and the passions.

The fear of God leads to the consciousness of sin and the need for *repentance*. The Fathers speak of two types of repentance: repentance as a mystery (i.e., a gift of God), and as a permanent action of the soul. Saint Isaac the Syrian writes:

> If we are all sinners and no one is above temptations, not one of the virtues is above repentance. Its work can never end … because it is forever suitable for all sinners and righteous, if they wish to gain salvation. And there is no end to their perfection, because the perfection even of the perfect is imperfection.[297]

Repentance, then, is the highest virtue; it is to be continual[298]; and it is a means to purification and perfection.[299] Emphasizing its importance,

---

296 Maximos, "Texts on Love," 62.

297 Saint Isaac the Syrian, "Ascetical Homilies" 55, quoted in Staniloae, *Orthodox Spirituality*, 136–37.

298 "Through repentance the filth of our foul actions is washed away. After this we participate in the Holy Spirit, not automatically, but according to faith, humility, and inner disposition of the repentance in which our whole soul is engaged … It is good to repent each day, in accordance with the commandment that tells us to do this; for the words, 'Repent, for the kingdom of heaven has drawn near' (Matt 3:2), indicate that the act of repentance is unending." Saint Symeon the New Theologian, "One Hundred and Fifty-three Practical and Theological Texts," in *The Philokalia: The Complete Text*, vol. 4, comp. Saint Nikodimos of the Holy Mountain and Saint Makarios of Corinth, trans. and ed. G. E. H. Palmer, Philip Sherrard, and Kallistos Ware (London: Faber & Faber, 1995), 40.

299 "It is always possible to make a new start by means of repentance. 'You fell,' it is written (cf. Prov 24:16) and if you fall again, then rise again without despairing at all of your salvation no matter what happens." Saint Peter of Damaskos, "The Great Benefit of

Saint John Climacus states, somewhat audaciously, "Greater than baptism itself is the fountain of tears after baptism ... for baptism is the washing away of evils that were in us before, but sins committed after baptism are washed away by tears [of repentance]."[300] Then he goes on to say that

> we will not be condemned at the end of our lives because we have failed to perform miracles. Nor because we failed to theologize. Neither will we be condemned because we have failed to achieve the divine vision. But because of one reason only: that we did not repent continuously.[301]

Repentance leads to a desire to avoid the sins of which we repent. To that end *self-control* or restraint is necessary as a path away from our addiction to material things. Saint Peter of Damaskos speaks of four forms of wisdom which protect the soul. The second is self-restraint, "whereby our moral purpose is safeguarded and kept free from all acts, thoughts and words that do not accord with God."[302] Restraint begins with limiting or eliminating possessions. This is followed by a taming of the natural appetites: for example, by fasting in order to overcome gluttony; through silence to defeat talkativeness and gossip, slander, and lying; by limiting sleep in order to overcome laziness. The hard work of self-control gradually leads to the weakening of the passions.

> Self-restraint is a sure and unfailing sense of discretion. It does not permit its possessor to lapse into either licentiousness or obduracy, but safely preserves the blessings reaped through moral judgement while rejecting all that is bad.

---

True Repentance," in *The Philokalia: The Complete Text*, vol. 3, comp. Saint Nikodimos of the Holy Mountain and Saint Makarios of Corinth, trans. and ed. G. E. H. Palmer, Philip Sherrard, and Kallistos Ware (London: Faber & Faber, 1984), 170.

300 Saint John Climacus, *The Ladder of Divine Ascent* (Boston: Holy Transfiguration Monastery, 1991), 71.

301 Ibid., 80.

302 Saint Peter of Damaskos, "Active Spiritual Knowledge," in *The Philokalia: The Complete Text*, vol. 3, comp. Saint Nikodimos of the Holy Mountain and Saint Makarios of Corinth, trans. and ed. G. E. H. Palmer, Philip Sherrard, and Kallistos Ware (London: Faber & Faber, 1984), 100.

> Self-restraint is born of the desiring power of the soul. Without it, should any good thing come to pass, it cannot be preserved; for without self-restraint the soul's three powers are carried either upward towards licentiousness or downwards toward stupidity … Self-restraint disciplines all things and bridles the mindless impulses of soul and body, directing them towards God.[303]

*Guarding the heart.* As we saw above, the mind is continually generating thoughts. Some of them may be honoring to God and should be immediately sacrificed to him in the heart. Some of the thoughts may be evil, either awakening the passions or themselves the result of the evil one or the passions. If we allow this reciprocal cycle to continue, the evil thoughts will gain strength and penetrate the heart, disrupting communion with Christ. So it is that we set up a continual watch and immediately reject the sinful thoughts, preventing them from getting into the heart. Saint Nikodomos states:

> True and unerring attentiveness and prayer mean that the intellect keeps watch over the heart while it prays; it should always be on patrol within the heart, and from within—from the depths of the heart—it should offer up its prayers to God.
>
> Our holy fathers hearkened to the Lord's words, "Out of the heart proceed evil thoughts, murderers, adulteries, unchastity, thefts, perjuries, blasphemies; these are the things that defile a man" (Matt. 15:19–20) … Hence they abandoned all other forms of spiritual labor and concentrated wholly on this one task of guarding the heart, convinced that through this practice they would

303 Saint Peter of Damaskos, "Self-restraint," in *The Philokalia: The Complete Text*, vol. 3, comp. Saint Nikodimos of the Holy Mountain and Saint Makarios of Corinth, trans. and ed. G. E. H. Palmer, Philip Sherrard, and Kallistos Ware (London: Faber & Faber, 1984), 257.

> also possess every other virtue, whereas without it no virtue could be firmly established.[304]

*Patience* is also called for in light of the pain and sufferings that have a significant place in the development of the spiritual life. There seem to be two ways of growing: one through voluntary, self-initiated actions, and the other as judgments, trials, sufferings imposed from without. Temptations, for example, are sent in order to help us conquer the passions of the appetites and make us stronger. Trials help us overcome anger and pride. So voluntary abstinence from pleasure as well as the patient bearing of pain both indicate a victory of the will and spiritual advance. Patience leads to *hope*; that is, the hope of blessings to come. "Hope is faith in an advanced stage."[305] As we free ourselves from worldly attachments, care and worry fade and the certainty of hope grows. Only when hope gains control is the heart opened to eternity and we escape the thoughts and cares of the world.

*Meekness* and *humility* are the fruits of patiently enduring trials, temptations, and humiliations. In them we have "a shelter to keep us from seeing our own accomplishments,"[306] reducing us to a form of nothingness. They are a kind of emptiness or darkness into which God can send his divine light. And if a man accepts this role of being nothing but a reflector and receiver of divine light, then he may expect to live with the infinite. "If he is ashamed of this role and is filled with his own smoke, he can no longer see anything even in himself."[307]

*Dispassion* is the ultimate goal of the spiritual life. It is a peaceful condition of the soul which defeats every temptation. The one who has reached this state no longer sins easily, is no longer tempted by the passions, not easily stirred up either by things, thoughts, or the remembrance of sinful deeds. Saint Isaac the Syrian writes:

> Dispassion doesn't mean to no longer feel the passions, but to no longer accept them. For by the multiple and varied virtues, evident and hidden, which he who has

---

304 Quoted in Saint Symeon, "Three Methods of Prayer," 70–71.

305 Staniloae, *Orthodox Spirituality*, 177.

306 Climacus, *Ladder of Divine Ascent*, 154.

307 Staniloae, *Orthodox Spirituality*, 184.

> reached it, has gained, the passions have been weakened and can no longer easily rise up in and against the soul. The mind therefore no longer needs to be constantly concerned with them because all the time is filled with good thoughts.[308]

There is a close connection between *love* and dispassion. In fact, love presupposes dispassion. At its highest level love is not only the freedom from passions, but is also a gift of God and the essence of union with God. Human beings do know something of love which develops through three stages: (1) the tendency toward natural sympathy even in a state fallen from grace; (2) Christian love which grows by divine grace and self-effort; and (3) the ecstasy of union with God, which is a gift from God.[309] This love is an uncreated energy of God communicated by the Holy Spirit, which allows us to participate in the life of the Trinity. It is complete victory over the self, it is unceasing, and it cannot be shaken. According to Saint John Climacus:

> Love by reason of its nature is resemblance to God, as far as is possible for mortals; in its activity it is inebriation of the soul; and by its distinctive property it is a fountain of faith, an abyss of patience, a sea of humility.[310]

### b. *Illumination*

The second stage of spiritual development is entered when the soul has been cleansed from the passions. Until then the gifts of the Spirit cannot flourish in our lives, even though they have been given to us with baptism and chrismation. But once purification has taken place, the gifts "blaze up in our consciousness, from the hidden part of the heart, in all their brilliance."[311] According to Staniloae, there are seven gifts of the Holy

308 Saint Isaac the Syrian, "Directions to Hesychasts," 86, quoted in ibid., 185.
309 Ibid., 305–6.
310 Climacus, *Ladder of Divine Ascent*, 225.
311 Staniloae, *Orthodox Spirituality*, 195.

Spirit[312] related to spiritual growth[313]: (1) the spirit of the *fear of God*, by which we carry out the commandments of God; (2) the spirit of *strength*, by which we seize the opportunity to obey God; (3) the spirit of *counsel*, by which we begin to understand which commandment is most suitable in each situation; (4) the gift of *understanding*, which teaches us how to realize the blessings revealed by the commandments; (5) the gift of *knowledge*, which reveals the deeper motivation of each command and virtue; (6) *comprehension*, which changes the most theoretical penetration of the *logoi* of the virtues and fuses them with our own natural powers; and (7) *wisdom*, which brings simple and exact contemplation of the truth in all things—the gift of seeing God through all things (nature becomes transparent) and the Scriptures mediate knowledge of God. Some of what is seen is then realized in the one who sees, the second phase of our ascent to deification, namely illumination.

This illumination facilitates the contemplation of God in nature and is the first step on the way to a contemplation of the Divine. Rooted in the idea that each entity of creation contains its own *logos*, the ideas of God, this inner meaning makes possible a partial understanding of God's wisdom. As Saint Maximus puts it, "Things hide divine *logoi* in them as so many rays of the supreme Logos. He who discovers them in things ascends on their thread to the knowledge of God and this knowledge must anticipate his direct knowledge."[314] This knowledge is a symbolic knowledge, the world being a symbol of the reality that created it, the symbol making the reality visible. In the West we generally access these meanings by means of rational, discursive, deductive reasoning. However, the mind clouded by the passions cannot see the truth, thus the need for the preparation of purification. Once that is done, the virtuous mind can come to the truth. By contemplating nature, we come to discern the *logoi* sometimes as a direct gift of God, sometimes as the result of long practice. We see what is truly good, beautiful, and true, not subjectively but with true objectivity. With increasing sharpness we are able to discern the true meaning of things (and people), both good and evil, and the relationships between them; we gain a spiritual vision of creation.

---

312 Ibid., 305–6.

313 Not to be confused with the gifts of the Spirit given to help equip the church for its work in the world (1 Cor 12:4).

314 Quoted in ibid., 205.

Illumination also facilitates our understanding of the Scriptures. It has long been the tradition of the Eastern Church to insist that only those who are worthy can gain an exact understanding of the Scriptures. While the Scriptures must also be considered to be a symbol, they are the direct action of God, his supernatural revelation, and thus have a more direct claim on us than the meanings or words of God contained in creation. To have a spiritual understanding of the text does not imply any kind of subjectivity. That is prevented by our being anchored in the fact that I only gain that understanding (a) when I have conformed to the objective standards of the church, and (b) when I take the time to read and meditate on the patristic spiritual commentaries.[315] The virtuous life is guided into the true meanings of the texts as they radiate from Christ and under the guidance of the Holy Spirit. The text mediates knowledge of God. These truths and events are then realized in my own life. The persons of Scripture become types, the events become present events. In this way the Scriptures become not only contemporary but a biography of our relationship with Christ. As we grow spiritually, our understanding of the text deepens.

In all of this we have been talking about gaining a knowledge of God. Dionysius, in his *Mystical Theology*, speaks of two ways of knowing God, a *cataphatic* or positive way, and an *apophatic* or negative way.[316] At the root of this distinction is the incomprehensibility of God, the fact that we cannot know him in his essence. This, however, does not mean that we cannot know him at all. At the lower reaches of the spiritual life, God is certainly almost unknowable. However, with the divine-human union and the purification from the passions, a new condition exists, a progression from the created to the uncreated; we ascend toward God, and at each stage of that ascent we are given increasingly lofty images and knowledge. So the two ways have to be joined in a dynamic relationship, so that we are able to express a grain of truth even though we know it is not all that there is to know.

---

315 Ibid., 226.

316 Dionysius the Areopagite, "Preface to *Mystic Theology*," in *Dionysius the Areopagite: Works (1897)*, trans. John Parker (Grand Rapids: Christian Classics Ethereal Library, n.d.), http://www.ccel.org/ccel/dionysius/works.i.iii.html. See also Vladimir Lossky, *The Mystical Theology of the Eastern Church* (Crestwood, NY: St. Vladimir's Seminary Press, 1976).

According to Eastern tradition, a fuller and more existential knowledge of God can be realized by what is called pure prayer. This is "an ecstasy of interior quietness, a total cessation of thought in the face of the divine mystery, before the divine light descends to the mind thus stopped by astonishment."[317] This perfect prayer is reached when the mind is able to expel any thought while it prays; it is a wordless, visionless state of pure peace. As such it is rightly called the prayer of the mind. In addition to dispassion, two conditions have to be met: (1) the mind must be brought back from things outside to within itself, to its heart; and (2) this state should be maintained by just a few words addressed to Jesus.[318] Pure (mental or noetic) prayer does not contribute to the knowledge of God through creation, but by the depths of its own soul.[319] It is a direct perception of God, an opening of the heart pierced by the very presence of God.

Throughout the centuries a number of methods have been suggested, designed to facilitate this pure state of prayer. In general they included two components: (1) physiological recommendations, like slowing the breathing, bringing the mind to the heart by means of breathing in through the nose and imagining the parallel movement of the mind, praying to the beat of the heart; and (2) the Jesus Prayer, said with increasing frequency, synchronized to the heartbeat and breathing, and finally, having it prayed unceasingly. One example of this thinking comes from Saint Nikiphoros the Monk. He writes:

> Seat yourself, then, concentrate on your intellect, and lead it into the respiratory passage through which your breath passes into your heart. Put pressure on your intellect and compel it to descend with your inhaled breath into your heart. Once it has entered there, what follows will be neither dismal nor glum. Just as a man, after being away from home on his return is overjoyed at being with his wife and children, so the intellect, once it is united with the soul, is filled with indescribable delight.[320]

---

317 Staniloae, *Orthodox Spirituality*, 255.

318 Ibid., 257.

319 Ibid., 259.

320 Nikiphoros the Monk, "On Watchfulness and the Guarding of the Heart," in *The*

Bringing the mind to the heart implies that we have abandoned all thoughts, all objects, and are actually contemplating our very own subject. We make a distinction between the mind and reason which comes from it. Reason (rational faculties) operates in terms of concepts. The mind, however, is pure thought without well-defined concepts. Thus, giving up those concepts, we enter the mind and bring it to the heart, the very center of our being. There, without objects, thoughts, and concepts, we are faced with our own subject. When this happens, the mind becomes transparent and we are able to see God. So in overcoming thoughts and objects, we are at the same time contemplating God, who is the absolute subject. Put differently, Jesus is already present in us, and when we are able to abandon all objects and thoughts, and bring the mind to transparency, we are in fact contemplating him.

This then is the second step on the way to perfect stillness, and it has several distinct characteristics: (1) it is a standstill of mental activity because the mind has reached the peak of all objects received by thought and has given up all understanding, no matter how well defined; (2) the experience of God is in the motionlessness of the mind; (3) the mind has left behind all things including its own activity; (4) the soul is filled with a great love for the divine infinity; (5) the warmth of prayer has reached a state in which pure prayer is possible; and (6) it is overcome by the boundless mystery of the divine.[321]

### c. *Perfection*

Between those joined in love there is no separation. Obviously this mutual communication takes place differently between two people than between God and human being. Nevertheless the comparison is useful. This kind of love is realized when two subjects (not subject and object) meet each other in a full, mutual experience, in their qualities as subjects; that is, without the reciprocal reduction of each other to the state of objects, but revealing themselves to each other to the maximum, as subjects nevertheless with complete freedom. Love penetrates two

*Philokalia: The Complete Text*, vol. 4, comp. Saint Nikodimos of the Holy Mountain and Saint Makarios of Corinth, trans. and ed. G. E. H. Palmer, Philip Sherrard, and Kallistos Ware (London: Faber & Faber, 1995), 205.

321 Staniloae, *Orthodox Spirituality*, 295–97.

subjects reciprocally in their intimacy without ceasing to be sovereign and autonomous.[322] This interpenetration brings with it an increase in knowledge, realizing by direct experience the treasure that is the other subject. This is not a knowledge captured in concepts, but is rather the idea of imagination, by which the image of the one loved becomes a transformative force beautifying and strengthening one's own virtues and opening the unlimited depths of one's subject. This brings the feeling of fullness, of overflowing of infinity, of blessed intoxication, and it can be prolonged at the height of prayer, even though this union is beyond prayer. Those who love each other dwell one in the other. Not only do we enter into God, but God into us. In addition the intoxication of the love of God experienced at the height of pure prayer fills me with the impulse to love all people, to accept all in my heart, who are found in the heart of God.[323]

As we have already seen, the height of pure prayer brings with it a cessation of thought, the standstill of every mental movement. However, this does not mean the suspension of every operation of the mind, but simply that the mind does not produce and discover its own thoughts. Rather the Holy Spirit is at work, and the mind participates in this work by receiving that which is given, surpassing itself. In other words, the mind has the capacity to enter into a union with God. Saint Gregory Palamas writes:

> If our mind couldn't surpass its own self, there would be no vision or understanding above mental activities … And that the mind has the power to surpass itself and by this power to unite with things higher than it … the power to understand the union which surpasses the nature of the mind and by which it is joined to the things beyond it.[324]

This active role of the mind in the union with God is also seen in the vision of the divine light. Listen to Saint Maximus:

---

322 Ibid., 315.

323 Ibid., 326.

324 Saint Gregory Palamas, "In Defence of the Hesychasts," quoted in ibid., 328.

> When the mind borne by the eros of love goes out of itself to go toward God, it knows neither itself, nor anything else that exists. For illumined by the divine and infinite light, it no longer perceives things created by him, just as the physical eye no longer sees the stars when the sun comes up.[325]

This light is, of course, the light of knowledge; it is not a physical light but rather a spiritual light seen in ecstasy that comes at the height of pure prayer. It is beyond the senses. Saint Palamas says:

> Those who see it are able to penetrate by the power of the Spirit in them beyond the plane of physical realities. They find themselves raised to an order of Spirit. Their eyes are open and they seek a target somewhere outside. But this means only that the light from the order of spiritual realities has overwhelmed the surrounding realities; their senses have become full of the power of the Spirit.[326]

As already mentioned, this light of knowledge surpasses the mind and thus all knowledge that can be reached by natural abilities. Again the words of Palamas:

> Because this union surpasses the power of the mind it is higher than all mental functions and it isn't a kind of superior knowledge ... It is something incomparably higher than the power which ties the mind with things created ... Such union with God is beyond all knowledge.[327]

This experience is superior to knowledge, and we could even call it unknowing, a darkness, not only because it is received by the power of the Spirit and represents a quantitative and qualitative surplus which

---

325 Maximos, "Texts on Love," 54.

326 Saint Gregory Palamas, "In Defence of the Hesychasts," quoted in ibid., 340.

327 Saint Gregory Palamas, *The Triads*, 2.3.33, quoted in Staniloae, *Orthodox Spirituality*, 341.

exceeds our natural intellectual capabilities as well as all concepts.[328] So what does one see? What did Moses see when he penetrated the darkness on the mountain?

> But precisely there he saw the immaterial tabernacle which he showed to those below by a material imitation. Now this tabernacle, according to the words of the saints, could be Jesus Christ, the power and the immaterial autohypostatic wisdom of God, which being immaterial and uncreated by nature, He showed in anticipation of the Mosaic tabernacle that He, the super-essential and formless Word, would someday accept a structure that would come in form and essence. He would become the tabernacle which is above and before all things, in which all things were created and are sustained, both visible and invisible.[329]

So the one who is purified of the passions reaches the height of pure prayer, sees the divine light, has spiritualized his own nature to such an extent that it has become the warmth and the light of the love of God. For that reason Saint Symeon the New exclaims:

> O Drink of light!
> O Movement of fire!
> O Stirring of flames
> Which burn in me a sinner,
> Which come from Thy glory!
> This Glory, I say it and I proclaim it,
> Is Thy Spirit, Thy Holy Spirit,
> The Partaker of the same fire and glory with Thee,
> O Word![330]

This, then, is the ultimate goal of humanity: godlikeness as the transformation which spills over into the world we inhabit, freeing us from the cares of this world, enabling us to see divine meaning in everything, to

328 Ibid., 343.
329 Saint Gregory Palamas, "In Defence of the Heychasts," 2.3.55, quoted in ibid., 348.
330 Saint Symeon the New Theologian, "Hymns," quoted in ibid., 359.

love with the love of God. In a particular sense as partakers of the divine nature (2 Pet 1:4), so spiritualized, so divinized, so sanctified, that we are holy like he is holy, communing intimately with him, knowing him directly, radiating the divine light that is now within us.

## 2. Human-to-human Communion

Knowing God in this personal way puts the believer in a position to introduce Christ to someone else. In fact, I would suggest that this knowledge, this advanced level of spiritual development, is a prerequisite for effective witness. For it is only in this state that the believer is able to transcend the self, to truly love the other, to do so in complete freedom, to establish the intimate bond of human-human communion needed for an invitation. Saint Theophan the Recluse confirms this idea when commenting on Zechariah 8:22. "Those who live always according to the Spirit of Christ are, without the use of words, the best preachers of Christ and the most convincing apostles of Christianity."[331]

It might be argued that this level of spiritual growth is not readily available to anyone other than a monk or an extreme ascetic. However, as Saint Symeon the New Theologian puts it:

> It is good that we make God's mercy known to all
> and speak to those close to us of the compassion and
> inexpressible bounty He has shown us. For as you know
> I neither fasted, nor kept vigils, nor slept on bare ground,
> but—to borrow the Psalmist's words—"I humbled myself"
> and, in short, "the Lord saved me."
>
> Or, to put it even more briefly, I did no more than believe
> and the Lord accepted me (Ps 16:6,10; 27:10 LXX). Many
> things stand in the way of our acquiring humility, but
> there is nothing that prevents us from having faith.[332]

---

331 Saint Theophan the Recluse, *Thoughts for Each Day of the Year* (Platina: St. Herman of Alaska Brotherhood, 2010), 53.

332 Saint Symeon the New Theologian, "On Faith," in *The Philokalia: The Complete Text*, vol. 4, comp. Saint Nikodimos of the Holy Mountain and Saint Makarios of Corinth, trans. and ed. G. E. H. Palmer, Philip Sherrard, and Kallistos Ware (London: Faber & Faber, 1995), 16.

In other words, the blessings of spiritual union with God are available to anyone embedded in the church by faith,[333] and it is that union with God that enables the inviter to be fully present to the invitee through self-transcendence, kenotic love, and complete freedom.

Yet it could also be argued that the spiritual path outlined above is something that will be nearly incomprehensible, unattainable, even unavailing in the late or postmodern environment of North America—for believers and unbelievers alike. On the one hand, many of the concepts assumed and needed for the discussion of spirituality are disappearing from the modern imaginary. For example, in our discussion of the path of spiritual growth we have made much of the soul and its faculties, but according to some, "souls are already obsolete."[334]

> Hardly anyone, even religious leaders and theologians, mentions "souls" any more. The notion of souls important in Christianity and taken for granted in medieval Christianity began to lose its key importance as a religious concept and moral consideration with the growth of psychology in the latter 1800s and early 1900s in the waning of formal institutional religion. Psychology's portrayal of human nature composed of complexes, subconsciousness, emotions, superego, and such for the most part replaced the concept of soul as an individual's spiritual center. Even before this, the Protestant Reformation of the sixteenth and seventeenth centuries and the rise of capitalism in the increasingly mercantile, secular societies of the eighteenth and nineteenth centuries eroded the concept of the soul. With today's studies in neuroscience, biology, physiology. chemistry and other sciences and new theories about altruism, love, and social bonds, the concept of the soul has been practically totally overshadowed and may be forever lost.[335]

333 Saint Symeon's understanding of faith is clearly centered on the church and its sacraments.

334 Henry Berry, *Let There Be Links: The Sources and Nature of Internet Religion* (CreateSpace, 2011), 10.

335 Ibid.

On the other hand, as much of traditional Christianity becomes irrelevant and unattractive, it is replaced with ideas and institutions rooted in the concept of service (mostly customer service) that "meet seamlessly with the narcissism—self-centeredness—of postmodern individuals."[336] Take, for example, contemporary and mostly unsuccessful attempts to reconstitute the ailing structures.

> Newly-minted religions, however, were often barely more than social clubs with a spiritual facet of evangelical self-help. As groups of wealthy individuals or a corporation or other organization would establish a country club with a golf course or a pleasant rural retreat, so would groups of affluent suburbanites establish a local or regional organization in the name of a vaguely humanistic religion. Like the country club of the well-to-do, with the newly-minted religious organization—often with new building looking like a high school in an affluent town—filled a social desire for neighborliness, setting for meeting new people, recreation of children, and continuing education, self-improvement, and exercise classes for adults. Such newly-founded religions of suburbia—as most of them were—attended to mental, emotional, and physical well-being but with a faint assimilation of religion as this has been ordinarily historically and culturally defined.[337]

These attempts at religion mirror the present-day fascination with the self, leisure, materialism, and all manner of so-called and self-serving spiritualities. They are, in fact, part of the whole late-modern project which seems to be a highly reflexive exercise in self-monitoring, whereby we continually evaluate the state of our own being in order to insure maximum levels of pleasure and happiness. This contemporary preoccupation with the self pushes biblical ideas such as the soul, self-restraint, self-denial, self-transcendence beyond understanding and practice, and has transformed many a Christian community into society-emulating, pleasure-seeking associations. However, these adaptations of religion

336 Ibid., 12.

337 Ibid., 16.

> were not fully satisfying spiritually, whatever their ultimate ambitions. Once-a-week feel-good talks filled with encouragements and exhortations fell short of evoking or confirming the deepest, most private, abiding, affirmative, and sustaining feelings and inklings which are the source of religion.[338]

Having bought into the prevailing self-centeredness, these Christians are themselves unfulfilled, unable to enjoy communion with God, and are understandably having a hard time introducing Christ to the world around them. As incomprehensible as they might be, without the fruits of the spiritual life described above, no true communion with God or others can be established. In the absence of self-transcendence, kenotic love, and complete freedom, the spiritually immature simply cannot be fully present to others, and as a result no invitation to Christ is or can be issued. Let me illustrate.

I was recently relaxing at my favorite pub. I had had my dinner and, with my laptop open in front of me, I was tinkering with a writing project while watching a rather exciting soccer match. All of a sudden one of the other regulars came in, sat at my table, and started a conversation. Initially I was a bit distracted, annoyed, and torn between what he was saying, my computer, and the big-screen TV. The most I was willing to offer was partial attention, but he carried on as if in the background. When I heard him say some disturbingly inaccurate things about Christianity, my interest was piqued, and I shifted some of my resources to what he was saying. I was tempted to offer a corrective, but I still didn't want to get into an extended discussion. I also felt awkward and somehow inhibited, afraid to assert even what I knew to be the truth. Eventually he left, the encounter unsatisfying for both of us.

Upon reflection, it was clear that, to the extent that I was preoccupied with myself and my own projects, I could not be fully present to him. Without the temperance of unqualified, kenotic love, a correction of his error would not have been well received. In the resultant absence of complete freedom, I could not bring myself to fully engage or correct, much less talk about Christ.

338 Ibid.

Another way of looking at this would be to say that the whole encounter passed off without ever reaching the stage of communion. Obviously the impulse for that could not come from the person who did not yet know Christ. But for his apparent spiritual immaturity, it should have been the believer who put into place the components of communion, presence, participation, and interpenetration, by embodying their respective conditions—self-transcendence, love, and freedom. The problem, then, is self-love, the hallmark of our society and much of our religion. As countercultural as it might be, a mature Christian spirituality is the only practical solution, since it alone can conquer narcissism and replace self-centeredness with conditions that facilitate interpersonal communion.

## *a. Transcending the Self*

The first of these conditions is self-transcendence, a state of being in which self-love has been overcome. As mentioned above, the soul, which is a unified whole, possesses three distinct faculties: the intellect, the will, and the emotions. When the soul loves itself, the intellect uses all of its powers to insure that its own desires are fulfilled and that its emotions remain pleasurable. To this end intellect needs to constantly monitor the state of its emotions and its desires. As a result it is unable to give anything but a passing attention to anyone else, even while engaged in conversation.Overcoming this self-addiction involves two things. First, it means taking the path of detachment, disengaging the self from all those things to which it is attached, all those things which bring it carnal pleasure. This includes not only our material possessions but our desires for the sensual, for recognition and amusement. It is a radical state in which no personal desire can compete with and supplant the will of God. As Saint Palamas puts it:

> These are persons who have been initiated by actual experience, who have renounced the possessions, human glory and the ugly pleasures of the body for the sake of the evangelical life; and not only this, but they have also: strengthened their renunciation by submitting themselves

> to those who have attained spiritual maturity in Christ. Through the practice of the life of stillness they devote their attention undistractedly to themselves and to God, and by transcending themselves through sincere prayer and by establishing themselves in God through their mystical and supra-intellectual union with Him they have been initiated into what surpasses the intellect.[339]

In other words, the focus of the will's desires has been shifted away from the self and is focused on another, initially on God. This is the second step. Conforming itself to the will of God, the intellect directs the will and the emotions to find joy and love in God. His heart now

> burns constantly with the fire of love and clings to God with an irresistible longing, since he has once and for all transcended self-love in his love for God.[340]

> It is through this union that divine realities are apprehended, not by means of our own natural capacities, but by virtues of the fact that we entirely transcend ourselves and belong entirely to God.[341]

It is this path of self-transcendence that enables the believer to be fully present to God and thus to experience divine presence. Moreover, the same dynamic will be at work in the believer's encounters with other human beings. If there are no desires that hold us, we will be naturally, spontaneously free to focus our intellect on the desires of the other. As

339 Saint Gregory Palamas, "The Declaration of the Holy Mountain in Defence of Those who Devoutly Practise a Life of Stillness," in *The Philokalia: The Complete Text*, vol. 4, comp. Saint Nikodimos of the Holy Mountain and Saint Makarios of Corinth, trans. and ed. G. E. H. Palmer, Philip Sherrard, and Kallistos Ware (London: Faber & Faber, 1995), 419.

340 Saint Diadochos of Photiki, "On Spiritual Knowledge and Discrimination," in *The Philokalia: The Complete Text*, vol. 1, comp. Saint Nikodimos of the Holy Mountain and Saint Makarios of Corinth, trans. and ed. G. E. H. Palmer, Philip Sherrard, and Kallistos Ware (London: Faber & Faber, 1983), 256.

341 Saint Maximos the Confessor, "Various Texts on Theology, the Divine Economy, and Virtue and Vice," in *The Philokalia: The Complete Text*, vol. 2, comp. Saint Nikodimos of the Holy Mountain and Saint Makarios of Corinth, trans. and ed. G. E. H. Palmer, Philip Sherrard, and Kallistos Ware (London: Faber & Faber, 1984), 276.

Saint Paul writes to the Philippians, "Let nothing be done through selfish ambition or conceit, but in lowliness of mind let each esteem others better than himself. Let each of you look out not only for his own interests, but also for the interests of others" (2:3,4 NKJV). Self-transcendence is the secret of Christian witness, the first step toward building a context of communion through presence.

### *b. Kenotic Love*

The second condition of communion is a self-emptying love. In an encounter between a believer and a nonbeliever it is sometimes difficult for the believer to truly love the other person. This could be rooted in our own self-interest, or even the way the other person is treating us, perhaps with disrespect, ridicule, or the like. It may also have to do with behaviors that do not conform to the will of God, with opinions with which we disagree, or with factually incorrect understandings of our faith, the Scriptures, the church. But "if you are not indifferent to both fame and dishonor, riches and poverty, pleasure and distress, you have not yet acquired perfect love."[342] Once again we see that it is our relationship to God, our spiritual maturity, that makes this kind of love possible. Consider the words of Saint Maximus the Confessor:

> The person who loves God cannot help loving every man as himself, even though he is grieved by the passions of those who are not yet purified. But, when they amend their lives, his delight is indescribable and knows no bounds ... Blessed is he who can love all men equally.[343]
>
> You have not yet acquired perfect love if your regard for people is still swayed by their characters—for example, if, for some particular reason, you love one person and hate another, or if for the same reason you sometimes love and sometimes hate the same person. Perfect love does not split up the single human nature, common to all,

342 Maximos, "Texts on Love," 61.

343 Ibid., 55.

> according to the diverse characteristics of individuals; but, fixing attention always on this single nature, it loves all men equally.[344]

This consistent and unconditioned love is essential to the witnessing context because it puts into place the second component of communion, participation. Saint Diadochos suggests that "when a man begins to perceive the love of God in all its richness, he begins also to love his neighbor with spiritual perception."[345] Another way of seeing this idea of spiritual perception would be as participation in the life of the other. With genuine love the intellect engages by making the other's desires and emotions its own. It goes beyond the superficial exchange of pleasantries, seeking to love the other person by sharing in the primary aspects of his or her soul and, as communion begins to grow, by sharing with the other its own burning love of God. This interpersonal union is not simply a knowledge of the other's concerns, an understanding of fears, but a joining of souls whereby the witnessing intellect invests all its energy in ensuring that the other encounter Christ and the joy and peace of knowing its deepest longings fulfilled in God.

### c. *Complete Freedom*

The third condition of communion is freedom. Not all the interests, opinions, desires of a nonbeliever are going to be pleasing to God. At some point communion will have to involve an interpenetration of truth, something which will have to be done in the freedom purchased by love. If the witness is completely freed from attachments to possessions, fame, honor, and pleasure, and if she has developed perfect love for God and man, then she will be able to introduce Christ and his teachings without reservation, without fear. The witness will be able to invite the listener to "come and see" without concern for the privatization of religion, challenge the other person's beliefs, engage in dialogue in spite of the lost art of discussion, even "require" the abandonment of self-love while showing love, and suggest corrections and redefinition of self-actualization while

344 Ibid., 60.

345 Diadochos, "Spiritual Knowledge and Discrimination," 256.

promoting a new kind of freedom. At the same time, the witness need not fear the challenges and possible corrections that will come from the listener. No tension, no offense is taken in either direction because of a natural freedom that allows interpenetration.

Another pub story. Again, relaxing after dinner, one of the waiters that I have gotten to know well comes out of his way to see if I happen to be having dinner and if he can join me. He does. I close my laptop, disengage from the soccer match, put aside my own interests, and attend fully to what he needs. In the course of our conversation he tells me some of his exploits during a recent bar crawl and relates the general aimlessness of his life. I listen, participate in his life. Having, with God's help, transcended my own self, loving him as I should, I have complete freedom to point out the downside of his bar-crawl antics. I criticize his self-centeredness. I am able to give him access to my own love of Christ and offer him a life-fulfilling introduction to Christ. We talk for several hours. He takes no offense, doesn't even defend himself, and promises to think about turning his life over to Christ.

Aided by a more successful season in my own spiritual journey, and guided by the Holy Spirit, I was able to put into place presence through self-transcendence, participation through love, and interpenetration in freedom, thus creating a context of communion. So why should we make the effort to grow spiritually, to apply the wisdom of the fathers and mothers of the church? Because it is good for us and our salvation, and because the very things that make it hard for late moderns to understand the gospel are overcome by spiritual maturity, enabling us to be fully present to others and introduce them to Christ, who is perceptibly present in our lives.

## 3. Human-to-divine Communion

The ultimate goal of the missionary situation is to see the invitee come to faith in Christ and grow into communion with him and with the members of his body, the church. Assuming that the core context of the church has been established, that the witness has been adequately contextualized, or rather spiritualized, and that the witness has initiated nascent communion with the invitee, an invitation to "come and see" can be confidently issued. The confidence is not only that the person invited will come to the church, but that they will, while there, become aware of Christ's presence in the Eucharist and in the faithful. While communion with the faithful has already begun in the person of the witness, its full impact is realized within the church. So the initial "come and see" visit needs to be followed up with repeated invitations to negotiate intimacy with Christ using all the gifts of tradition.

To facilitate this the invitee is brought into the catechumenate, which gives them a special status within the church, not fully a member but nevertheless part of the family. Among other things, this usually includes a period of time devoted to the study of the practices and teachings of the church using a set catechesis explored in a class-like environment.[346] It is during this phase that the newly invited are exposed to the Holy Scriptures, both in the Liturgy and the daily readings. This is the time when regular attendance at the services of the church is encouraged. The dogmatic assertions of the church are explored as is its interaction with social issues. This is the time for drawing closer to Christ through the holy icons and the Lives of the Saints. All of this towards the development of faith in Christ and eventual incorporation into the church through baptism and chrismation. The hope that the faithful have for the catechumens is captured in a prayer said for them during the Divine Liturgy.

> O Lord our God, who dwellest on high and lookest upon the humble, who has sent forth as the salvation of the race of men thine only-begotten Son, and God, our Lord Jesus Christ, look upon thy servants the catechumens, who have bowed their necks before thee. Vouchsafe unto them in due time the laver of regeneration, the forgiveness of sins, and the robe of incorruption. Unite them to thy Holy Catholic and Apostolic Church and number them with thine elect flock– that with us they also may glorify thine all-honorable and magnificent name, of the Father, and of the Son, and of the Holy Spirit, now and ever, and unto ages of ages. Amen.[347]

346 *Living God.*

347 Orthodox Church in America, *The Priest's Service Book,* 130–31.

This, then, is the path of the seeker, introduced to Christ, drawn into intimacy with him during the catechumenate, and then to inclusion in his own body. It is rooted in an understanding of contextualization that involves an invitation issued to a relationship with the ascended Christ, given in the presence of Christ, which is to be found in the church and particularly in its sacraments, given within the core context of missions (the church), which is established with the help of the gifts of tradition, and proffered it by a witness of sufficient spiritual maturity to facilitate interpersonal communion and ultimately the invitation to Christ. What remains to be discussed is whether or not this approach can be implemented on the various fields of human presence. In other words, is it possible to establish the core context in any field and then effectively issue an invitation growing out of and into communion? It is to that question that I now turn.

## Chapter 5

# Engaging the Fields of Personal Presence

An essential aspect of my understanding of contextualization is the implementation of everything I have presented so far by its extension into extra-ecclesial fields of human presence. As defined above, a field is the space around a body radiating personal presence, within which it can exert force on similar bodies. They are spheres of human existence into which aspects of the core context can be extended, settings where communion can flourish. These fields inhabit the broad expanses of whole cultures, people groups, national entities, geographic units. They are also to be found in the more narrowly defined spaces of institutions such as schools, pubs, restaurants, families, businesses.

The prerequisites for this extension have been laid out above. To begin with, we will need a place of divine presence to which we can call people to "come and see." This is nothing other than the church with its sacraments. In most cases this initial projection will be accomplished in keeping with the structures associated with apostolic succession. Second, that core context (the church) needs to be firmly established with the help of the six gifts of tradition: the Holy Scriptures, apostolic succession, liturgical structures, councils (dogma and canons), hagiography, and iconography. Third, we will need to navigate the fields of personal presence and initiate communion with the invitee by means of self-transcendence, kenotic love, and complete freedom.

Unfortunately not all fields of presence are equally situated. Some, such as people groups, are so open and generous of purpose that, absent anti-ecclesial laws and outright persecution, the extension of everything I have described is easily conceived of. In other cases, such as the pub mentioned above, we are limited by the purpose of the field's parent context. Obviously we can be personally present to others in a pub, but its primary function makes the extension of some of what we have been talking about either impossible or even inappropriate. So for every proposed projection we will have to carefully examine the field and its parent context to see if an invitational engagement is even possible.

From the standpoint of the church's mission in the world, one of today's more intriguing and challenging collection of personal presence fields is what we have come to call cyberspace, the Internet with all its attendant forms of computer-mediated communication. CMC has become so widely available that today it may well be considered our primary form of communication. "The rate of growth has been staggering. Worldwide, the number of Internet users is estimated to have been 16 million in 1995, 378 million in 2000 (Castells 2001: 260), more than 500 million in 2002 (Wellman and Haythornthwaite 2002: 11),"[348] and an estimated 2 billion in 2011.[349] It affects so many people that the church can simply not afford to ignore it.

While communication in cyberspace presents an amazing opportunity for the dissemination of information, it does pose unique challenges since it is done in the absence of many of the cues we take for granted in face-to-face communication. Here there are no (or few) facial expressions, no body language, little in terms of those aspects of communication that radiate off the participants. How, then, can the gospel-as-person be communicated in this depersonalized, disembodied medium? How do you introduce a person in this space? What do identity, friendship, intimacy, love, community look like in this environment? What happens to the self, the person, in this context?

Because of its presence and popularity CMC is generally taken for granted. It is simply part of the world in which we operate, the air we breathe. We simply use it, and that mostly uncritically. As a result, there are few who ask of it the kinds of questions I am posing. Few who challenge

---

348 Dawson and Cowan, *Religion Online*, 5; citing Manuel Castells, *The Internet Galaxy: Reflections on the Internet, Business, and Society* (Oxford: Oxford University Press, 2001), and Barry Wellman and Caroline Haythornthwaite, eds., *The Internet in Everyday Life*, The Information Age Series (Malden, MA: Blackwell, 2002).

349 Agence France-Presse (AFP), "Number of Internet Users Worldwide Reaches Two Billion," Phys.Org, January 26, 2011, http://www.physorg.com/news/2011-01-internet-users-worldwide-billion.html.

it, who wonder about the implications for the church and the gospel. There are, of course, some who find it

> troubling that so many communities of faith are in hot pursuit of these technologies. The Internet is seen as the Holy Grail of "building community." However, churches will find the unintended consequences of this medium coming back to bite them. The Internet is a lot of things, but it is emphatically *not* a neutral aid. Digital social networking inoculates people against the desire to be *physically present* with others in real social networks—networks like a church or a meal at someone's home. Being together becomes nice but nonessential.[350]

But most people assume a kind of neutral (mindless) stance and simply use it. In what follows I would like to examine those assumptions and ask if and under what circumstances Christian witness can hope to engage the personal fields of cyberspace, if that's really what they are. We could start by asking if cyberspace is a context or a field of personal presence. For the purposes of our discussion the primary act or event is the invitation to Christ, and the facts and circumstances surrounding it are what I have been calling the core context of mission, the church. For that reason I want to see cyberspace as a collection of fields in which human beings attempt to engage each other. There are, of course, other online events, such as the sale of books, which are regulated by the context of the booksellers. There are certainly other contexts within cyberspace, but in this discussion they are secondary to the primary event of invitation. My question is: can the presence of Christ in the sacraments, the core context of the church, and the conditions of communion be extended into the fields of cyberspace? Based on the answers to these questions, I will make some recommendations on how I think the church should make use of this space. However, before we proceed with that, let me make a few preliminary observations.

350 Shane Hipps, *Flickering Pixels: How Technology Shapes Your Faith* (Grand Rapids: Zondervan, 2009), 115.

## 1. Preliminary Observations

### *a. On the Nature of Cyberspace*

The primary metaphor used to describe the space where emails, chat rooms, and bulletin boards exist is cyberspace. This comes from the Greek word, να ελέγχει, (to control), as in cybernetics—creating, at least, the illusion of complete freedom and control. We talk of cyberspace as if it were an actual place, using an array of geographic images. We speak of the World Wide Web, navigating this space, visiting different sites, and surfing. For all intents and purposes we treat it as any other space we have to deal with. But what kind of space is it? It is interesting that we do make a distinction between the cyberworld and the real world. So there is a tacit admission that cyberspace is in some sense possessed of a degree of unreality. William Gibson in his novel *Necromancer* goes so far as to suggest that cyberspace is

> a consensual hallucination experienced by billions of operators, in every nation … a graphic representation of data extracted from every computer in the human system. Unthinkable complexity. Lines of light arranged in the nonspace of the mind, cluster and combinations of data. Like city lights receding.[351]

Others have suggested that it is the mind taken to the next level or something like the nonlinear reality of mind-altering drugs.[352] Some have defined it as a conceptual space where "words, human relationships, data, wealth, and power are manifest by people using CMC."[353] In any case, it is an imagined, as opposed to a real, space. If that is the case, how can we speak of fields of personal presence? In what sense are things, in particular people, present in cyberspace? What is real in that environment?

351 Quoted in Andrew F. Wood and Matthew J. Smith, *Online Communication: Linking Technology, Identity, and Culture*, 2nd ed., Lea's Communication Series (Mahwah, NJ: Lawrence Erlbaum Associates, 2005), 18.

352 Ibid.

353 Ibid., 19.

The objects that exist in cyberspace are actually simulacra of those objects presented in the form of text, pictures and, in some cases, audio and video clips. Some of these representations could be said to possess a degree of quasi reality if they correspond to actual objects existing in the real world, as in the descriptions of an item actually sold and delivered via e-commerce. Other objects are completely unreal in that there is no correspondence to actual things; they are purely imaginary or fictional as in the case of gaming characters (avatars), where we are dealing with pure simulation, unreal characters. What then of human persons, can they exist in cyberspace? The first condition of personhood, their dual mode of existence, rules this out, since in order to be a person one has to exist as embodied in the real world. However, like all other cyberobjects, persons can be represented by the several media available in cyberspace; that is, information about the person can be provided. Does that mean that the person represented has some kind of quasi-real, cyberspatial presence? Well, no more than does the computer depicted for sale on eBay. Or is this not a case of presence-in-absence where the person puts something of themselves (e.g., a resume, a picture) into the void created by their physical absence? No different really than the presence of an absent artist in her own painting. While this is generally true, it is important to make a distinction between the way Christ is present in the world through the Holy Spirit and the way a person is present in cyberspace through something like Facebook. In the case of Christ, he has put something of himself, another member of the Godhead, into the void. But that is not simply a description or some form of information, it is the actual person of the Holy Spirit. Christ is *personally* present-in-absence. In the case of the person on Facebook, it is not a person but rather information in the form of pictures and text that are put into the void. So in this case we would have to say that the person is *informationally* present-in-absence. But is that form of presence enough for us to then speak of cyberfields of personal presence? What is the difference between this and a real-world field of presence; for example, the difference between two people facing each other in conversation over a table at the pub and two people in conversation in a chat room on the Internet? We said that a field is the space created by a body radiating personhood and affecting similar bodies. In the case of the pub the field is obvious with all of the common markers of human interaction such as facial expressions, tone of voice, body language. None of that exists in cyberspace; they are limited to information about each other. Nevertheless, the two persons in the chat room are affecting one another; there is some, at least, quasi presence involved. So we may need to make yet another distinction between a personal field of presence (the pub) and an informational field of presence (the chat room). In the one case, presence expressed directly by persons, and in the other case, presence mediated by something other than person.

### b. On the Nature of CMC

This place we call cyberspace is, of course, the realm of computer-mediated communication. In speaking of CMC we are making a distinction between immediate and the mediated communication or, as Ong has described it, the difference between orality and textuality.[354] Immediate or direct communication is communication without the use of alphabets, writing, print, or computer: primarily *oral*, relying on the sense of *hearing*. Since it requires the participation of at least two individuals, it is also *communal*.

> The word in its natural, oral habitat is a part of a real, existential present. Spoken utterance is addressed by a real, living person to another real, living person or real, living persons, at a specific time in a real setting which includes always much more than mere words. Spoken words are always modifications of a total situation which is more than verbal. They never occur alone, in a context simply of words.[355]

Mediated or indirect communication, on the other hand, is facilitated by writing, print, and computers and relies on the sense of *sight*.[356] Interestingly, it does not require the physical presence of another person

---

354 Walter J. Ong, *Orality and Literacy: The Technologizing of the Word* (New York: Routledge, 2002).

355 Ibid., 99.

356 The computer has become the new cultural symbol of the things that Rousseau feared from the pen: loss of direct contact with other people, the construction of a private world, a flight from real things to their representations. Cf. Jean-Jacques Rousseau, *Essay on the Origin of Writing*, trans. John Moran (New York: Frederick Ungar, 1966).

and is thus a basically individualistic medium, as can be seen from the act of reading. As a result mediated communication tends to isolate its participants. According to Ong:

> Writing and print isolate. There is no collective noun or concept for readers corresponding to "audience." The collective "readership"—this magazine has a readership of two million—is a far-gone abstraction. To think of readers as a united group, we have to fall back on calling them an "audience," as though they were in fact listeners.[357]

However, adding the computer as the vehicle of mediated communication seems to muddy the waters of these simple distinctions. Although it is a primarily print-oriented device, what it accomplishes goes way beyond the mediation achieved by straight printed materials. It actually provides a hybridized form of mediation. Not simply the text as a foundation or background to communication, but a machine that itself takes up a quasi-personal, active role, demanding attention, assuming authority. Speaking of the late-modern individual, Sherry Turkle observes that many

> are lonely and isolated, but when they have a computer around it can feel like somebody is always there, always ready, always responsive, but without the responsibility of having to deal with another person. The computer offers a unique mixture of being alone and yet not feeling alone.[358]

> Computers, with their reactivity and interactivity, stand in a novel and evocative relationship between the living and the inanimate. They make it increasingly tempting to project our feelings onto objects and to treat things as though they were people—an impulse I called the "Eliza effect" after the early AI program that was designed to seem like a solicitous psychotherapist.[359]

357 Ong, *Orality and Literacy*, 72.
358 Turkle, *The Second Self*, 146.
359 Ibid.

## c. Personal Identity in Cyberspace

If computers are "relational artifacts [that] ask their users to see them not as tools, but as companions, as subjects in their own right,"[360] we might reasonably ask how the quasi-personal nature of the machine affects the identity and self-awareness of the user. The question of identity is closely related to the issue of being and involves answers to the question "Who am I?" as opposed to "What or how am I?" Obviously identity is a complex, puzzling structure which involves personal (private, psychological) and public aspects and has both historical and momentary elements.[361]

> Online life became a social location for the projection and exploration of self. Virtual space not only made it possible for people who had never met physically to relate to one another (in anonymity if they wished), but also made it possible for individual users to assume multiple identities. In online life, computer users cycle through personae, cutting across "real life" distinctions of gender, race, class, and culture.[362]

But what are these identities? "A digital identity contains data that uniquely describes a person or thing (called the subject or entity in the language of digital identity) but also contains information about the subject's relationships to other entities."[363] Its basic function is to identify an entity, the subject (person, organization, computer), that is asking for access to a particular resource.

*Identities* are collections of data about a subject that represent attributes, preferences, and traits. *Attributes* are acquired, describing information about a subject such as medical history, past purchasing behavior, bank balance, credit rating, dress size, age, and so on. *Preferences* represent desires such as preferred seating on an airline, favorite brand of

---

360 Ibid, 316.

361 However, I do not wish to imply that identity is mere performance or only the result of human decisions. We, created in the image of God, are given *qua* creation some of what defines us as individuals.

362 Ibid., 316.

363 Phillip J. Windley, *Digital Identity* (Sebastopol, CA: O'Reilly, 2005), 8.

hot dog, use of one encryption standard over another, preferred currency, and so on. *Traits* are like attributes, features of the subject, but they are inherent rather than acquired [such as the color of your eyes].[364]

We usually speak of identity in the singular but, in fact, subjects can have multiple identities. One's multiple identities are linked by one's self and little else.

> These multiple identities, or personas, as they are sometimes called, are tied together by a few common data elements that are used, imperfectly, as keys for accessing them: my name, my address, my social security number, and my birthday.[365]

As you can see, all of this requires a certain level of *trust*; i.e., every authorization made using a digital identity infrastructure is dependent on trusting that an identity and its attributes are correct. Trust in a digital identity is ultimately based on some set of *evidence*.

> For example, when you log into your computer, you present an identity in the form of a user ID and evidence that you are the person to whom that ID refers by typing in a password. The password is evidence that the computer should trust that you are who you say you are.[366]

In any case, a digital identity is, with the exception of biometrics, divorced from the actual identity of the individual and relies on certain levels of trust rather than an actual identification of the person. It is an abstraction, depersonalized, and requires that the individual place his or her trust in some abstract system. So online identity is less a question of who I actually am as it is an issue of how and what I present online. Motivated by what others think of us, we spend countless hours perfecting our presentations, our profiles, our pictures, even to the point of being deceptive. I can use my real name and some information that is true of my person. I can use a pseudonym to mask my identity, or I can try to

364 Ibid., 9.
365 Ibid., 12.
366 Ibid., 17.

remain completely anonymous. In what way can this be considered a true identity?

I find it interesting that the literature on digital identity refers not to persons but to subjects. This seems to be a purely functional description of one aspect of a person's activity. As such it presents a truncated picture of the individual. I may be erommen + password to the university's server, but that is not all that I am. In fact, that represents very little of who I am. It has nothing to do with me as a person, but simply a digital identity that allows a preprogramed computer to give me access to some resource. In any case, the interaction between me and the server does not constitute a field of personal presence.

The possibility of multiple identities plays directly into the identity fragmentation so prevalent in the modern world.[367] Now I can set up online identities for every conceivable interest I have. But which one is me and is it really me? Online identity is open to abuse in several forms. One is the deception that is made possible and even encouraged by the lack of physical cues. I can, in theory, identify myself in ways that do not conform to my actual person: gender, age, education, expertise, and desires. Having multiple identities leads to what Sherry Turkle calls the "tethered self," the necessity of monitoring all of one's identities by being connected at all times.[368] However, this can easily lead to a kind of information overload because the individual is—between Twitter, Facebook, cell phone, and texting—required to engage in what some have called continuous partial attention.[369] Motivated by a desire not to miss anything, this creates a constant state of crisis or high alert. "Ever-

367 "What templates from the history of psychiatry might help us understand the fracturing of identity that seems to be taking place, albeit to different levels, among them? Might 'dissociation,' a well-known clinical phenomenon wherein thoughts and behaviors are not adequately integrated into consciousness and memory, be relevant to their experiences? For people who transform into something very different online, and for the many among us who transform to lesser degrees in front of our browsers, might e-personality represent a twenty-first-century 'alter' of sorts." Elias Aboujaoude, *Virtually You: The Dangerous Powers of the E-Personality* (New York: W. W. Norton, 2011), 33.

368 Sherry Turkle, http://sodacity.net/system/files/Sherry-Turkle_The-Tethered-Self.pdf Ssherry Turkel. Always on? Always-on-you: The Tethered Self.

369 Linda Stone, "Continuous Partial Attention—Not the Same as Multi-tasking," *Business Week*, July 23, 2008.

connected to everywhere but the here and now,"[370] losing the ability to be fully present to any single moment or person.

This mode of being, for all its desire to engage others, is ultimately isolating and works against self-awareness.[371] It is only over against another self that the self can begin to answer the question of who it is. Identity is then created in response to others in a matrix of mutual recognition.[372] But what is it we face in cyberspace, another consciousness or simply disembodied information? Take email as an example: logon, read mail, respond. In what sense are we aware of the other or even ourselves in that kind of transaction? It is at best an informational presence-in-absence. The same might be said of the so-called social networking sites. What are you engaging? Another person or information about another person? Even a visual representation usually serves only as a mnemonic device that triggers a memory unique to a human mind.[373] Jesse Rice, in his recent book *The Church of Facebook* (which, by the way, has nothing whatsoever to do with the church), suggests that there are two ways which blur our sense of self: (1) the desire to be always-on "reinforces the belief that an invisible entourage follows us wherever we go" and leads to the anxiety caused by the fact that someone is always watching, and (b) the fact that we cannot be fully present in the moment.[374]

## *d. Intimacy, Friendship, and Community in Cyberspace*

If the multiple-identity, always-on, constant-partial-attention aspects of CMC make personal presence in cyberspace difficult, what must that say about the possibility of intimacy, friendship, and community? Some time ago I read Brian McLaren's book *A New Kind of Christian*. In the book the author describes in some detail an ongoing, face-to-face discussion he was having with a nonbeliever. At one point in their encounter they

370 Jesse Rice, *The Church of Facebook: How the Hyperconnected Are Redefining Community* (Colorado Springs: David C. Cook, 2009), 146.

371 Keith Hampton et al., *Social Isolation and New Technology* (Annenburg: University of Pennsylvania Press, 2009); Miller McPherson and Lynn Smith-Lovin, "Social Isolation in America: Changes in Core Discussion Networks over Two Decades," *American Sociological Review* 71, no. 3 (June 2006): 353–75.

372 Stone, "Continuous Partial Attention," 112.

373 John R. Searle, *Mind: A Brief Introduction*, Fundamentals of Philosophy Series (Oxford: Oxford University Press, 2004).

374 Rice, *The Church of Facebook*, 142–44.

switched over to the computer and continued their dialogue by email. He then described this new phase of their discussion as more intimate than the face-to-face phase.

> When Neo responded to my initial e-mail, it was as if our relationship instantly went to a deeper level. I was intrigued by this: as soon as he was so physically distant, we seemed to get closer. Somehow it seemed unavoidable to be more personal and open with each other via e-mail.[375]

I have often wondered about this statement and have asked myself what constitutes true human intimacy. I think of it in terms of what one would call a closeness that involves the exclusivity of personal knowledge.[376] And so I tend to answer that it cannot be achieved by identifying ourselves to some list server. It will not happen even if we are authenticated by someone's blog. Email just won't do. Not even Facebook.[377]

Nevertheless, there is talk of online intimacy. Often it is associated with the possession of intimate knowledge of another in the physical absence of that person. But, unless I am mistaken, this amounts to a redefinition of the concept of intimacy. One interesting example of redefinition comes from the world of Twitter. In a piece entitled "17 Ways You Can Use Twitter," Leisa Reichelt's concept of "ambient intimacy" is referenced.

> It is about being able to keep in touch with people with a level of regularity and intimacy that you wouldn't usually have access to, because time and space conspire to make it

375 Brian D. McLaren, *A New Kind of Christian* (San Francisco: Jossy-Bass, 2001), 111.

376 "Intimacy happens the moment we are invited into the exclusive VIP room of another person's life. Intimacy always follows the statement, 'I'm going to tell you something I've never told anyone before.' These are risky words of deep trust and vulnerability. The exclusivity of personal information creates the conditions of intimacy. That intimacy is preserved in that relationship as long as the information remains exclusive. The moment it is available to anyone and everyone is the moment intimacy begins to evaporate." Hipps, *Flickering Pixels*, 113.

377 Benedict XVI, "New Technologies, New Relationships: Promoting a Culture of Respect, Dialogue and Friendship," Libreria Editrice Vaticana, January 24, 2009, http://www.vatican.va/holy_father/benedict_xvi/messages/communications/documents/hf_ben-xvi_mes_20090124_43rd-world-communications-day_en.html.

> impossible ... It makes us feel closer to people we care for but in whose lives we're not able to participate as closely as we'd like. Knowing details creates intimacy.[378]

So maybe we have to call this a kind of anonymous intimacy, which "provides just enough connection to keep us from pursuing real intimacy."[379] But again, is having knowledge, even intimate detailed knowledge, of a person in whose life we do not otherwise participate, to whom I am not fully present, the same thing as personal, face-to-face intimacy? Does ambient intimacy provide enough strength of personal presence to constitute a field of personal presence? Yet many would claim to have just such cyberintimacy. Something is taking place and it probably falls within the realm of what I called an informationally based presence of person.

Until recently the ideas of intimacy and close friendship have been associated with a relatively small number of acquaintances. Current research suggests that North Americans usually have more than one thousand interpersonal relationships,[380] but that only a half dozen of them are intimate and no more than fifty are significantly strong.[381] Another study seems to confirm this:

> Make a list of all the people you know whose death would leave you truly devastated. Chances are you will come up with around 12 names. That, at least, is the average answer that most people give to that question. Those names make up what psychologists call our sympathy group. Why aren't groups any larger? Partly it's a question of time. If you look at the names on your sympathy list, they are probably the people whom you devote the most attention

---

378 Leisa Reichelt, "17 Ways You Can Use Twitter," http://www.doshdosh.com/ways-you-can-use-twitter/ (accessed 11/20/2009).

379 Ibid.

380 Manfred Kochen, *The Small World* (Norwood, NJ: Ablex, 1989); Barry Wellman, "Which Types of Ties and Network Give What Kinds of Social Support?" *Advances in Group Processes* 9 (1992): 207–35.

381 Of course there is also the famous "Dunbar's number" that puts it at a much higher 150. Cf. Malcolm Gladwell, *The Tipping Point: How Little Things Can Make A Big Difference* (New York: Little, Brown, & Company, 2000), 177.

> to—either on the telephone, in person, or thinking and worrying about. If your list was twice as long, if it had 30 names on it, and, as a result, you spent only half as much time with everyone on it, would you still be as close to everyone? Probably not. To be someone's best friend requires a minimum investment of time. More than that, though, it takes emotional energy. Caring about someone deeply is exhausting. At a certain point, at somewhere between 10 and 15 people, we begin to overload, just as we begin to overload when we have to distinguish between too many tones.[382]

In other words, there is only so much relational information that a human being can process at once without becoming overwhelmed.

> If you belong to a group of five people, Dunbar points out, you have to keep track of ten separate relationships: your relationships with the four others in your circle and the six other two-way relationships between the others. That's what it means to know everyone in the circle.
>
> If you belong to a group of twenty people, however, there are now 190 two-way relationships to keep track of: 19 involving yourself and 171 involving the rest of the group. That's a fivefold increase in the size of the group, but a twentyfold increase in the amount of information processing needed to "know" the other members of the group.[383]

Yet the speed and the resources of CMC seem to be altering these conceptions of intimacy and friendship. It was said, for example, that in 2007 then-Senator Barack Obama had an impressive 128,859 friends on various social networking sites.[384] Can we really call these online connections friendships? I suppose we have to recognizing the desire

382 Ibid., 175.
383 Ibid.
384 Rosen, "Virtual Friendship," 18.

for friendship, which is no doubt one of the driving forces behind the phenomenal growth of Facebook. Started in 2004, it has grown from a directory of a few universities to an almost unbelievable 500 million participants by July of 2010.[385] But in spite of all the talk of friends, friending, friend finding, and the like, some are more skeptical and have warned against the unreality of social networking in cyberspace. Consider the words of Pope Benedict:

> The concept of *friendship* has enjoyed a renewed prominence in the vocabulary of the new digital social networks that have emerged in the last few years. The concept is one of the noblest achievements of human culture. It is in and through our friendships that we grow and develop as humans. For this reason, true friendship has always been seen as one of the greatest goods any human person can experience. We should be careful, therefore, never to trivialize the concept or the experience of friendship. It would be sad if our desire to sustain and develop *on-line* friendships were to be at the cost of our availability to engage with our families, our neighbors and those we meet in the daily reality of our places of work, education and recreation. If the desire for virtual connectedness becomes obsessive, it may in fact function to isolate individuals from real social interaction while also disrupting the patterns of rest, silence and reflection that are necessary for healthy human development.[386]

Indeed this may be happening; that is, there may be a "trend toward giving up face-to-face for virtual contact—and, in some cases, a preference for the latter."[387] At the very least, online social networking seems to have changed the way we understand friendship. Christine Rosen suggests that we are dealing with a new taxonomy of friendship. She writes:

---

385 http://money.cnn.com/2012/10/04/technology/facebook-billion-users/index.html.

386 Benedict XVI, "New Technologies."

387 Rosen, "Virtual Friendship," 30.

> "Friendship" in these virtual spaces is thoroughly different from real-world friendship. In its traditional sense, friendship is a relationship which, broadly speaking, involves the sharing of mutual interests, reciprocity, trust, and the revelation of intimate details over time and within specific social (and cultural) contexts. Because friendship depends on mutual revelations that are concealed from the rest of the world, it can only flourish within the boundaries of privacy; the idea of public friendship is an oxymoron.
>
> The hypertext link called "friendship" on social networking sites is very different: public, fluid, and promiscuous, yet oddly bureaucratized. Friendship on these sites focuses a great deal on collecting, managing, and ranking the people you know. Everything about MySpace, for example, is designed to encourage users to gather as many friends as possible, as though friendship were philately.
>
> The use of the word "friend" on social networking sites is a dilution and a debasement … The impulse to collect as many "friends" as possible on a MySpace page is not an expression of the human need for companionship, but of a different need no less profound and pressing: the need for status.[388]

So friendship is a mixed and fluid concept that is being redefined. So what does all of this say about the possibility of community?[389] If the ideas of both friendship and intimacy are fundamentally altered, what are we to say about the larger concept of community? Here again we encounter a redefinition of terminology. Recent research indicates that "virtual communities differ from real-life communities on the basis upon which participants perceive their relationships to be intimate."[390] In cyberspace

388 Ibid., 11–12.

389 Marc A. Smith and Peter Kollock, *Communities in Cyberspace* (New York: Routledge, 1999).

390 Ibid., 185.

there is a tendency to base feelings of closeness on shared interests rather than shared social characteristics, such as gender, age, race. Yet cyberspace is not the great leveler that we once thought it would be. The cartoon with two dogs in front of a monitor, the one saying, "On the Internet, no one knows you are a dog," does not hold true. Race, gender, financial status, supposed expertise are all very much a part of what goes on. "Far from being a site where race, racism, ethnocentrism, or stereotyping are banished, these phenomena flourish in newsgroups."[391] Perhaps one of the reasons for the confusing mix of coarseness, vulgarity, and intimacy commonplace on social networking sites is that we are dealing with a dislocation of mind and body. Uninhibited by the conventions of everyday embodied life,[392] users are "both more intimate and more hostile with each other than would be socially acceptable in everyday life."[393] For these reasons some have suggested that online community is a fantasy, an illusion.

But there is no need to be quite that skeptical. After all, can 500 million people all be wrong? Obviously there is such a thing as a virtual community; it is just a matter of definition. Rheingold, for example, argues that these communities "are social aggregations that emerge from the Net when enough people carry on … public discussions long enough, with sufficient human feeling, to form webs of personal relationships in cyberspace."[394] Again we seem to be dealing with an informationally based field of human presence. This has led Lorne Dawson to propose that we accept the existence of a virtual community as community to the degree that it displays six elements: (1) interactivity, (2) stability of membership,

---

391 Ibid., 72.

392 "Regardless of the neuotransmitter cocktail at work, one downstream effect is certain and seems to characterize every e-personality: We all have less inhibitions online and act out more frequently and more intensely than we would 'in person.' The normal brake system, which under usual circumstances helps keep thoughts and behaviors in check, constantly malfunctions on the information superhighway. This chronic malfunction has been called the 'online disinhibition effect.'" Aboujaoude, *Virtually You*, 40.

393 Smith and Kollock, *Communities in Cyberspace*, 111.

394 Howard Rheingold, *The Virtual Community: Homesteading on the Electronic Frontier* (Reading, MA: Addison-Wesley, 1993), 5, quoted in Dawson and Cowan, *Religion Online*, 74.

(3) stability of identity, (4) netizenship and social control, (5) personal concern, (6) and occurrence in a public space.[395]

So, if we can, if only tentatively, conclude that there is such a thing as a virtual community, we are still left asking if

> individuals communicating by computer from the comfort of their homes [can] practice their religion? We are told that new forms of community are coming into being, "virtual communities" free of any meetings in the flesh in any real place. If these communities exist, can religion happen in them?[396]

## e. *Religion in Cyberspace*

To say that religion is flourishing online is a bit of an understatement. According to some researchers, there are over 1 million active religious sites. As Brenda Brasher observes:

> That something spawned by the military, cultivated by academia, and colonized by commerce would come to house an enormous quantity of sites dedicated to religious expression is an amazing, if little known, fact. From the Vatican to Buddhist mediation to the Dark Lair of Infinite Evil, online religion flourishes.[397]

As Hadden and Cowan note:

> There is scarcely a religious tradition, movement, group, or phenomenon absent entirely from the Net. From the Norse neopaganism of Asatru to Christian countercult refutations of it, from Tibetan Buddhist prayer bowls and thangka paintings to Wiccan scrying bowls that come with easy-to-follow instructions, from a disenfranchised

---

395 Dawson and Cowan, *Religion Online*, 83.

396 Ibid., 75–76.

397 Brenda E. Brasher, *Give Me That Online Religion* (San Francisco: Jossey-Bass, 2001), 10.

> Catholic bishop exiled to a non-existent North African diocese to a cyber-monastery established exclusively for non-resident students of Zen.[398]

Most religious sites can be classified either as presenting information about a religion or as inviting the visitor to participate in some form of religious practice. In the literature this distinction is captured in the phrases "religion online" as opposed to "online religion."

The first category is clear and unproblematic. An example would be the website of our parish. It is exclusively informative. One potential difficulty arises from the fact that many of these informative sites are also commercialized, are actually online stores.

The second category is what interests me most since they give the appearance of simulating real-world activities. In many cases the websites of Christian churches offer a section on prayer. The simplest form offers an opportunity to type in a prayer request, which is then forwarded to some prayer groups within the church or organization. This can be taken a step further. In some cases, you are not only asked to write a request, you are offered a prayerful "environment" (music, visuals, instructions) and asked to pray while in a virtual chapel.

Another way in which participation is encouraged is through links to ongoing projects that the visitor can engage in. For example, one site (UMC) offers a link to a "clean energy" initiative with several ways of participating. Of course it is not really clear whether this is online participation or just the implementation in the real world of suggestions made online.

The most ambitious of these sites offer a worship experience, Communion, baptism, and even confession online. Worship amounts to viewing an actual service via video stream, or joining other gaming characters in a virtual church, or a guided session through various parts of a liturgy with text, prayers, sermons, music and, of course, visuals. This, of course, raises the question of whether the corporate worship of the church can be practiced in this way. In what sense is "being there" a

---

398 J. K. Hadden and D. E. Cowan, "The Promised Land or Electronic Chaos? Toward Understanding Religion on the Internet," in *Religion on the Internet: Research Prospects and Promises*, ed. J. K. Hadden and D. E. Cowan (London: JAI Press / Elsevier Science, 2000), 8, quoted in Dawson and Cowan, *Religion Online*, 5.

requirement? In what sense is the individual on the Net actually there? Can "being there" be mediated, contextualized? And if we should conclude that the sacraments are among the givens that predetermine the shape of contextualization, then we are forced to ask if those offering them in cyberspace are contextualizing or violating the gospel.

Based on these preliminary considerations, I have concluded that cyberspace is an evolving, fluid realm of quasi reality and personhood. It is an imaginary or conceptual space in which objects and persons can be represented by information. It is a place in which persons do not and cannot exist, but in which they can be informationally present-in-absence, radiating information rather than personhood in fields of human engagement. Given the nature of human cyberpresence, the concepts of intimacy, friendship, and communion have had to be reconceptualized. The question now is: can the invitational core context of the church be extended into this space?

## 2. Can the Invitational Context Exist in Cyberspace?

### *a. The Church and Its Sacraments*

The first prerequisite for this extension has to be the presence of Christ in the privileged mode of his manifestation today, the sacraments. We need, then, to ask if the sacraments can be practiced in cyberspace and if Christ can be present there in them. Let me begin by pointing out that there are plenty of people who believe that this is possible. For example, at a website called Church for All, which purports to be "a real church" using the Internet for its communication, you will find a page entitled "Worship Time."[399] There the viewer is provided with an outline of a worship service that includes sections on prayer, hymns, Scriptures, a sermon, and the Lord's Supper.[400] The link for the Lord's Supper takes you to a series of instructions on how to celebrate the sacrament.[401] These are introduced with the following statements:

399 Church for All, http://www.churchforall.org.
400 Church for All, "Worship with Us," http://www.churchforall.org/worship.htm.
401 Church for All, "Lord's Supper," http://www.churchforall.org/lordssup.htm.

> The Lord's Supper is observed in many churches as a solemn ceremony conducted by "official and ordained" members of the clergy. Such ceremony and restrictions may be helpful for some people but are not essential.
>
> It was originally celebrated by Jesus and his disciples in a home, in an informal setting and manner, and you may choose to celebrate it that way yourself.[402]

After some further discussion about the worthiness of the one partaking, a series of "simple instructions" are given:

> If there are other believers with you, you should celebrate with them. If not, you can do this as an individual.
>
> The important thing is our focus on Jesus, not the literal elements of food used, or the special words spoken.
>
> It is good if you have red grape juice because that easily reminds us of Jesus['] precious blood. If you don't have any, use water or some other liquid.
>
> Use unleavened bread if you have it, if not then use any bread, cracker, or whatever you have.
>
> Keep your attention on the wonderful, finished work of Jesus—not on the portion of food you are eating. The efficacy is in Jesus, and our relationship of faith in Him—not in some "magic" that happens when we eat a cracker and/or sip some grape juice.
>
> I suggest you read the Scripture (Matthew 26:26–28 or Luke 22:19,20 or 1 Corinthians 11:23–26) aloud and partake of the juice and bread in a prayerful, thankful, and happy manner.[403]

402 Ibid.
403 Ibid.

Obviously the practice proposed on this website is radically different from the one I presented above. In addition to the question concerning the authenticity of the rite itself, which I will get to below, this site also raises the questions of religious authority.

***i. Authority***

Authority is a primary concern here.

> Because there is no mechanism by which information posted to or claims made on the Internet may be vetted beforehand, the World Wide Web produces what some have either lauded or deplored as the phenomenon of "instant experts."[404]

As is obvious on the Church for All site, CMC "accommodates those individuals and groups who wish to 'be' religious outside the control of an organized religious institution."[405] It is also clear that anyone with the requisite skill can challenge the expertise of professionals and flaunt the recognized authorities.[406] Even though the vast majority of the world's Christians think otherwise, this site claims that you don't need "'official and ordained' members of the clergy" and that you can celebrate the Eucharist by your self in your own home. But by what authority are these claims made? There is no appeal to Scripture, no appeal to tradition, nothing. Just the personal opinion of an "instant expert" with the resources to create a website which translates his opinion, *qua* cyberspace, into an "authoritative" doctrinal assertion, true simply because he says it is so.[407]

Now, on the one hand, this reflects the prevailing postenlightenment individualism, the conviction that every person has the freedom to form and assert their own opinions, as well as the general belief that the whims of the contemporary moment trump the inheritance of historical continuity, giving us the right to change that inheritance at will. Accordingly, if you

404 Dawson and Cowan, *Religion Online*, 2.

405 Christopher Helland, "Popular Religion and the World Wide Web: A Match Made in (Cyber) Heaven," in ibid., 23.

406 "When a new technology unleashes massive cultural change, the challenge to traditional religion is immense." Brasher, *That Online Religion*, 12.

407 Obviously you don't need the Internet to make such claims. But the speed and ubiquity of CMC makes for instant and wide distribution of even baseless claims.

don't think clergy are necessary for the celebration of the Eucharist, then they can without any other justification be declared nonessential.[408] Similarly, if you don't see the need for the corporate gathering of the faithful around the celebration of the Eucharist, you can dispense with that "option" and do it on your own.

On the other hand, I wonder, as some have speculated, if this cavalier treatment of tradition is encouraged by the new medium of CMC and if it might not represent a radical shift in the way these "instant experts" view the speech (print) act itself. We know from past experience that Christianity has been profoundly affected by the introduction of new media and new theories of speech. Take as an example the liturgical changes introduced by the Protestant Reformation. In the case of the Catholic liturgy, much depended on aural and tactile imagination. In particular, the words of institution spoken by the priest over the bread and the wine.

> What is important to stress here is the theory of language that underlies this ritual. For believers, the words of institution, "this is my body," authorized and commanded by Christ himself, were (and are) literally true; when performed by a duly ordained priest, they effected the miracle of transubstantiation by which the bread and wine served as vehicles of the Real Presence.[409]

In language theory this is known (after Austin)[410] as a performative use of language. That is, something actually happens as a result of a speech act. However,

> the liturgies devised by Calvin, Zwingli, and other reformers enacted a theory of language that differed

---

408 The following statement is typical of this sentiment: "Any religion that relies on ecclesial authority and hierarchy, as well as on sacraments, is going to have a hard go on the Net." Jeffrey P. Zaleski, *The Soul of Cyberspace: How New Technology Is Changing Our Spiritual Lives* (San Francisco: HarperEdge, 1997), 100.

409 Stephen D. O'Leary, "Cyberspace as Sacred Space," in Dawson and Cowan, *Religion Online*, 42.

410 J. L. Austin, *How to Do Things with Words*, The William James Lectures (Oxford: Clarendon, 1962).

> radically from the Roman Catholic conception of the relationship of Word and sacrament; they reach their climax, their symbolic payoff not in the Communion but in the sermon, a discourse which is delivered orally but which lacks the supernatural efficacy of the Catholic priest's speech over the Eucharistic elements. In contrast to the Catholic, the Protestant liturgy was enacted in the vernacular tongues; in its most austere forms, it eschewed ornament and visual representation and minimized all sensory input that might lead to idolatry; it focused on the sermon and the words of Scripture to the exclusion of other messages; and it denied the performative character of liturgical speech acts altogether, characterizing the ritual action of the priest as, in Calvin's words, "murmuring and gesticulating in the manner of sorcerers."[411]

The Church for All website still reflects this general understanding. Note that the celebration of the Lord's Supper is governed by a few "simple instructions," whereas the worship time's centerpiece—the sermon—was, at least on the day I accessed the site, eighty minutes long. But at the same time, this site assumes a performative understanding of its own language in that it posits truth of a statement based simply on its being stated. It seems that the speech act itself and not some biblical, traditional, or logical justification is what renders the statements true. I suppose one could question the use of the term "speech act" in connection with cyberspace. But it seems that in CMC, aspects of orality and literacy are combined into a hybrid form of communication that

> is both talking and writing yet isn't completely either one. It's talking by writing. It's writing because you type it on a keyboard and people read it. But because of the ephemeral nature of luminescent letters on a screen, and because it has such a quick—sometimes instant—turn-around, it's more like talking.[412]

411 O'Leary, "Cyberspace," in Dawson and Cowan, *Religion Online*, 43.
412 Ibid., 41.

In any case, the statement that clergy are unessential is considered true by virtue of having been stated. You do not need to use bread and wine, but can substitute any "food" you have available, including crackers and water. The speech act itself seems to verify the statement. The fact that it appears in cyberspace somehow makes it true. Perhaps CMC is bringing us full circle.

> Just as Protestant congregations and reformers, influenced by the culture of printing, reformed the liturgy in ways that privileged textuality over gesture and performance as the vehicle of symbolic meaning, so too modern religious practitioners rebel against current religious orthodoxy by devising new rituals that employ new technology to reassert the power of language as performative utterance.[413]

Although this may be the way in which the "instant experts" are using the language of CMC, language does not function that way. Language is not self-authenticating. It is a tool, a vehicle, a set of symbols that can carry or mediate truth if the content of the statement conforms to a real state of affairs, to the way things actually are. Thus the veracity of the role claimed for the clergy or the nature of the elements is not determined by the assertion itself, but by the correspondence between those claims and the actual teaching of the Scriptures, the church, and tradition. This raises the question of authenticity. Under what circumstances can the practice of the sacraments be considered authentic?

***ii. Authenticity***

According to the teaching of the Eastern Church, the celebration of the Eucharist is to take place within the field of personal presence created by the gathering of the faithful, under the administration of a priest duly ordained by a canonical bishop, according to the rubrics of Scripture and tradition, and by the power and descent of the Holy Spirit. Can these conditions be met in cyberspace?

---

413 Ibid., 49.

As already mentioned, the church is constituted by the gathering (sunaxis) of the faithful for the celebration of the Eucharist.[414] That this gathering is of a personal nature is clear from the fact that the thus-constituted group of faithful is also called the body of Christ; that is, they are unified by the person of the fully present Christ. By partaking of one cup and of one bread (1 Cor 10:16,17) the many become one. In order for that to happen, the faithful have to be physically present in the place where one Eucharistic Lamb (bread) is being offered and received. This presence, this gathering, is taken so seriously that the Eucharist cannot be celebrated unless some of the faithful have come together. A priest may not celebrate alone. In other words, the faithful have to be personally present to one another and to Christ. This kind of gathering can, of course, not take place in cyberspace. There is indeed the possibility of being informationally present to others on the Internet, as in a chat room, but that is not the kind of intimate, personal presence and community required for the constitution of the body or for the unity established by participation in the Eucharist. There are some who have attempted cybercommunity by establishing a game-like environment where you download software that allows you to create a character (avatar) that can then participate in a simulation of a worship service.[415] Second Life[416] churches, for example, invite you into spaces for prayer, meditation, music, and worship. In some cases the avatars are seated in simulated pews, sing, and listen to sermons.[417] But since the gaming characters are themselves completely imaginary, inventions that do not reflect and may even purposely distort the persons behind them, whatever community the characters might think they enjoy is an illusion, even further removed from reality than the informational presence possible in a chat room.[418]

414 Cf. Alexander Schmemann, *The Eucharist: Sacrament of the Kingdom* (Crestwood, NY: St. Vladimir's Seminary Press, 2003), 15–16.

415 Church of Fools, http://www.churchoffools.com.

416 Second Life is a virtual world in which you are present in the form of a gaming character, an avatar. That character can be anything you want it to be; in particular, what you are not in the real world but would like to be. In this world you can relate to other avatars, visit locations, buy and sell, even marry and cohabitate. Second Life, http://www.secondlife.com.

417 For example: Friends of the Coptic Church, http://world.secondlife.com/group/7def79e2-9851-dd22-29d0-3b130fc613ec.

418 Another aspect of these communities is a lack of personal responsibility. "These sites make certain kinds of connections easier, but because they are governed

Either way, a *gathering* cannot take place in cyberspace, and without it there is no church and therefore no sacrament.

From the earliest days of the church, Eucharistic celebrations were presided over by specially appointed members of the body who each had their own set of responsibilities.[419] Clement of Rome, as early as the year 96, reminded the Christians of the special ordinances that governed the celebrant (bishop), the priests, the deacons, and the laity and seems to imply that these rules of institution came from Christ himself.[420] Justin, in the second century, refers to the bishop as the one who "'eucharistises' the bread and the wine as the 'president.'"[421] The Lord's Supper, as practiced by the early church, was a corporate, "ecclesiastical occasion at which the clergy were indispensable."[422] This practice has been carried forth through the centuries and is still expressed during the Liturgy in a prayer said by the priest just before the Great Entrance.

> Thou didst become a man and didst take the name of our High Priest, and deliver unto us the priestly rite of this liturgical and bloodless sacrifice … I implore thee, therefore, who alone art good and ready to listen, look down upon me a sinner and thine unprofitable servant, and purify my soul and heart from an evil conscience, and, by the power of thy Holy Spirit, enable me, who am clothed with the grace of the priesthood, to stand before this thy holy table and to perform the sacred rite of thy holy, immaculate Body and precious Blood.[423]

---

not by geography or community mores but by personal whim, they free users from the responsibilities that tend to come with membership in a community. This fundamentally changes the tenor of the relationships that form there, something best observed in the way social networks treat friendship." Rosen, "Virtual Friendship," 26.

419 "The 'presider' προιστάμενος, whose primary function was to stand at the head of the assembly as the 'president of the brethren.'" Schmemann, *The Eucharist*, 15.

420 Dix, *Shape of the Liturgy*, 1.

421 Quoted in ibid., 60.

422 Ibid., 84.

423 Orthodox Church in America, *The Priest's Service Book*, 134–35. Similarly during the Prayers of Entrance before the service of preparation, the priest prays that God will look down from his holy dwelling place and "strengthen me for this thine appointed service." Ibid., 98.

Performing or celebrating this sacred rite has always been the specific responsibility of the clergy. Why would that practice be so suddenly abandoned? But even if the need for an ordained priest were accepted, one could still ask if that service could be performed in cyberspace. Certainly a priest could be informationally present-in-absence to a group "gathered" in a cybercommunity. But that gathering cannot be the church, and this informational mode of presence falls far short of the personal presence required by an active administration of a rite that involves concrete actions and specific objects (the elements). That, more than anything, prevents the celebration of the rite in cyberspace. The reality of the divine mystery is tied to the actual presence of the gifts, which are actually—not virtually—prepared, consecrated, fractured, and distributed by the priest. I should also point out that the way in which these actions are done is not left up to the individual preferences of the priest. We have exact instructions, rubrics, as to what kind of bread (leavened wheat bread not crackers)[424] and wine (pure red wine with no additives, not water or some other liquid)[425] we are to use, as to how to cut the Lamb, pierce the Lamb, pour wine and water into the chalice, and so on. In other words, the individual is not free to improvise but is bound and thus protected by tradition.

It has been suggested that faithful viewing a live video feed of an actual Liturgy could place bread and wine before the monitor allowing them to be consecrated along with the Lamb in the service.[426] Apparently the idea is that the Holy Spirit who sanctifies the gifts and is not limited by place could simultaneously sanctify the remote bread. But the Liturgy does not call for a multipronged descent of the Spirit. Consider the words of the priest just before the *epiclesis*: "Again we offer unto thee this rational and bloodless worship, and we call upon thee and pray thee, and supplicate thee: send down thy Holy Spirit upon us and *upon these Gifts here set*

424 Erickson, *Challenge of Our Past*, 133–55.

425 The use of water for the Eucharist is an ancient problem and was resolved early on. See Cyprian, "Epistle 62: Cæcilius, on the Sacrament of the Cup of the Lord," in *Hippolytus, Cyprian, Caius, Novatian, Appendix*, vol. 5 of *Ante-Nicene Fathers*, edited by Alexander Roberts, James Donaldson, and A. Cleveland Coxe (Grand Rapids: Eerdmans, 1957), http://www.ccel.org/ccel/schaff/anf05.iv.iv.lxii.html.

426 Gregory S. Neal, "Holy Communion on the Web: Liturgical, Theological, Photographic, and Video Resources for Laity and Clergy," Grace Incarnate Ministries, 2009, http://www.revneal.org/page5/page5.html.

*forth*" (italics added).[427] Outside of the gathering and beyond the action of the priest and the descent of the Holy Spirit, there are no gifts and thus no Eucharist.

So the Liturgy is something that is done and not just said. The faithful do their part by gathering. The priest does his part by offering the gifts according to the rubrics and then calling upon the Holy Spirit. But the gifts are not consecrated by virtue of some performative quality of the clerical speech act, but rather by the power, the descent, the action of the Holy Spirit. A video feed is, of course, not an action. It may depict but it does not constitute a gathering of the faithful. It may represent the priest, but it cannot mediate his real presence and enact his concrete liturgical movements. It can picture but cannot affect the consecration of the gifts. Because the cyberrepresentation is only "said" and not done, it effectively excludes the observer from all active, sacramental participation in the Liturgy shown.[428] Furthermore, the representation of the gifts being consecrated is symbolically removed from the actual signifier/signified unity that exists in a real celebration of the Eucharist. A representation of the signifier cannot signify, cannot do anything.[429] That is, the depiction cannot participate in the sacred act of consecration, cannot be the object of the Holy Spirit's power and descent, and is thus sacramentally powerless.

It would appear, then, that online Eucharist is an impossibility. First, because it would circumvent the first act of the Eucharist, the real gathering of the faithful. Second, because it would obviate the priest's administrative role, the doing rather than the mere saying of the Liturgy. Third, because it would destroy the Spirit-enacted harmony between signified and signifier that is at the core of sacramental symbolism. So if a cyber-Eucharist is not possible, we must also conclude that Christ cannot manifest himself in it; that is, that he is not personally present on the Internet, in which case he cannot be introduced to anyone in cyberspace; there is no presence to "come and see."

---

427 Orthodox Church in America, *The Priest's Service Book*, 147.

428 Dix, *Shape of the Liturgy*, 12–14.

429 I am not suggesting that cyberspace representations such as chat, text, pictures, videos have no power at all. Obviously they can evoke emotions, and lead to decisions and actions in real time. What has to be emphasized is that whatever response they do elicit takes place in the life of the person observing and not in cyberspace.

The same things can be said about the other sacraments.[430] In the case of baptism, the rite requires the real presence of water and the action of a personally present priest who calls upon the Holy Spirit to come and sanctify the water, into which a personally present individual descends to die with Christ and rise to new life. Another sacrament in the Eastern Church is confession. Here one of the faithful, joined by a priest, confesses their sins to Christ. That done, the priest lays his stole on the person's head, places his hand over the stole, and prays a prayer of absolution in which the one confessing is assured of God's forgiveness. Obviously, there can be no cybersubstitute for this personal, intimate, and physical exchange. The laying on of hands is simply not possible outside a field of personal presence.[431]

### *b. The Core Context*

The second prerequisite for the possible extension of the invitational context into the personal fields of cyberspace would be firmly establishing the core context (the church) with the help of the six gifts of tradition. Now I have already established that the gathering of the faithful cannot exist in cyberspace, that the church does not exist in cyberspace, and that Christ cannot be present in the "sacraments" presented on the Web. So that form of extension into cyberspace is not possible. However, given the representational nature of cyberspatial presence, its potential could be matched with certain aspects of the gifts of tradition and used to help establish core context in the real world.

The textual nature of the Holy Scriptures allows them to be stored, presented, disseminated on the Internet. The website of the OCA's Diocese of the South, for example, makes the text of the daily readings available to the faithful according to the lectionary.[432] CMC can also be used to send the readings electronically. Other sites provide various translations of

---

430 There is even online ordination; see Universal Life Church Monastery, http://www.themonastery.org.

431 "With online rituals we are still at arms-length from the sacred space." Michael Sellers, quoted in Stephen O'Leary, "Utopian and Dysutopian Possibilities," in Morten T. Højsgaard and Margit Warburg, *Religion and Cyberspace* (New York: Routledge, 2005), 44.

432 The Diocese of the South, http://dosoca.org.

the whole Bible.[433] And there are hundreds of sites that offer online Bible commentary. But which ones can you trust? Any unverified "expert" can claim to interpret the Scriptures. The difficulty here is that, while there are many legitimate sites that offer the text of well-known commentaries,[434] there are also a host of "private" commentaries.[435] Since the Scriptures need to be interpreted according to the "mind" of the church, the faithful will need to be educated as to the dangers of the many extra-ecclesial and individual commentary sites and steered to the interpretations available from legitimate church sites, such as the Greek Orthodox site that provides sermon texts for the lectionary readings throughout the year.[436]

Apostolic succession itself is obviously something that is established and experienced in person and offline. However, the hierarchs can use the Web and CMC to stay in touch, inform, and instruct their flocks. A good example comes from the website of the OCA's Diocese of the South.[437] Here you will find information on the bishop, the administration, the finances, and the programs of the diocese. Of particular importance are the pastoral messages, teaching that the hierarch provides for his people. Such sites help create a sense of belonging and unity among the many parishes of a given diocese. This said, there is, however, no substitute for the personal presence of the bishop during his visits to the parish. His being with us, present to us, celebrating the Liturgy with us, we are joined to his person and the historical and didactic continuity that he represents.

Liturgical structures, as we have seen, can only have legitimacy in personal fields of presence, such as the gathering of the faithful. The informational nature of cyberspace precludes the actual celebration of even the simplest service. However, many of the resources needed for those services can be made available on the Web. This could include the text of the services, the rubrics that guide their celebration, and any temporary changes made in response to real world events, such as the

---

433 For example, BibleGateway.com, http://www.biblegateway.com.

434 For example, Matthew Henry, "Matthew Henry's Commentary on the Whole Bible," Christian Classics Ethereal Library, http://www.ccel.org/ccel/henry/mhc.i.html.

435 For example, Bob Utley, "Free Bible Commentary," http://www.freebiblecommentary.org.

436 Greek Orthodox Archdiocese of America, "Sermons," http://goarch.org/resources/sermons/sermons.

437 Diocese of the South, http://dosoca.org.

petitions added to the Great Litany during a time of crisis.[438] Another form of support is the OCA's central site, which provides music for the movable parts of the services.[439] In these ways the informational potential and technologies of cyberspace support the establishment of the real-world core context.

Councils (dogma and canons) are obviously text-based materials that can be presented and disseminated on the Web. The texts of the ecumenical councils, for example, are available online along with their canons.[440] Modern interpretations and applications of the canons are also available through the websites in the form of minutes and encyclicals of the holy synod.[441] Having this information on the Net gives the faithful a, albeit limited, share in the bishops' struggle to address contemporary issues. Here again cyberspace's function seems to be educational, informational, guiding the faithful in the application of their faith to the real world.

---

438 The OCA, for example, offers petitions that can be added to our litanies during times of particular crisis; for example, for the people of Japan during the 2011 tsunami disaster. "In light of the ongoing tragedy in Japan and requests for intensified prayers, the following approved petitions may be added to the [Augmented] Litany at divine services.

"'Again we pray for the suffering people of Japan: for the families, friends and communities enduring bitter sorrow and tragic loss: for the wounded and the grieving; that the Lord Our God will look upon them with mercy and will heal, comfort, strengthen and shelter them in his love.

"'Again we pray to Thee, O Lord and God, for the repose of the thousands of precious souls departed this life in the earthquake; specially those whose earthly sojourns have ended suddenly, without repentance; give them rest where all sickness, sorrow and sighing have passed away: hear us, O Lord, and have mercy.

"'Again we pray for all those working for Japan's relief and recovery; specially our Orthodox brethren ministering in behalf of all to those in desperate need: and for all who are anxious and fearful; that they may persevere in their struggles and find consolation, hope and courage in Jesus Christ, Our Savior and Our God.

"'Again we pray that we may be preserved from wrath, pestilence, earthquake, flood, fire, the sword, terrorist attack, civil war and sudden death: and that Our God, Who loves mankind, may be gracious, merciful and easy to be reconciled to us: that He may deliver us from the righteous judgment impending against us, and have mercy on us.'" Orthodox Church in America, "Petitions for Those Suffering in Japan," March 18, 2011, http://oca.org/news/2474.

439 Orthodox Church in America, "Liturgical Music and Texts," http://oca.org/MDIndex.html?SID=13.

440 Henry R. Percival, ed., *The Seven Ecumenical Councils*, vol. 14 of *A Select Library of the Nicene and Post-Nicene Fathers of the Christian Church*, 2nd series, edited by Philip Schaff and Henry Wace (Grand Rapids: Eerdmans, 1975), http://www.ccel.org/ccel/schaff/npnf214.toc.html.

441 See http://oca.org/holy-synod/encyclicals.

Hagiography is similarly situated. The Lives of the Saints are available online and can be used by the faithful in their own lives.[442] Of course the presence of the saints on the Internet is exclusively informational, knowledge about, not the intimate, personal presence of communion with the saint. The real contact between a believer and a saint is mediated as personal presence-in-absence through prayer and, in most cases, through icons.

Iconography presents a bit of a dilemma, since icons are images both in the real world and in cyberspace. It might be argued that computer-generated images are just another way to render the iconographic content, no different than wood and paint. However, as we saw above, an icon is a real, concrete object that is both holy and sacred. In the case of cyberspace, what we are dealing with are insubstantial representations, not objects that continue to "exist" once the site is abandoned or the power cut. Having no concrete existence, the electronic image has no special, sacred status or inherent holiness. This distinction is most obvious in the case of the images shown by a business that sells icons on the Internet.[443] The depictions are just that, and not actual icons. But what of their use in an online virtual chapel? Here the visitor is offered a quiet space replete with the text of prayers, icons, flickering candles, and even music—a simulation of a real world place of prayer.[444] I have no doubt that the images thus presented could help move the individual to a quiet state of prayer. But, because these images have no material substance, they cannot be sanctified and are thus not able to mediate personal presence. I think that what happens in this case is that the one praying is reminded of real icons and the personal, specific presence of Christ mediated through them and is thus moved to reflect on the divine, the Scriptures, or address a prayer to the generally ever-present Lord.

Although presence in cyberspace is limited to the informational, it does have great potential for helping the faithful establish the core missionary context, the church. Since many of the gifts of tradition come

---

442 Orthodox Church in America, "Lives of the Saints," http://oca.org/fslives.asp.

443 Skete.com, "Beautiful Hand-painted Icons," http://www.skete.com/index.cfm?fuseaction=category.display&category_id=100.

444 Holy Transfiguration Orthodox Church, "Virtual Chapel for Orthodox Christian Prayer," http://holyTransfiguration-oca.org/vchapel.htm.

to us in the form of text, they can easily be adapted for use on the Internet where they could facilitate wider involvement.

### c. *Communion*

The third stage of the extension of the invitational context is carried out by the faithful, who are dismissed from the Liturgy into the world as witnesses to what they have heard and seen. As mentioned above, this task requires an advanced state of spiritual development. That, of course, is not something that can be acquired through the Internet or CMC. Certainly the informational resources of cyberspace could be used to support spiritual growth. Chat groups and blogs could help answer questions. Online libraries and resources may add to the individual's knowledge and understanding. But growing intimacy with God will take place in the church as a result of divine-human communion mediated personally by the Holy Spirit. Assuming that this spiritual state has been achieved, the witness is able to enter fields of personal presence and initiate communion by being fully present to another through self-transcendence, kenotic love, and complete freedom, all of which is made possible by the presence of Christ evident in their life. But can these conditions of communion be effectively expressed in the depersonalized, disembodied environment of cyberspace? Can Christ be seen in us there?

The only human presence possible in cyberspace is some form of presence-in-absence. As we have seen, this kind of presence is established when the person absent puts something of their own into the void created by the absence. In the case of the ascended Christ, he put the person of the Holy Spirit in the void to mediate his personal presence. Human beings cannot put their own person into the void and still be absent. That is, in situations where you can insert your person, you are no longer absent. But in situations where that is not possible, we rely on objects like an artist's painting, representations such as pictures, and information; i.e., all its mediated, as opposed to direct, forms. In cyberspace these things are further limited to representations and information. In other words, no personal presence-in-absence is possible in cyberspace—you cannot be fully present to someone on the Internet—leaving us with a representational or informational presence-in-absence.

This raises some doubt about the cyberspatial expression of the conditions needed for human-human communion. How can something like self-transcendence, which overcomes all self-centeredness, be expressed in the limited context of an informational presence-in-absence? Maybe they can't be. Some have pointed out that the Web itself nurtures the opposite, narcissism, creating "self-worshipers" who are "'interpersonally exploitive,' which means they will ignore the needs of others."[445] That this is not an isolated phenomenon can be seen from the fact that social networking sites provide "the perfect forum for ... narcissistic tendencies." "They are very effective outlets of self-promotion[446] through heavily edited biographical information, flattering pictures, and the large numbers of shallow Web-based relationships advertised on people's profiles."[447] Perhaps the best we can hope for is a partial expression of the conditions of communion. Things as simple as giving full attention to the chat-room partner (that is, not surfing, typing, texting while engaged in the discussion or waiting for a reply), and the way in which we treat the people contacted through CMC. Self-transcendence would make it impossible for the user to engage in the crudeness, sensuality, and vulgarity so often displayed in cyberspace. With the other's interests and well-being paramount, there could be no hurtful outbursts of anger, sarcasm, or the infamous practice of flaming.[448]

The same things could be said about love. The love of which I speak is a self-emptying participation in the life of the other. A love that radiates out from the faithful's communion with God and fully accepts and acknowledges the other person. A personal presence in which love is recognizable as the love of God. Cyberspace offers only limited opportunity to express that kind of love. Love will certainly observe certain standards of etiquette, treating with respect everyone they encounter. It can be

---

445 Aboujaoude, *Virtually You*, 68–69.

446 With few exceptions this is true of blogs, the assumption of which is that it is important for the world to hear what I have to say. This is even true of purportedly Christian sites which appear to promote individuals rather than the church or Christ. See for example: Grace Incarnate Ministries, http://www.revneal.org. One refreshing example of how the church might use this medium is Stephen Freeman, *Glory to God for All Things* (blog), http://glory2godforallthings.com.

447 Referring to a 2008 study on Facebook narcissism conducted by Laura Buffardi and Keith Campbell of the University of Georgia in Athens. Aboujaoude, *Virtually You*, 72–73.

448 Ibid., 252–53.

given limited voice through appropriate words in a chat session or an email, as you might in a card or letter. This could even be an indicator of real love if it were based on the memory of an actual or the anticipation of a likely encounter with the real person being addressed. But one way or the other, love requires personal, embodied presence in order to be fully realized. Some do speak of cyberlove claiming, for example, that their gaming character (avatar) has fallen in love with another one. In some cases this leads to discussions that reveal intimate aspects of the avatar's supposed life, to marriage, even by those already married in real life, to cohabitation, and even sex.[449] In some cases the chat and the images seem to make up for what has not been experienced in real life, hence the "second life." In other cases it represents raw sensuality and lust triggered by text and image. But whatever else these activities might seem to be, they are imaginary fantasies which have nothing to do with real love. In cyberspace you can fall in "love" with a representation, but not with a person. For that to happen, both parties would have to be fully, personally present.

What, then, of freedom? Here, too, cyberspace provides only limited means of expression. If we are engaged in a witnessing encounter with nonbelievers, we will at some point have to offer teachings and truths that contradict those of the invitee. We can speak the truth hoping that our expressions of love have earned us the freedom to do so. But does the limited expression of love create an environment of sufficient freedom? Or does it simply encourage an endless debate in which everyone is an expert. Appealing to the informational aspects of the core context such as the Scriptures or the canons can only take us so far, since doing so does not engage all of the conditions of personhood. In the absence of the power of divinely inspired personal presence, there is little hope of adjudicating differences. Moreover, in the absence of physical clues, it is very difficult to assess the impact that our contradictory statements might have on the other. We may well unknowingly or unintentionally offend the other. In any case, our freedom to invite is limited. If the conditions of communion can only be partially realized in cyberspace, and if there can be no personal presence, then it is not possible to establish the

449 Sherry Turkle, *Alone Together: Why We Expect More from Technology and Less from Each Other* (New York: Basic Books, 2011), 159.

human-human communion needed for an introduction of Christ. The other user will not be able to see Christ in the witness. The best we can hope for is to relay information about the teachings and practices of the church and issue an invitation to "come and see."

So I have tried to examine the fields of personal presence available to us in cyberspace in order to assess the possibility and the appropriateness of an extension of the invitational core context, and I have concluded that the opportunity is quite limited. From what I have seen, it seems clear that there are some places CMC simply cannot take us. This is certainly an expression of what has been called a romantic reaction to the presence of the computer.[450] Sherry Turkle sums it up by saying, "Simulated thinking might be thinking, but simulated feeling is not feeling; simulated love is never love."[451] That being the case, the conditions that facilitate communion are also not fully available to us online. However, the Web does offer some practical help in promoting and disseminating the informational aspects of the faith. But given the fact that human presence on the Web is limited to a representational presence-in-absence (i.e., the fact that church cannot gather and the sacraments cannot be celebrated there), we must also conclude that Christ does not personally manifest himself in cyberspace. For that reason, the Internet is not a place to which we can invite others to "come and see." It is however, a place from which we can, in a limited way, invite others to the church and an encounter with Christ.

---

450 Of course many dream about the places that CMC may one day take us and the "romantic reaction has largely given way to a new pragmatism. Computers 'understand' as little as ever about human experience—for example, what it means to envy a sibling or to miss a deceased parent. They do, however, perform understanding better than ever, and we play our part. After all, our online lives are all about performance. We perform on social networks and direct the performances of our avatars in virtual worlds. A premium on performance is the cornerstone of the robotic moment. We live the robotic moment not because we have companionate robots in our lives, but because the way we contemplate them on the horizon says much about who we are and who we are willing to become." Ibid., 26.

451 Ibid., 289.

# Conclusions: A Reversal of Perspective

I began this study with the intention of revisiting the work on contextualization that I started decades ago under the guidance of David Hesselgrave. I shared with him an unshakable faith in Christ; a firm commitment to the church, its Scriptures and teachings; and a deep desire to communicate my faith to others. None of that has changed. But I did want to see how my perspective might change if I considered some of the things I did not or could not have explored earlier; things like the personal nature of the gospel and human beings, the nature and the role of the sacraments, and the opportunities afforded by cyberspace. I wondered what might change if I broadened the ecclesial perspective to include not only the Free Churches but the Orthodox Church that I am now a part of. I puzzled over the implications of my impression that the witness was in need of as much contextualization as the message. And my perspective has indeed changed. I might say that in many respects it has been reversed. Now I understand the gospel not so much as information about Christ, but rather the person of Christ. I consider the church to be the focal point of missions and not simply the result of missionary effort. I now believe that the introduction of Christ is to take place in a universal core context established between the two axes of ecclesial tradition and the conditions of human personhood, and that it is not to be adapted to every new context we encounter. And I believe that the advanced spiritual state of the witness is more important than the adaptation of the message. So what does this all say about my understanding of the process of contextualization? What are the principles that now guide my approach to this essential aspect of the missionary task?

## 1. Basic Principles of Contextualization

### *a. The Gospel Is a Person*

This is the most fundamental principle of the process of contextualization. It is rooted in the conviction that, in the end, it is a relationship to the person of Christ, an intimate divine-human communion, that is initiated by our faith. God has created us as personal beings, and he has demonstrated his desire for personal communion through the Incarnation. Thus the desired outcome of all evangelism is this life-changing, saving relationship with the person of Christ.

### *b. The Evangelistic Task Is to Introduce the Person of Christ*

If what I have just said is true, then the ultimate task of missionary outreach is to introduce the person of Christ. Yes, we do that in part by relaying the facts of his life as presented in the Gospels and anticipated by the Prophets. But the basic act of the church's mission is to introduce, in a perceptible way, the person of our Lord and issue an invitation to, by faith, enter into a relationship with him and live in the intimacy of that communion.

### *c. The Church Is the Focal Point of That Activity*

In order for that introduction to take place, Christ has to be present. We know that he is generally present in the world through the work of the Holy Spirit. We also know that, by the power of that same Spirit, Christ is specifically and personally present in the celebration of the Eucharist. Since that happens in the church, it is one place that we know that Christ is present, and thus it becomes both the place of departure as well as the place of invitation. That is, the faithful gather and behold Christ's presence and are then dismissed into the world to be witnesses of what they have seen and heard. Those who do not yet know Christ can be invited to "come and see" and, because they have been created as persons by a personal God who desires communion with them, they are capable of perceiving the divine presence in the church and in the faithful gathered.

### d. The Sacraments Are the Privileged Place of Christ's Presence in the World Today

A sacrament involves the sanctification of some created matter (bread, wine, oil, water) by the descent and the power of the Holy Spirit. When Christ commanded his followers to celebrate the Eucharist and baptize new believers, he promised to be with them. In other words, the personal presence-in-absence of the risen and ascended Lord is mediated by the Holy Spirit. Such is Christ's presence that in the Eucharist we really partake of his body and blood, and during baptism we actually die and rise again with him. It is to these loci of divine presence that we confidently invite others to "come and see" Christ.

### e. The Core Invitational Context Needs to Be Established

The church, then, is the core invitational context and must be established in a way that engages the conditions of human personhood. Fortunately, we have been give a set of tools to do just that. The gifts of ecclesial tradition not only define the church, but do so in ways that address human personhood. So the task of contextualization is not to adapt the gospel to every new situation we encounter, but rather to use those tools to establish the core context wherever the missional path takes us. The catholicity of the church and the universality of human personhood allow this core context to be established without the imposition of things extraneous or unknown. Under the guidance of the Holy Spirit the combination of tradition and personhood bring about the creation of a new reality within which the invitation can be effectively and worthily given.

### f. The Invitational Context Has to Be Projected onto Fields of Human Presence

Obviously this core context will have to be projected onto fields of human presence—those spaces where we can be present to others and invite them into the presence of Christ. In some cases this involves a new planting of the church. In other cases it means engaging in intimate exchange in extra-ecclesial settings. Unfortunately not all fields are conducive to or worthy of such presence. So part of the task will be to carefully evaluate the potential and appropriateness of available fields, asking if and what kind of personal presence is possible.

### g. *The Witness Needs to Be "Spiritualized"*

It is, for the most part, the faithful who will be issuing the invitation and, in order to do so, they will need to develop and maintain an advanced state of spiritual maturity. Personal sin, not contexts in and of themselves, is what prevents people from following Christ. If we are going to invite people to a life with him, our relationship with him will have to show discernible fruits of knowing him. If the passions are raging in our lives, we will not be in any position to initiate communion with nonbelievers or challenge their thoughts and behavior. But if our own spiritual growth leads us to a knowledge of God, then we will also be able to love others and treat them in such a way as to facilitate communion with them and the invitation to Christ.

## 2. The Task of Contextualization

As I see it, the primary task of contextualization is to *establish an invitational core context*, the church, which (a) is host to the presence of the Divine Person, (b) is defined with the help of personhood-engaging gifts of ecclesial tradition, (c) enables conditions that facilitate communion, and (d) engages extra-ecclesial fields of personal presence. Now I have heard it said that contextual theology is a theology

> which takes as its starting point not statements about God but the context where people are engaging with God, and the religious thinking that occurs as a result of the particular characteristics of the context.[452]

But I wonder if that is not the greatest reversal of all. What we must never forget is that the gospel is the person of Christ and that contextualization begins with an invitation to a relationship with Christ and ends with the intimacy of divine-human communion.

---

452 Højsgaard and Warburg, *Religion and Cyberspace*, 149.

# Bibliography

Aboujaoude, Elias. *Virtually You: The Dangerous Powers of the E-Personality.* New York: W. W. Norton, 2011.

Agence France-Presse (AFP). "Number of Internet Users Worldwide Reaches Two Billion." Phys.Org. January 26, 2011. http://www.physorg.com/news/2011-01-internet-users-worldwide-billion.html.

All Saints of North America. "Alaskan Orthodox Texts." http://www.asna.ca/alaska.

Andrew of Crete. *The Great Canon.* Jordanville, NY: Holy Trinity Monastery, n.d.

Anonymous. "Chronicon Paschale." In *Patrologia Graeco-Latina*, vol. 92, col. 989. Turnhout, Belgium: Brepolis.

Arndt, William, F. Wilbur Gingrich, Frederick W. Danker, and Walter Bauer. *A Greek-English Lexicon of the New Testament and Other Early Christian Literature: A Translation and Adaptation of the Fourth Revised and Augmented Edition of Walter Bauer's* Griechisch-Deutsches Wörterbuch zu den Schriften des Neuen Testaments und der Übrigen Urchristlichen Literatur. 2nd ed. Chicago: University of Chicago Press, 1979.

Austin, J. L. *How to Do Things with Words.* The William James Lectures. Oxford: Clarendon, 1962.

Bajis, Jordan. *Common Ground: An Introduction to Eastern Christianity for the American Christian.* 2nd ed. Minneapolis: Light & Life, 1996.

Banana, Caanan. "The Lord's Prayer—in the Ghetto." In *Mission Trends No. 3: Third World Theologies; Asian, African, and Latin American Contributions to a Radical, Theological Realignment in the Church*, edited by Gerald Anderson and Thomas F. Stransky, 156–57. New York: Paulist, 1976.

Basil, Saint. Ch. 27 in "The Book of Saint Basil on the Spirit." In *Basil: Letters and Select Works.* Vol. 8 of *A Select Library of the Nicene and Post-Nicene Fathers of the Christian Church*, 2nd series, edited by Philip Schaff and Henry Wace. Grand Rapids: Eerdmans, 1975. http://www.ccel.org/ccel/schaff/npnf208.vii.xxviii.html.

Bebis, George. *The Mind of the Fathers*. Brookline, MA: Holy Cross Orthodox Press, 1994.

———. "The Saints of the Orthodox Church." Greek Orthodox Archdiocese of America. http://goarch.org/resources/saints.

Benedict XVI. "New Technologies, New Relationships: Promoting a Culture of Respect, Dialogue and Friendship." Libreria Editrice Vaticana. January 24, 2009. http://www.vatican.va/holy_father/benedict_xvi/messages/communications/documents/hf_ben-xvi_mes_20090124_43rd-world-communications-day_en.html.

Berry, Henry. *Let There Be Links: The Sources and Nature of Internet Religion*. CreateSpace, 2011.

Bertsch, Ludwig, ed. *Der neue Meßritus im Zaire*. Vol. 18 of *Theologie der Dritten Welt*. Freiburg, Germany: Herder, 1993.

BibleGateway.com. http://www.biblegateway.com.

Bonino, Jose Miguez. *Doing Theology in a Revolutionary Situation*. Philadelphia: Fortress, 1975.

Brasher, Brenda E. *Give Me That Online Religion*. San Francisco: Jossey-Bass, 2001.

Breck, John. "Orthodox Principles of Biblical Interpretation." *St. Vladimir's Theological Quarterly* 40, no. 1–2 (1996): 77–93.

Brierley, Michael W. "Naming a Quiet Revolution: The Pantheistic Turn in Modern Theology." In *In Whom We Live and Move and Have Our Being: Panentheistic Reflections on God's Presence in a Scientific World*, edited by Philip Clayton and A. R. Peacocke, 1–15. Grand Rapids: Eerdmans, 2004.

Brom, Robert H., ed. "Apostolic Succession." Catholic Answers. 2004. http://www.catholic.com/tracts/apostolic-succession.

Bulgakov, Sergius. *The Bride of the Lamb*. Translated by Boris Jakim. Grand Rapids: Eerdmans, 2002.

———. *The Comforter*. Translated by Boris Jakim. Grand Rapids: Eerdmans, 2004.

———. *The Lamb of God*. Translated by Boris Jakim. Grand Rapids: Eerdmans, 2008.

———. *Relics and Miracles: Two Theological Essays*. Translated by Boris Jakim. Grand Rapids: Eerdmans, 2011.

Byassee, Jason. "Looking East: The Impact of Orthodox Theology." *Christian Century*, December 28, 2004, 24–25.

Cassian, John. "On the Eight Vices." In *The Philokalia: The Complete Text*. Vol. 1. Compiled by Saint Nikodimos of the Holy Mountain and Saint Makarios of Corinth, translated and edited by G. E. H. Palmer, Philip Sherrard, and Kallistos Ware, 73–93. London: Faber & Faber, 1983.

Castells, Manuel. *The Internet Galaxy: Reflections on the Internet, Business, and Society*. Oxford: Oxford University Press, 2001.

Cavarnos, Constantine. *Holiness: Man's Supreme Destiny*. Belmont, MA: Institute for Byzantine and Modern Greek Studies, 2001.

Chondropoulos, Sotos. *Saint Nectarias: A Saint for Our Times*. Brookline, MA: Holy Cross Orthodox Press, 1989.

Chrysostom, Saint. "Homily 2." In *Saint Chrysostom: On the Priesthood; Ascetic Treatises; Select Homilies and Letters; Homilies on the Statues*. Vol. 9 of *A Select Library of the Nicene and Post-Nicene Fathers of the Christian Church*, edited by Philip Schaff. Grand Rapids: Eerdmans, 1975. http://www.ccel.org/ccel/schaff/npnf109.xv.iv.html.

Church for All. http://www.churchforall.org.

———. "Lord's Supper." http://www.churchforall.org/lordssup.htm.

———. "Worship with Us." http://www.churchforall.org/worship.htm.

Church of Fools. http://www.churchoffools.com.

Clayton, Philip, and P. C. W. Davies. *The Re-Emergence of Emergence: The Emergentist Hypothesis from Science to Religion*. New York: Oxford University Press, 2006.

Clement I, Pope. "Letter to the Corinthians" (AD 80). In "Apostolic Succession," edited by Robert H. Brom. Catholic Answers, 2004. http://www.catholic.com/library/Apostolic_Succession.asp.

Climacus, Saint John. *The Ladder of Divine Ascent*. Boston: Holy Transfiguration Monastery, 1991.

Confessor, Maximus. "The Four Hundred Chapters on Love." In *Maximus Confessor: Selected Writings*, edited by George Berthold, 33–98. New York: Paulist, 1985.

Cyprian. "Epistle 62: Cæcilius, on the Sacrament of the Cup of the Lord." In *Hippolytus, Cyprian, Caius, Novatian, Appendix*. Vol. 5 of *Ante-Nicene Fathers*, edited by Alexander Roberts, James Donaldson, and A. Cleveland Coxe. Grand Rapids: Eerdmans, 1957. http://www.ccel.org/ccel/schaff/anf05.iv.iv.lxii.html.

Davis, Leo Donald. *The First Seven Ecumenical Councils (325–787): Their History and Theology*. Collegeville, MN: Liturgical Press, 1990.

Dawson, Lorne L., and Douglas E. Cowan, eds. *Religion Online: Finding Faith on the Internet*. New York: Routledge, 2004.

de Silva, Lynn A. *Mit Buddha und Christus auf dem Weg*. Vol. 24 of *Theologie der Dritten Welt*. Freiburg, Germany: Herder, 1998.

Diadochos of Photiki, Saint. "On Spiritual Knowledge and Discrimination." In *The Philokalia: The Complete Text*. Vol. 1. Compiled by Saint Nikodimos of the Holy Mountain and Saint Makarios of Corinth, translated and edited by G. E. H. Palmer, Philip Sherrard, and Kallistos Ware. London: Faber & Faber, 1983.

The Diocese of the South. http://dosoca.org.

Dionysius the Areopagite. "Preface to *Mystic Theology*." In *Dionysius the Areopagite: Works (1897)*, translated by John Parker. Grand Rapids: Christian Classics Ethereal Library, n.d. http://www.ccel.org/ccel/dionysius/works.i.iii.html.

Dix, Dom Gregory. *The Shape of the Liturgy*. Westminster, England: Dacre, 1945.

Downey, Michael. *Understanding Christian Spirituality*. New York: Paulist, 1997.

Ende, Michael. *Momo*. New York: Penguin Books, 1986.

Erickson, John H. *The Challenge of Our Past: Studies in Orthodox Canon Law and Church History*. Crestwood, NY: St. Vladimir's Seminary Press, 1991.

———. *Orthodox Christians in America: A Short History*. New York: Oxford University Press, 2008.

Erickson, Millard J. *Christian Theology*. 2nd ed. Grand Rapids: Baker Book House, 1998.

Evnine, Simon. *Epistemic Dimensions of Personhood*. New York: Oxford University Press, 2008.

Fairbairn, Donald. "Orthodoxy and Nationalism." In *Eastern Orthodoxy through Western Eyes*, 143–51. Louisville: Westminster John Knox Press, 2002.

Florovsky, Georges. *Creation and Redemption*. Collected Works of Georges Florovsky, vol. 3. Belmont, MA: Nordland, 1976.

———. "The Idea of Creation in Christian Philosophy." Holy Trinity Orthodox School. http://www.holytrinitymission.org/books/english/theology_creation_florovsky_e.htm.

Ford, David C. *Prayer and the Departed Saints*. Chesterton, IN: Conciliar, 1994. http://www.holy-trinity-church.org/index.php?option=com_content&task=view&id=70&Itemid=131&limit=1&limitstart=1.

Ford, Mary. "Towards the Restoration of Allegory: Christology, Epistemology and Narrative Structure." *St. Vladimir's Theological Quarterly* 34, no. 2–3 (1990): 161–95.

Frankfurt, Harry G. "Freedom of the Will and the Concept of a Person." In *What Is a Person?*, edited by Michael F. Goodman, 127–44. Contemporary Issues in Biomedicine, Ethics, and Society. Clifton, NJ: Humana, 1988.

Freeman, Stephen. *Glory to God for All Things* (blog). http://glory2godforallthings.com.

Friends of the Coptic Church. http://world.secondlife.com/group/7def79e2-9851-dd22-29d0-3b130fc613ec.

Gladwell, Malcolm. *The Tipping Point: How Little Things Can Make A Big Difference*. New York: Little, Brown, & Company, 2000.

Goodman, Michael F. *What Is a Person? Contemporary Issues in Biomedicine, Ethics, and Society*. Clifton, NJ: Humana, 1988.

Greek Orthodox Archdiocese of America. "Sermons." http://goarch.org/resources/sermons/sermons.

Grivec, Franz. *Konstantin und Method: Lehrer der Slaven*. Wiesbaden: Harrassowitz, 1960.

Hampton, Keith, Lauren Sessions, Eun Ja Her, and Lee Rainie. *Social Isolation and New Technology*. Annenburg: University of Pennsylvania Press, 2009.

Halton, Thomas. *The Church*. Message of the Fathers of the Church. Edited by Thomas Halton. Vol. 4, Wilmington Deleware: Michael Glazier, 1985.

Henry, Matthew. "Matthew Henry's Commentary on the Whole Bible." Christian Classics Ethereal Library. http://www.ccel.org/ccel/henry/mhc.i.html.

Hesselgrave, David J., and Edward Rommen. *Contextualization: Meanings, Methods, and Models*. Grand Rapids: Baker Book House, 1989.

Hesychios the Priest, Saint. "On Watchfulness and Holiness." In *The Philokalia: The Complete Text*. Vol. 1. Compiled by Saint Nikodimos of the Holy Mountain and Saint Makarios of Corinth, translated and edited by G. E. H. Palmer, Philip Sherrard, and Kallistos Ware, 162–98. London: Faber & Faber, 1983.

Hipps, Shane. *Flickering Pixels: How Technology Shapes Your Faith*. Grand Rapids: Zondervan, 2009.

Højsgaard, Morten T., and Margit Warburg. *Religion and Cyberspace*. New York: Routledge, 2005.

The Holy Synod of Bishops. "Encyclical Letter of the Holy Synod of Bishops of the Orthodox Church in America on Marriage." Orthodox Church in America. http://oca.org/holy-synod/encyclicals/on-marriage.

Holy Transfiguration Orthodox Church. "Information." http://holyTransfiguration-oca.org/information.htm.

———. "Virtual Chapel for Orthodox Christian Prayer." http://holyTransfiguration-oca.org/vchapel.htm.

Hopko, Thomas. *The Liturgy of the Presanctified Gifts*. New York: Orthodox Church in America, 1978.

Ignatius of Antioch. "The Epistle of Ignatius to the Ephesians." Translated by Alexander Roberts and James Donaldson. In *Ante-Nicene Fathers*, vol. 1, edited by Alexander Roberts, James Donaldson, and A. Cleveland Coxe. Buffalo, NY: Christian Literature Publishing, 1885. Revised and edited for New Advent by Kevin Knight. http://www.newadvent.org/fathers/0104.htm.

———. "The Epistle of Ignatius to the Smyrnaeans." Translated by Alexander Roberts and James Donaldson. In *Ante-Nicene Fathers*, vol. 1, edited by Alexander Roberts, James Donaldson, and A. Cleveland Coxe. Buffalo, NY: Christian Literature Publishing, 1885. Revised and edited for New Advent by Kevin Knight. http://www.newadvent.org/fathers/0109.htm.

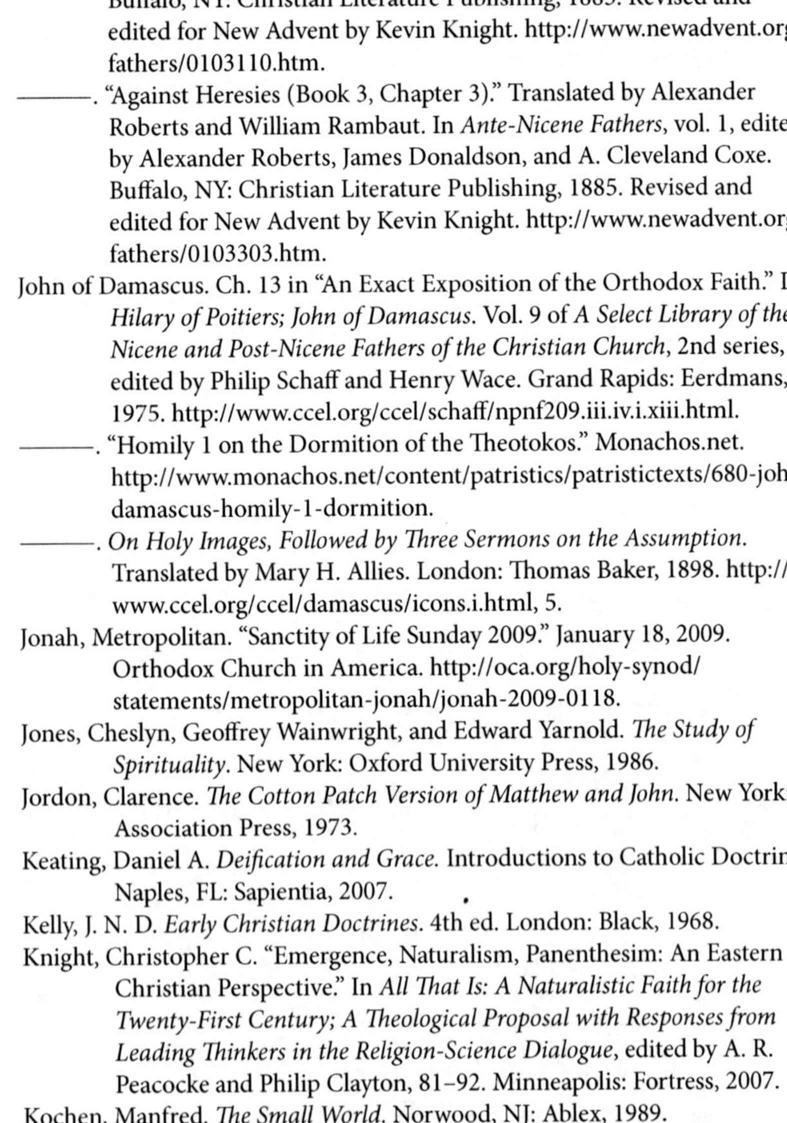

Irenaeus, Saint. "Against Heresies." In *Ante-Nicene Fathers*, vol. 1, edited by Alexander Roberts and James Donaldson. Peabody, MA: Hendrikson, 1995.

———. "Against Heresies (Book 1, Chapter 10)." Translated by Alexander Roberts and William Rambaut. In *Ante-Nicene Fathers*, vol. 1, edited by Alexander Roberts, James Donaldson, and A. Cleveland Coxe. Buffalo, NY: Christian Literature Publishing, 1885. Revised and edited for New Advent by Kevin Knight. http://www.newadvent.org/fathers/0103110.htm.

———. "Against Heresies (Book 3, Chapter 3)." Translated by Alexander Roberts and William Rambaut. In *Ante-Nicene Fathers*, vol. 1, edited by Alexander Roberts, James Donaldson, and A. Cleveland Coxe. Buffalo, NY: Christian Literature Publishing, 1885. Revised and edited for New Advent by Kevin Knight. http://www.newadvent.org/fathers/0103303.htm.

John of Damascus. Ch. 13 in "An Exact Exposition of the Orthodox Faith." In *Hilary of Poitiers; John of Damascus*. Vol. 9 of *A Select Library of the Nicene and Post-Nicene Fathers of the Christian Church*, 2nd series, edited by Philip Schaff and Henry Wace. Grand Rapids: Eerdmans, 1975. http://www.ccel.org/ccel/schaff/npnf209.iii.iv.i.xiii.html.

———. "Homily 1 on the Dormition of the Theotokos." Monachos.net. http://www.monachos.net/content/patristics/patristictexts/680-john-damascus-homily-1-dormition.

———. *On Holy Images, Followed by Three Sermons on the Assumption*. Translated by Mary H. Allies. London: Thomas Baker, 1898. http://www.ccel.org/ccel/damascus/icons.i.html, 5.

Jonah, Metropolitan. "Sanctity of Life Sunday 2009." January 18, 2009. Orthodox Church in America. http://oca.org/holy-synod/statements/metropolitan-jonah/jonah-2009-0118.

Jones, Cheslyn, Geoffrey Wainwright, and Edward Yarnold. *The Study of Spirituality*. New York: Oxford University Press, 1986.

Jordon, Clarence. *The Cotton Patch Version of Matthew and John*. New York: Association Press, 1973.

Keating, Daniel A. *Deification and Grace*. Introductions to Catholic Doctrine. Naples, FL: Sapientia, 2007.

Kelly, J. N. D. *Early Christian Doctrines*. 4th ed. London: Black, 1968.

Knight, Christopher C. "Emergence, Naturalism, Panenthesim: An Eastern Christian Perspective." In *All That Is: A Naturalistic Faith for the Twenty-First Century; A Theological Proposal with Responses from Leading Thinkers in the Religion-Science Dialogue*, edited by A. R. Peacocke and Philip Clayton, 81–92. Minneapolis: Fortress, 2007.

Kochen, Manfred. *The Small World*. Norwood, NJ: Ablex, 1989.

Leary, Mark R. *The Curse of the Self: Self-Awareness, Egotism, and the Quality of Human Life*. New York: Oxford University Press, 2004.

Lindbeck, George A. *The Church in a Postliberal Age: Radical Traditions.* Edited by James J. Buckley. Grand Rapids: Eerdmans, 2003.

*Living God: Catechism for the Christian Faith.* Crestwood, NY: St. Vladimir's Seminary Press, 1988.

Lossky, Vladimir. *The Mystical Theology of the Eastern Church.* Crestwood, NY: St. Vladimir's Seminary Press, 1976.

Louth, Andrew. "The Cosmic Vision of Saint Maximos the Confessor." In *In Whom We Live and Move and Have Our Being: Panentheistic Reflections on God's Presence in a Scientific World*, edited by Philip Clayton and A. R. Peacocke, 184–96. Grand Rapids: Eerdmans, 2004.

Manley, Johanna. *The Bible and the Holy Fathers for Orthodox: Daily Scripture Readings and Commentary for Orthodox Christians.* Menlo Park, CA: Monastery Books, 1990.

Mantzarides, Georgios I. *The Deification of Man: St. Gregory Palamas and the Orthodox Tradition.* Contemporary Greek Theologians. Crestwood, NY: St. Vladimir's Seminary Press, 1984.

"The Martyrdom of Ignatius." In *The Apostolic Fathers; Justin Martyr; Irenaeus.* Vol. 1 of *Ante-Nicene Fathers*, edited by Alexander Roberts, James Donaldson, and A. Cleveland Coxe. Buffalo, NY: Christian Literature Publishing, 1885. http://www.ccel.org/ccel/schaff/anf01.v.xxv.vii.html.

Maximos the Confessor, Saint. "Four Hundred Texts on Love." In *The Philokalia: The Complete Text.* Vol. 2. Compiled by Saint Nikodimos of the Holy Mountain and Saint Makarios of Corinth, translated and edited by G. E. H. Palmer, Philip Sherrard, and Kallistos Ware, 52–113. London: Faber & Faber, 1984.

———. "Various Texts on Theology, the Divine Economy, and Virtue and Vice." In *The Philokalia: The Complete Text.* Vol. 2. Compiled by Saint Nikodimos of the Holy Mountain and Saint Makarios of Corinth, translated and edited by G. E. H. Palmer, Philip Sherrard, and Kallistos Ware, 164–284. London: Faber & Faber, 1984.

McLaren, Brian D. *A New Kind of Christian.* San Francisco: Jossy-Bass, 2001.

McPherson, Miller, and Lynn Smith-Lovin. "Social Isolation in America: Changes in Core Discussion Networks over Two Decades." *American Sociological Review* 71, no. 3 (June 2006): 353–75.

Meyendorff, John. *Byzantine Theology: Historical Trends and Doctrinal Themes.* New York: Forham University Press, 1979.

———. *Rome, Constantinople, Moscow: Historical and Theological Studies.* Crestwood, NY: St. Vladimir's Seminary Press, 1996.

Moltmann, Jürgen. *A Theology of Hope.* New York: Harper & Row, 1967.

Mondzain, Marie-José. *Image, Icon, Economy: The Byzantine Origins of the Contemporary Imaginary.* Cultural Memory in the Present. Stanford, CA: Stanford University Press, 2005.

Nash, James A. "The Bible vs. Biodiversity: The Case against Moral Argument from Scripture." *Journal for the Study of Religion, Nature and Culture* 3, no. 2 (2009): 213–37.

Nasr, Constantine. *The Bible in the Liturgy*. Oklahoma City: Theosis, 1988.

Neal, Gregory S. "Holy Communion on the Web: Liturgical, Theological, Photographic, and Video Resources for Laity and Clergy." Grace Incarnate Ministries. 2009. http://www.revneal.org/page5/page5.html.

Nellas, Panayiotis. *Deification in Christ: The Nature of the Human Person*. Crestwood, NY: St. Vladimir's Seminary Press, 1997.

Nesteruk, Alexei V. "The Universe as Hypostatic Inherence in the Logos of God: Panentheism in the Eastern Orthodox Perspective." In *In Whom We Live and Move and Have Our Being*, edited by Philip Clayton and Arthur Peacocke, 169–83. Grand Rapids: Eerdmans, 2004.

Nikiphoros the Monk. "On Watchfulness and the Guarding of the Heart." In *The Philokalia: The Complete Text*. Vol. 4. Compiled by Saint Nikodimos of the Holy Mountain and Saint Makarios of Corinth, translated and edited by G. E. H. Palmer, Philip Sherrard, and Kallistos Ware, 194–206. London: Faber & Faber, 1995.

Nikodimos of the Holy Mountain, Saint, and Saint Makarios of Corinth, comps. *The Philokalia: The Complete Text*. 4 vols. Translated and edited by G. E. H. Palmer, Philip Sherrard, and Kallistos Ware. London: Faber & Faber, 1983–95.

Northcott, Michael S. "Loving Scripture and Nature." *Journal for the Study of Religion, Nature and Culture* 3, no. 2 (2009): 247–53.

Olson, Roger E. "Deification in Contemporary Theology." *Theology Today* 64, no. 2 (2007): 186–200.

Ong, Walter J. *Orality and Literacy: The Technologizing of the Word*. New York: Routledge, 2002.

Orthodox Church in America. *Baptism*. New York: Orthodox Church in America, Department of Religious Education, 1972.

———. "Liturgical Music and Texts." http://oca.org/MDIndex.html?SID=13.

———. "Lives of the Saints." http://oca.org/fslives.asp.

———. "Petitions for Those Suffering in Japan." March 18, 2011. http://oca.org/news/2474.

———. *The Priest's Service Book*. Translated by Archbishop Dmitri. Dallas: Diocese of the South, 2003.

*The Orthodox New Testament*. Vol. 2. Buena Vista, CO: Holy Apostles Convent, 2000.

Palamas, Saint Gregory. "The Declaration of the Holy Mountain in Defence of Those who Devoutly Practise a Life of Stillness." In *The Philokalia: The Complete Text*. Vol. 4. Compiled by Saint Nikodimos of the Holy Mountain and Saint Makarios of Corinth, translated and edited by G. E. H. Palmer, Philip Sherrard, and Kallistos Ware, 418–26. London: Faber & Faber, 1995.

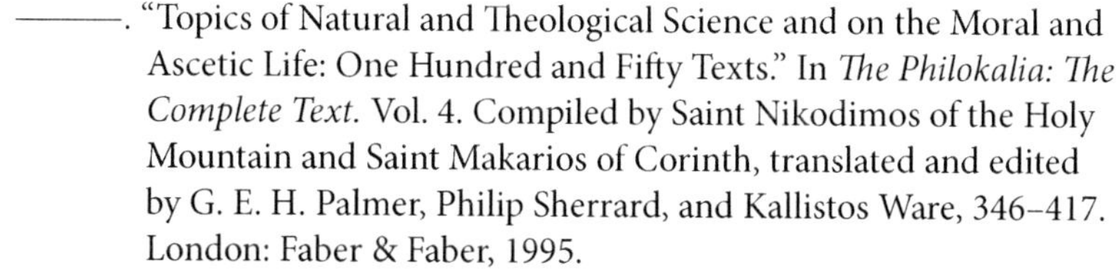

———. "Topics of Natural and Theological Science and on the Moral and Ascetic Life: One Hundred and Fifty Texts." In *The Philokalia: The Complete Text.* Vol. 4. Compiled by Saint Nikodimos of the Holy Mountain and Saint Makarios of Corinth, translated and edited by G. E. H. Palmer, Philip Sherrard, and Kallistos Ware, 346–417. London: Faber & Faber, 1995.

———. *The Triads.* The Classics of Western Spirituality. Mahwah, NJ: Paulist, 1983.

Pamphilius, Eusebius. Ch. 1 in "Church History." In *Eusebius Pamphilus: Church History; Life of Constantine; Oration in Praise of Constantine.* Vol. 1 of *A Select Library of the Nicene and Post-Nicene Fathers of the Christian Church*, 2nd series, edited by Philip Schaff and Henry Wace. Grand Rapids: Eerdmans, 1975. http://www.ccel.org/ccel/schaff/npnf201.iii.vii.ii.html.

Pannenberg, Wolfhart. "Ecumenical Tasks in Relationship to the Roman Catholic Church." *Pro Ecclesia* 15, no. 2 (2006): 161–71.

———, and Niels Henrik Gregersen. *The Historicity of Nature: Essays on Science and Theology.* West Conshohocken, PA: Templeton Foundation Press, 2008.

Peacocke, A. R., and Philip Clayton. *All That Is: A Naturalistic Faith for the Twenty-First Century; A Theological Proposal with Responses from Leading Thinkers in the Religion-Science Dialogue.* Minneapolis: Fortress, 2007.

Percival, Henry R., ed. *The Seven Ecumenical Councils.* Vol. 14 of *A Select Library of the Nicene and Post-Nicene Fathers of the Christian Church*, 2nd series, edited by Philip Schaff and Henry Wace. Grand Rapids: Eerdmans, 1975. http://www.ccel.org/ccel/schaff/npnf214.toc.html.

Peter of Damaskos, Saint. "Active Spiritual Knowledge." In *The Philokalia: The Complete Text.* Vol. 3. Compiled by Saint Nikodimos of the Holy Mountain and Saint Makarios of Corinth, translated and edited by G. E. H. Palmer, Philip Sherrard, and Kallistos Ware, 101–103. London: Faber & Faber, 1984.

———. "The Great Benefit of True Repentance." In *The Philokalia: The Complete Text.* Vol. 3. Compiled by Saint Nikodimos of the Holy Mountain and Saint Makarios of Corinth, translated and edited by G. E. H. Palmer, Philip Sherrard, and Kallistos Ware, 170–71. London: Faber & Faber, 1984.

———. "Self-restraint." In *The Philokalia: The Complete Text.* Vol. 3. Compiled by Saint Nikodimos of the Holy Mountain and Saint Makarios of Corinth, translated and edited by G. E. H. Palmer, Philip Sherrard, and Kallistos Ware, 257. London: Faber & Faber, 1984.

Polanyi, Michael. *Personal Knowledge: Towards a Post-Critical Philosophy.* Chicago: University of Chicago Press, 1958.

Popovich, Saint Justin. "The Attributes of the Church." Orthodox Christian Information Center. http://orthodoxinfo.com/general/attributes.aspx.

Reichelt, Leisa. "17 Ways You Can Use Twitter." http://www.doshdosh.com/ways-you-can-use-twitter/ (accessed 11/20/2009).

Rice, Jesse. *The Church of Facebook: How the Hyperconnected Are Redefining Community*. Colorado Springs: David C. Cook, 2009.

Robichau, B. Peter. "From District to Diocese: An Examination of the Founding and Missionary Methods of the OCA Diocese of the South." St. Vladimir's Orthodox Theological Seminary, 2010.

Rodger, Symeon. "The Soteriology of Anselm of Canterbury: An Orthodox Perspective." *Greek Orthodox Theological Review* 34, no. 1 (1989): 19–43.

Rommen, Edward. *Get Real: On Evangelism in the Late Modern World*. Pasadena: William Carey Library, 2010.

Rosen, Christine. "Virtual Friendship and the New Narcissism." *New Atlantis* (2007): 15–31.

Rousseau, Jean-Jacques. *Essay on the Origin of Writing*. Translated by John Moran. New York: Frederick Ungar, 1966.

Schaff, Philip. Ch. 13 in "Prolegomena." In *Saint Chrysostom: On the Priesthood; Ascetic Treatises; Select Homilies and Letters; Homilies On the Statues*. Vol. 9 of *A Select Library of the Nicene and Post-Nicene Fathers of the Christian Church*, edited by Philip Schaff. Grand Rapids: Eerdmans, 1975. http://www.ccel.org/ccel/schaff/npnf109.iii.xiii.html.

Schmemann, Alexander. *The Eucharist: Sacrament of the Kingdom*. Crestwood, NY: St. Vladimir's Seminary Press, 2003.

———. *For the Life of the World: Sacraments and Orthodoxy*. Crestwood, NY: St. Vladimir's Seminary Press, 2004.

———. *Great Lent: Journey to Pascha*. Rev. ed. Crestwood, NY: St. Vladimir's Seminary Press, 1974.

———. *Introduction to Liturgical Theology*. 3rd ed. Crestwood, NY: St. Vladimir's Seminary Press, 1986.

———. *Introduction to Liturgical Theology*. 4th ed. Crestwood, NY: St. Vladimir's Seminary Press, 2003.

———. *Liturgy and Tradition: Theological Reflections of Alexander Schmemann*. Edited by Thomas Fisch. Crestwood, NY: St. Vladimir's Seminary Press, 2003.

———. *Of Water and the Spirit*. Crestwood, NY: St. Vladimir's Seminary Press, 2003.

Searle, John R. *Mind: A Brief Introduction*. Fundamentals of Philosophy Series. New York: Oxford University Press, 2004.

The Second Ecumenical Council. "The Holy Creed Which the 150 Holy Fathers Set Forth, Which Is Consonant with the Holy and Great Synod of Nice." In Henry R. Percival, ed. *The Seven Ecumenical Councils*. Vol. 14 of *A Select Library of the Nicene and Post-Nicene Fathers of the Christian Church*, 2nd series, edited by Philip Schaff and Henry Wace. Grand Rapids: Eerdmans, 1975. http://www.ccel.org/ccel/schaff/ npnf214.ix.iii. html.

Second Life. http://www.secondlife.com.

Serfes, Nektarios. "The Life of [Saint] Edward the Martyr, King of England." Spiritual Nourishment for the Soul. http://www.serfes.org/lives/stedward.htm.

Skete.com. "Beautiful Hand-painted Icons." http://www.skete.com/index.cfm?fuseaction= category.display&category_id=100.

Smith, Christian. *Moral, Believing Animals: Human Personhood and Culture*. New York: Oxford University Press, 2003.

———. *What Is a Person? Rethinking Humanity, Social Life, and the Moral Good from the Person Up*. Chicago: University of Chicago Press, 2010.

Smith, Marc A., and Peter Kollock. *Communities in Cyberspace*. New York: Routledge, 1999.

Solovyov, Vladimir Sergeyevich, and Boris Jakim. *Lectures on Divine Humanity*. Hudson, NY: Lindisfarne, 1995.

St. Tikhon's Monastery, trans. *The Great Book of Needs: Expanded and Supplemented*. 4 vols. South Canaan, PA: St. Tikhon's Seminary Press, 1998.

Staniloae, Dumitru. *Orthodox Spirituality: A Practical Guide for the Faithful and a Definitive Manual for the Scholar*. South Canaan, PA: St. Tikhon's Seminary Press, 2002.

Stavropoulos, Christoforos. *Partakers of Divine Nature*. Minneapolis: Light & Life, 1976.

Stokoe, Mark, and Leonid Kishkovsky. "Orthodox Christians in North America (1794–1994)." Orthodox Church in America. http://oca.org/MVorthchristiansnamerica.asp?SID=1&Chap=CH1.

Stone, Linda. "Continuous Partial Attention—Not the Same as Multi-tasking." *Business Week*, July 23, 2008.

Sullivan, Francis A. *From Apostles to Bishops: The Development of the Episcopacy in the Early Church*. Mahwah, NJ: Newman, 2001.

Symeon the New Theologian, Saint. "One Hundred and Fifty-three Practical and Theological Texts." In *The Philokalia: The Complete Text*. Vol. 4. Compiled by Saint Nikodimos of the Holy Mountain and Saint Makarios of Corinth, translated and edited by G. E. H. Palmer, Philip Sherrard, and Kallistos Ware, 25–63. London: Faber & Faber, 1995.

———. "On Faith." In *The Philokalia: The Complete Text.* Vol. 4. Compiled by Saint Nikodimos of the Holy Mountain and Saint Makarios of Corinth, translated and edited by G. E. H. Palmer, Philip Sherrard, and Kallistos Ware, 16–24. London: Faber & Faber, 1995.

———. "The Three Methods of Prayer." In *The Philokalia: The Complete Text.* Vol. 4. Compiled by Saint Nikodimos of the Holy Mountain and Saint Makarios of Corinth, translated and edited by G. E. H. Palmer, Philip Sherrard, and Kallistos Ware, 64–75. London: Faber & Faber, 1995.

Tertullian. "Demurrer against the Heretics" (AD 200). In "Apostolic Succession," edited by Robert H. Brom. Catholic Answers, 2004. http://www.catholic.com/library/Apostolic_Succession.asp.

———. *Prescription Against Heretics.* http://www.newadvent.org/fathers/0311.htm, chpt. 32.

Theophan the Recluse, Saint. *Thoughts for Each Day of the Year.* Platina: St. Herman of Alaska Brotherhood, 2010.

Thunberg, Lars. *Microcosm and Mediator: The Theological Anthropology of Maximus the Confessor.* 2nd ed. Chicago: Open Court, 1995.

Turkle, Sherry. *Alone Together: Why We Expect More from Technology and Less from Each Other.* New York: Basic Books, 2011.

———. *The Second Self: Computers and the Human Spirit.* 20th anniversary ed. Cambridge, MA: MIT Press, 2005.

———. http://sodacity.net/system/files/Sherry-Turkle_The-Tethered-Self.pdf Ssherry Turkel. Always on? Always-on-you: The Tethered Self.

Universal Life Church Monastery. http://www.themonastery.org/.

Utley, Bob. "Free Bible Commentary." http://www.freebiblecommentary.org.

Vasileios. *Hymn of Entry: Liturgy and Life in the Orthodox Church.* Contemporary Greek Theologians 1. Crestwood, NY: St. Vladimir's Seminary Press, 1984.

Vassiliadis, Petros. *Eucharist and Witness: Orthodox Perspectives on the Unity and Mission of the Church.* Brookline, MA: Holy Cross Orthodox Press, 1998.

Velimirovic, Nikolaj. *The Prologue from Ochrid.* 4 vols. Birmingham, England: Lazarica, 1985.

Veronis, Luke. *Go Forth: Stories of Mission and Resurrection in Albania.* Ben Lomond: Conciliar, 2009.

Vincent of Lerins. "Commonitorium." Translated by C. A. Heurtley. In *Nicene and Post-Nicene Fathers,* 2nd series, vol. 11, edited by Philip Schaff and Henry Wace. Buffalo, NY: Christian Literature Publishing, 1894. Revised and edited for New Advent by Kevin Knight. http://www.newadvent.org/fathers/3506.htm.

Ware, Kallistos. "God Immanent yet Transcendent: The Divine Energies according to Saint Gregory Palamas." In *In Whom We Live and Move and Have Our Being: Panentheistic Reflections on God's Presence in a Scientific World*, edited by Philip Clayton and A. R. Peacocke, 157–68. Grand Rapids: Eerdmans, 2004.

Webber, Meletios. *Bread and Water, Wine and Oil*. Chesterton, IN: Conciliar, 2007.

Wellman, Barry. "Which Types of Ties and Network Give What Kinds of Social Support?" *Advances in Group Processes* 9 (1992): 207–35.

———, and Caroline Haythornthwaite, eds. *The Internet in Everyday Life*. The Information Age Series. Malden, MA: Blackwell, 2002.

Windley, Phillip J. *Digital Identity*. Sebastopol, CA: O'Reilly, 2005.

Winkler, Gabriele. "Der Geschichtlich Hintergrund der Presanctienvesper." *Origens Christianus* 56 (1975): 185–206.

Wood, Andrew F., and Matthew J. Smith. *Online Communication: Linking Technology, Identity, and Culture*. 2nd ed. Lea's Communication Series. Mahwah, NJ: Lawrence Erlbaum Associates, 2005.

Wybrew, Hugh. *Orthodox Feasts of Jesus Christ and the Virgin Mary: Liturgical Texts with Commentary*. Crestwood, NY: St. Vladimir's Seminary Press, 2000.

Wysochansky, Demetrius. *Divine Office: Horologion, Octoechos, Triodion, Menaion*. Stamford, CT: Ukrainian Catholic Eparchy of Stamford, 2003.

Zaleski, Jeffrey P. *The Soul of Cyberspace: How New Technology Is Changing Our Spiritual Lives*. San Francisco: HarperEdge, 1997.

Zizioulas, Jean. *Being as Communion: Studies in Personhood and the Church*. London: Darton, Longman & Todd, 2004.

———, and Paul McPartland. *Communion and Otherness: Further Studies in Personhood and the Church*. New York: T & T Clark, 2006.

# Index

## D



## E

## F



## G



## H

## N



## O

## P



## R



## S

## T



## U



## V



## W

## Z